An Anthology of
African American Women

CONFIRMATION

◊

Amiri Baraka (LeRoi Jones)
&
Amina Baraka

QUILL
New York 1983

Library of Congress Cataloging in Publication Data
Main entry under title:

Confirmation, an anthology of African American women.

1. American literature—Afro-American authors.
2. American literature—Women authors.   3. American literature—20th century.   4. Afro-American women—Literary collections.   I. Baraka, Imamu Amiri, 1934–   .   II. Baraka, Amina.   III. Title:
Confirmation, an anthology of African American women.
[PS508.N3C66   1983b]   810'.8'09287   82-21425
ISBN 0-688-01580-8
ISBN 0-688-01582-4 (pbk.)

Printed in the United States of America

First Quill Edition

1   2   3   4   5   6   7   8   9   10

BOOK DESIGN BY MARIA EPES

For Charlie Parker
Billie Holiday
John Coltrane
& Sarah Vaughan

that kind of CONFIRMATION!

to our mothers

Anna Lois Jones
& Ruth Mae Richardson

Contents

◊ 7

   ◊ 9

◊ 10

◊ 13

◊ 14

INTRODUCTION

In 1968, Larry Neal and I edited an anthology of AfroAmerican Writing, *Black Fire*. It was meant to show that a new generation of black writers was emerging. This was not just a matter of chronological or generational distinction. In the main, the *Black Fire* writers were trying to create with their work a line of demarcation between themselves, and the ideas they had grown to hold and which had shaped their work, and what had passed for "Negro writing" in the generation just ahead of them.

Black Fire meant to present not only black writing but writing by young writers that clearly, in most cases, took the stand of the most militant and progressive tradition of AfricanAmerican letters. *Black Fire* was a loud and clear putdown of the "art for art's sake" mystique that had tried to mute and distort black writing after the forties when the big publishers made famous those usual "couple" of bloods they always do, but this time those that would denounce Richard Wright's most positive aspect, particularly in his earlier writings, his commitment to a critical-realist literature that reflected the struggles of the AfricanAmerican people for democracy and Self Determination.

Confirmation is not, in this sense, a line of demarcation. Nor is it intended, in the same way that *Black Fire* was, to attack the house-negro appropriation of bourgeois aesthetics. Rather the purpose of this volume is to draw attention to the existence and excellence of black women writers. There is no single generational theme (although all of the writers are still very active), in fact, the collection covers the considerable ground between Margaret Walker and the youngest writers published here for the first time.

Actually, this calling attention is itself a point of demarcation, since it is in distinct contrast to the norm in American letters where "American Literature" is for the most part white and male and bourgeois. To study American Literature, then, is to be exposed to a white male bourgeois world—with perhaps, as Bruce Franklin has pointed out in his book, *The Criminal As Victim And Artist*, a smattering of black men recently, and next to no Latino, Asian, or Native American presence, and just a few white women. The black woman is usually and notoriously absent (as are the other third-world women).

This fact alone would justify the publication of *Confirmation*—to "confirm" that a whole body of American Literature has been consistently ignored or hidden. And though it has been dawning on more people (myself included) how thorough this repression has been, there is still not a wide enough understanding of the entire problem in its full social context. Usually one hears people discussing the effects but only rarely the real causes—the lightest weight social commentators can say "racism and sexism" and leave the overall complexity of such social reaction mostly unanalyzed and not completely understood. And besides, effects can be tolerated much better than causes—to catalog effects is even the partial work of academic American sociologists. A chant of such terrors can even titillate certain dilettantes, be they publishers or producers or politicians or artists or other ghetto tourists, but to speak of *cause* is to *accuse* and there is no room for accusation on the Great White Way, unless it be accusing the victims.

Black women in the United States are at the very bottom of the American social ladder—as someone has said, "the slaves of slaves." But even this bitter characterization hides the real nature of the evil we are confronting. Black working women are *triple* losers in United States society. For, simultaneously, they must face the violent attacks of *class* exploitation, as workers under monopoly capitalism; *national* oppression as AfricanAmericans (with its attendant horror of racism—repression because of physical characteristics); and as well the horrors of *sexual* oppression as women. It is true that all third-world working women are up against the same triple oppression; but it should be pointed out that there is a *caste* system as well as a class system operating in the United States, or at least a caste aspect to the class system, so that racism is most terrifying the darker one is.

The term "sexism" does not speak to what is really involved with the oppression of women (just as "racism" does not fully explain what is involved with the oppression of the AfroAmerican Nation). The oppression of women developed with the advent of class society—from ancient world slavery until today's capitalist societies—and it will never be fully eliminated until the elimination of class society. The same is true of national oppression; it can not really be totally annihi-

◊ 16

lated until the elimination of class society. Oppression of women, like national oppression, like class exploitation, is a source of profit for a small class of exploiters, though certainly the ideas and ideology of this tiny ruling class are made ubiquitous by the power of their stolen wealth. The rulers can infect even their victims with their own ruling class ideology, to the victims' detriment. Although monopoly capitalism, national oppression, and the oppression of women benefits only a tiny few, many many of the people whose lives are attacked and made ugly by these systems nevertheless walk around upholding the same ideas as their oppressors and exploiters. Working people have anti-worker philosophies they pick up from the newspapers or television or movies; black people have anti-black philosophies they pick up from the very fabric of this white supremist society—in school, the media, etc.; women who uphold anti-woman ideology, gained from the same places. Alas, as Lenin said, there is no wall between the exploited and the exploiters, and the exploiters have the power to make their ideas not only ubiquitous but *attractive*!

So to destroy the oppression of women, the material base, the economic foundation upon which such a system depends for its life and replication, must be destroyed. To destroy the oppression of women necessitates the destruction of monopoly capitalism. Not until this economic foundation is eliminated will the system of social organization that stifles women become just a set of bad *ideas*. The same is true with racism. The rulers make superprofits from racism too. They exploit all workers, but they can superexploit black and third-world workers and women workers with the justification that this is just "their place" in the order of things.

The destruction of monopoly capitalism will not *automatically* end the oppression of women (nor national oppression and racism), but without its economic base, what was once a form of social (and economic and political, etc.) organization becomes merely a bad idea that can be eliminated with education. For these social disorders to be isolated as merely backward notions, the profit motive must be removed. As long as one class profits from the oppression of women and national oppression, they will continue to exist. And while we must fight specific inequities right now, our fight is part of a series of democratic struggles that provide the fuel for the majority of people in society to come to fully *revolutionary* positions and eventually rise up and smash monopoly capitalism forever!

What often complicates the struggle against the oppression of women for some people is the confusion of the feminist sector of resistance to this oppression with the whole of the resistance. Feminism, as much as it can be focused on as a specific trend, is an expression, in the main, of petty bourgeois (middle class) and mainly white, women's resistance to the oppression of women. It is the expression of the white professional women against their exclusion from all the benefits of this sector because of their sex. It can be summed up, but not totally, by the *Ms* magazine sector of women who cry out at being passed over historically from the full fruits of United States middle-class prosperity because they are women. This is a class stand basically, and some black and third-world women share this same class outlook.

The conflict between the masses of black women and the feminist movement is chiefly one of class antagonism [most black women and men are not petty bourgeois but workers]. In addition, enthusiastic white feminists can be guilty of as much white chauvinism as any other racist white person.

Feminism, in some of its aspects and expressions, reminds one not a little of certain kinds of nationalism! Some black nationalists, for instance, cry out because they are excluded from being in charge of the exploitation of the black sector of the American pie. They would like black secretaries of state in monopoly capitalist America. They are not interested in taking this oppressive system down, they just want to get in on it! And usually a few spaces are made for these tokens so the ruling class can play at democracy. A certain segment of feminists strike the same pose with the same expectation. They do not want to tear this whole playhouse down, they just want to get in on the ripoff they have been excluded from because they are women.

In the same vein, just as there are those nationalists who are separatists and do not understand the *generally* exploitative nature of monopoly capitalism and that their national oppression can never be ended until this entire system is destroyed and that this must be done, in this multinational state, by all nationalities *together*, there are feminists who are separatists as well, who believe that the enemy is men and not the system that has shaped them, just as those black people who believe that the enemy is white people. So that such feminists believe that the answer is to have nothing to do with men, just as such black separatists believe that having nothing to do with white people is obligatory. Such stances cover the essence of both the system that has enslaved us and the nature of the struggle that must be waged against it to reduce it to a historical curiosity!

Yet, to a certain extent, it has been society's attention to the feminist movement that has brought a more focused appreciation to the struggles of women in general. Though, certainly, anyone mildly acquainted with the history of democratic struggles in the United States realizes that there has always been a strong movement against the oppression of women, in whatever form it took, most notably the various "Suffragette" movements. The division between the struggle of black women and these movements has been a class division, and inevitably a division based on the continuing white chauvinism of the women's movements. But then even the United States Marxist-Leninist movement has always suffered from the split that white chauvinism among so-called Marxists causes.

So *Confirmation* is not feminist, per se, but it does mean to point out by its appearance, the injustice of black women's low profile in the world of literature—and at the same time to do something about it. It also means to let black women speak for themselves about such a world as they find themselves in, and to register their reactions multidimensionally. So that what we find in these pages in total is a heavy portrait of this world. This portrait emerges as the consequence of joining together so many diverse portraits or pieces of portrait, until we have a whole. Not that anyone could say that all the billions of ways of seeing the world have been registered. But from the forty-nine writers published here, a certain clarity of *place* emerges—the place in which AfricanAmerican women register their perception, rationale, and use of the world. The "America" that can be seen from this complex portrait will allow the willing to see much more clearly, especially as they can see where they themselves "are at" in such a world. Only the very insensitive or isolated would be "shocked" by the complex image that does emerge, or refuse to recognize this as the place where we all somehow live "together."

What is interesting, though, is that what becomes fairly obvious is that one element of that world that these authors do make reference to and evoke is the oppression and exploitation that sum up that world in all too many instances. Half of these authors make direct and open reference to oppression—most often as experienced by black people collectively, the women, the men, the children, the struggle of the AfricanAmerican people for life. Throughout, these women are not only recording this oppression but also making a leaping demand for justice, for democracy, that often is couched in the simplest of descriptions. Yes, there is a willingness to *fight*—these are no sad laments of hopelessness.

A clearly Pan-African, even international, consciousness is also evident. Quite a few pieces speak to the African struggle against colonialism, particularly black people raging against South African fascism. There is not only a moving solidarity but attempts to identify and understand what life must be for black people under apartheid, so that our commonality is more clearly expressed!

What is it like here in the United States to be a black woman under the hammer of national oppression? What does this poison do to the woman herself, her life, lovers, family? What does it take to survive? Can one "survive" and not survive at the same time? What does it take not only to survive but to triumph? How does one live under the rule and sway of national oppression, racism, and white supremacy? How does one keep one's sanity and balance in such a world, and how is this further complicated by being not just black, but a woman?

Overwhelmingly, the stance here is a kind of critical-realism that wants all of us not only to perceive this world, but to go past that to understanding it, making some rational appropriation of it—because finally it is the uses we make of the world, what we do in it, that remains significant. Though even a sharp enough registration of perception must force one to some further understanding.

The next largest category of response in the collection is historical. There is a recurrent need for people in struggle to try to gain an overview of their situation that only history can provide. We must see where we've been to know where we are—so we cannot be lied to. At the same time, within this historical view, many times a need arises to celebrate historical figures—not just famous persons, but people in our families, personal symbolic figures, others we have seen survive with

◊ 20

strength and dignity. So that a large part of this historical perspective is given to celebrating people, particularly women, who have served in some way to help these writing women, perhaps to guide them in their development. Other historical examples, personal and otherwise, are symbols of lost strength or life denied, paradigms of tragedy to be evoked as examples to be avoided. But what remains clear is how important history is to seeing and understanding what is real.

At another lower level of occurrence is the work meant to elevate perception itself, of experience, of life, and of one's own life, as constant revelation. What is real? What is relevant? What is my life for? What is its meaning? What is the use of the constant registration given us by our senses?

For still another group [or groups] the question of relationship to men is what is focused on. I say "groups" because some of the work explores particularly the *struggle* between men and women. Many superficial observers conclude with little real investigation that "women's literature" (whatever that actually means aside from the obvious and factual meaning) devotes itself mainly to the struggle between men and women. But study of this volume will quickly disprove that. In fact, I used "groups" because just as many of these writers have focused on their *love* relationships with men (though, granted, love itself is the heaviest of struggles). And taken together, the Ancestor-History group of work and the Man-Woman/Love & Struggle groups occur with the same incidence in this volume. Only the focus on oppression and the general struggle, and awareness of black national oppression receive more attention.

But even when works concentrate on national oppression and imperialism, we are strikingly aware that the consciousness drawing attention to some aspect of that reality or to itself is an AfricanAmerican woman. The focus on history or an ancestor is also drawn with that particular sensibility, and we are aware of that stance as the context of a particular feeling or meaning.

At another level of frequency there are works in which there is a conscious redefining of the black woman to herself and to all the rest of us. In these instances, the writer steps out of the "traditional" role of woman in a capitalist society to redefine herself in her own terms. The family under capitalism takes on the same relationships as exist in the economy. So, in the family structure, the Man is the bourgeois, the owner-capitalist, the "boss" and the woman is the worker, the exploited. The social relations are shaped by the economic structure, with the woman-worker not even getting paid for keeping the actual capitalist's worker (male) fed and becalmed, and at the same time breeding new workers for the pitiless maw of monopoly. So this redefinition, inevitably, is an attempt to step outside these capitalist relations to recreate oneself according to some new and higher level of perception, one that is more beneficial and fulfilling to that consciousness.

It is within and against the entire social organization shaped by monopoly capitalism that such redefinition must be worked out. It is the same social organization in which bourgeois ideologies like national chauvinism and male chauvinism exist ubiquitously as "the norm" or what is "traditional" and "American." We are always aware of these constant menaces to life and development in this volume, whether we are dealing with the struggle of AfroAmerican nation against national oppression or we are overhearing the back and forth of would-be lovers trying to make sense to each other in a world rendered almost senseless by a primitive social system.

And, as usual, the final "meaning" of these encounters comes to exist only to the degree we are able to take something away to use in our own lives. We even look, in a few instances, into the struggle between black and white women that occurs in the same distorted world and for the same reasons. We cannot be sisters or comrades too often, for the same reasons we cannot be lovers. And when we can create relationships that are satisfying and positive it means we have learned how to fight in this world and take away meaningful victories, no matter how seemingly small. Only the realization of "causal connections" in society, as Brecht says, prepares us to smash the old society and build a new one. This volume speaks of these causal connections as they manifest in hundreds of different ways. All of this is to show us "how this shit works," so that we can change it.

Historically, black women writers have a rich tradition. First, from the whole of American Literature (and no matter what the academies say, this is *not* England!). But also the legacy of AfroAmerican Litera-

◊ 22

ture, from its real development as a genre during the early part of the nineteenth century. I am not talking about the Phyllis Wheately-Jupiter Hammon slavemaster-sanctioned house-negro writing, but the emergence of the genre of AfroAmerican writing reflecting the ideology of the black masses such as the slave narratives, as well as the writing of the northern black abolitionists during the black convention movement located in the north and participated in mostly by the northern free blacks. During this period a distinct AfricanAmerican Literature appeared with enough frequency and with enough commonality so that an entire body (genre) of work was recognizable. The slave narratives showed America to the world with such staggering reality that the anti-slave stance became a rising tide in United States' life culminating in the Civil War. Ditto, the pre-Civil War revolutionary democrats like David Walker, Henry Highland Garnett. But the narratives, from Fred Douglass, Henry Bibb, H. Box Brown and the rest, are distinctly extended by Linda Brent's *Diary of A Slave Girl*, which was edited and introduced by the noted white fighter for women's rights L. Maria Child. This is one of the earliest documents showing how even the terror of slavery is made more hideous for a black woman who must endure not only slavery but the sexual assaults of the slave master as well.

Brent's narrative is especially interesting because it depicts not only the dimension of women's oppression to the depth of description of the slave society, but it also shows us how the slavemaster's wife, herself the victim of a male chauvinist society, too often took her frustration out on the black slave woman rather than fighting either the slave society or her husband!

Francis Watkins Harper, the brilliant poet of the Civil War, was the first black woman to publish a novel in the United States. Her *Iola Leroy* (1892), considered the first novel by an AfricanAmerican woman, appears not much after William Wells Brown's *Clotel* (1853), generally regarded as the first novel by an AfricanAmerican.

Just before the Harlem Renaissance, Angelina Grimke came into her own as both poet and playwright; and during the Renaissance itself (the twentieth-century flowering of a black intelligentsia outside the south that was urban and northern in reflection of the masses of blacks who had come up to the north seeking a new life), black women like

◊ 23

Zora Neale Hurston, Nella Larsen, and Jessie Fauset are the best known. But there were also women like Georgia Douglas Johnson, Anne Spencer, Helene Johnson.

In the late thirties the great Margaret Walker appears, *For My People* being published in 1941. This year (1982), Ms. Walker has two more books being published—a new book of poetry, *This Is My Century*, as well as a book on Richard Wright. We also associate the forties with Ann Petry (The Street, 1946).

The fifties established both the first black Pulitzer prize winner in poetry, Gwendolyn Brooks (Illinois' poet laureate), and the black writer whose works ran longest of any AfricanAmerican on Broadway—Lorraine Hansberry, whose *Raisin In The Sun* has become a classic. During the forties and fifties more black women writers than ever before began to surface, breaking through into print. Paule Marshall, Dorothy West, and Alice Childress are some who come to mind. This was only a preface to the sixties and the seventies and the eighties in which even more black women published and were identified by the public as writers.

Women like Mari Evans, Sonia Sanchez, Carolyn Rodgers, Adrienne Kennedy, Johari Amini, Nikki Grimes, Mae Jackson, June Jordan, Audre Lorde, Alice Walker, Vertamae Grosvenor, Toni Cade Bambara, Lucille Clifton, Maya Angelou, Toni Morrison all appear in the sixties. Nikki Giovanni and Jayne Cortez, Aishah Rahman, and Sherley Anne Williams begin to become known in the seventies. And the eighties already have brought us a host of new names, many of which appear in this volume. This decade perhaps will be especially rich because of the added emphasis on women's struggle and feminism carried by the media and the ongoing fight to pass the ERA.

This volume, *Confirmation*, provides a continuum of black women writers. Most of the writers named above are still writing and have works represented in this volume. Also included are the newer writers like Janus Adams, Brenda Conner-Bey, Amina Baraka, Alexis De Veaux, Lois Griffith, Safiya Henderson, Akua Hope, Rashidah Ismaili, Adrienne Ingrum, Gayl Jones, Esther Louise, Rosemari Mealy, Margaret Porter, Michelle Wallace, Regina Williams, Nzadi Zimele-Keita—some of whom, though young, have already achieved national recognition (DeVeaux, Jones and Wallace), plus others who are already spoken of by other writers as people to be reckoned with.

◊ 24

So the book means to be a continuum, a gift of the whole genre—
the writing of AfricanAmerican women circa 1982. Here are the *giants*
Margaret Walker and Gwendolyn Brooks. Here are the well-known
and important names, Toni Morrison and Maya Angelou, plus names
that must be spoken when one mentions seriousness and high quality—women who are also well known but certainly not well known
enough in the white-supremacist, male-oriented United States: Amini,
Bambara, Cortez, Evans, Grosvenor, Jones, June Jordan, Lorde, Marshall, Meriwether, Rodgers, Sanchez, Alice Walker, Clifton, Wallace
and for the first time in this context the incredibly beautiful singer,
Abbey Lincoln (Aminata Moseka).

Some names are missing (Ntozake Shange, who wrote that she did
"not have anything" for the anthology and Julia Fields who did not respond)* but for the most part the inclusiveness, united front aspect, and
high quality of the volume speak for themselves.

Obviously, there is a lot of poetry in this volume, but that is because
my wife and I, being poets, value poetry a great deal. I know that for
me poetry is the first articulation of everything else that will be said or
that is being said. It is the wellspring of the whole story the earliest
song of perception, recognition, response. But at the same time, ten of
the writers chose short pieces of fiction and two of them plays, but only
two sent critical works of nonfiction. Although this certainly is a po-
lemical period in the woman's movement, these writers obviously feel
that they want their creative work to speak for itself in this instance.

So the volume speaks of Being, in the face of, in spite of, in the
midst of ... whatever. *Confirmation* is its title and, in a sense, its
theme. It is dedicated to the confirmation of AfricanAmerican history
and tradition—a history and tradition of resistance and struggle—but
at the same time to the spirit of innovation and populist high art. It
wants to come from "way back" with a spirit of black modernism
(Bop, New Music, etc.), and for this reason the book must be dedicated to those who represent that to us, *Bird, Sassy, Trane, Lady Day.*
Yes, beauty and truth in the face of, sensitivity in spite of, intelligence
in the midst of ... monopoly capitalism, white supremacy, women's
oppression.

What is being confirmed is that these qualities, beauty, truth, sensi-

* At press time we heard from Nikki Giovanni, but we decided against including her work because of her trip to South Africa.

tivity and intelligence, continue to be the truest legacy of African-American artists. At the same time these qualities can only exist because of the intense resistance and *struggle* that must be waged against the enemies of human life and development who continue to rule our lives who are also the enemies of beauty, truth, sensitivity and intelligence. As I said in *In The Tradition*, a long poem dedicated to altoist Arthur Blythe, "We are the Artists!" it is the slave/ex-slave/oppressed nation speaking, "We are the Artists"! You want to know what the United States of North America was really like during slavery days, can you ask the slave master? No, finally, we must ask Linda Brent!

Likewise, you want to know what this place has been like since . . . ? "We are the Artists," tell us Bird, tell us Sassy, tell us Trane, tell us Lady Day, what it was really all about. At the very bottom of United States society, beneath all mystification, are the slaves, and at the bottom of the slaves' society is the black working woman—it is here that the ultimate description is given, that region of life and feeling in which truly there is nothing to lose but chains.

—AMIRI BARAKA

July 1982
Community Correctional
Facility—N.Y.C.

◊ 26

CONFIRMATION

Janus Adams

St. Stephen: A Passion Play (Act I) (excerpt)

The play is a performance piece for actors, dancers, singers, and drummer.

The action takes place everywhere and anywhere in a time of need.

The set is bare, open, vulnerable—in wait. The only piece of scenery is a large scaffold that can be used to create a multipurpose, multilevel area. Somewhere in the distance a projection screen periodically appears for slides and shadow lighting effects.

Masks are used to give flexibility to the characters of the passion play—especially to the PILGRIMS.

The characters are:
> LADY/MARINETTE
> KEEPER/HOUNGAN
> STEVE
> DOCTOR/VICTIM
> PILGRIMS
> MESSENGERS

Act I, Scene 1: Prologue

It is the evening of our humanity. LADY enters softly. Like a general displaying her medals, LADY is shrouded in the details of the ages. From the clothes she wears to the piercing look, there is madness about her. She looks the space over. She pauses, resisting the temptations of fatigue. She knows. This is no place for her to stay.

LADY: Promises. Who can keep them?
Silence. Such silence.
Yes. And even the silence calls you liar. But you try. You must. Learn. To keep pace with all that there is. To the silence. You find yourself daily. Waiting. Until finally, you will learn, he said, to make it. Disappear. I will try.

◊ 29

I will try, I said, leaving with an empty stare. My hands feeling for
the touch again, emptier still but uncompared to the awful wanting, the constant joyless dance of my heart. Shouts searing my
head. Leaving me breathless. And alone.
I will try.

In her hands she fondles crumpled, old shopping bags.

These. Craters of grief that once bulged mountains of memory.
Oddly deflated now. They crave future. I will try.
I try to make them stand for something again. Open. Full. To make
them remember. Red, red cloth. I kept my passage. Bush for tea
and presence. Orange peel. Always. You must never be without
orange peel. Ashes. Log. And ointment. Blue. I search my
pockets.
Where to look. Back to go forward. Perhaps. Forward to go back.
And so she picks them. One by one. Centuries. Generations. Yes-
terdays. Tomorrow. Each a reason. Possibility. Searching.
Searching. Searching. Longing toward home.
Another day's journey. Yes now. Another day's journey traveling
along.

LADY *exits.*

Act I, Scene 2: CONSECRATED GROUND

*A lone drum calls through time. The beat is slow and deliberate.
The tenor, low and flat. Gradually the pulse quickens and its speech
grows more intense. History. Tradition. Warnings. The talking drum.
The ritual begins.*

*From a distant corner a candle flickers in darkness. It circles the air
as though moving by its own energy. It speaks with foreboding. It
lights a face—painted, passionate. There is an aura.*

*A sliver of light further invades the darkness. As it widens, ever so
slightly, we are awed by the magnitude of the presence. Light and*

sound merge. KEEPER. *A blaze of reds and orange. The image is indelibly fixed.*

His chant pours forth. The words are unknown to us at first, but the sounds are unmistakable. He prophesies, commands.

KEEPER: The drum has cleansed this space. With my masks and mystery I come. One spirit. Many realities I am. Keeper. Installed.

Keeper. Of time and faith and flame. Houngan. In this temple. Guide. To those who wish to know. Houngan. For those who choose to see. To hear. To speak. We wait and watch together. Plan. In this temple wishful time.

The drums slow to silence. He stands, taking it all in. Surveying the land he waits for the precise moment to make his move. This is his dance. His message. This is his world. Every finite space. And when he has assessed it, he is not pleased.

As he taunts the tides, masks emerge in the darkness behind him like visions. Dimly lit, they come through and remain—one at a time as he identifies them—until they form a tableau in the distance. Each expression tells a tale of time and generations.

Ibo. Ife. Christian. Jew.
Moslem. Muslim. Buddhist.
Eta. Czech. Arawak. Carib. Gaul.
Democrat. Fascist. Communist. All.

Each who knows higher reason than the rest.
Come. Savior. Saved. Come.
Guerrilla. Militant. Soldier. Peaceful one.
Come. Licensed. Passionate. All.

And KEEPER *further beseeches. And when his voice has swelled to encompass every region, the light focuses more narrowly upon him as if to assure that even the faintest wisp of his energy is not diffused. He calls again. Chanting words unknown.*

◊ 31

Act I, Scene 3: INCANTATION

From the distance a vague, gray sound nears. Voices chant in far-off regions. The PILGRIMS. The way has been cleared for their arrival. Many tongues respond.

A weight of chains. Clanging persecution. Dregs. This is the trail of souls trudging a landscape of pain and despair.

As the voices approach, the strains layer and merge in a cacophony of ill-conceived sound. They are desperate. Careless. They bring their claims.

PILGRIMS: Tired. Thirsty. Troubled. Worn. Abused. Misused. Empty. Scorned.

They repeat their claims over and over in chant. KEEPER appears before them and there is quiet. Searching their faces, KEEPER approaches them cautiously. He chants his offer. Taking a mask from the backdrop, he goes to each of them.

KEEPER: Take watch with me. What is your plan?

Afraid, they cower.

Will you outlive the silence?

As KEEPER walks among the PILGRIMS, a lone presence emerges almost imperceptibly from the side. LADY. Defiant. Disbelieving. She looks on. The shopping bags she carries bulge with the vestiges of history. And she clings to them as to life itself.

As KEEPER turns away disillusioned and bewildered, LADY tries to keep him from leaving. LADY, this lone woman of rags and pain. Drawing from her bags, she holds heritage before each of the PILGRIMS. Pictures, bits of clothing, stones, rags, papers, children's toys, books, records, a mirror.

LADY: But me you remember?
Sharpesville. Hiroshima. Dachau . . . ? I at Canboulay give flesh not
for sport.
Remember.

*She questions and commands. Coursing the fragments of their circle,
she continues her prayer of remembrance. Sometimes in English.
Sometimes in French patois.*

Johannesburg. Amritsar. Scottsboro. My Lai.

In a counterchant, the PILGRIMS *begin to answer her. They shun
her. They deny her as they have long denied themselves. They take up
their work: planting, tilling, moving on from spot to spot.* LADY
challenges them, speaking above them.

PILGRIMS: Freedom. Glory. Wealth. Power. Plenty. Money. Food.
Luxury. Now.

LADY: How? Future? 'Tis empty seed.

PILGRIMS (*Continuing the chant*):   Freedom. Glory. Wealth.
Power. Plenty. Money. Food. Luxury. Work.

LADY: It is not good enough.

Giving up, a wilted KEEPER *replaces the mask.*

KEEPER: Ashantis know: it is the calm and silent water that drowns
the man.

KEEPER *exits.*

As the PILGRIMS *continue their work,* LADY *moves among them.*

LADY: How long . . . ? How long . . . ?

◊ 33

She moves to the masks and takes the one of greatest pain. Putting it on, she moans under the weight of it and then screams in defiance.

LADY: NOOOOOOOooooooo . . .

Slow fade to black with a dim light on LADY.

Act I, Scene 4: EPISTLE

A telegraph is heard through the darkness tapping out its code. Trains come and go with their headlights and roar. The PILGRIMS *bustle about the terminal.*
   KEEPER *enters wearing his stationmaster's hat and jacket. His arms are full. Signs. Tickets. He lays out the terminal. Calls the train departures and arrivals. Sells tickets. Manages the terminal.*

KEEPER: Crossroads! Anywhere! Arriving!
                    (*To himself*)
   Going. Going. For years I've watched them. Called them out. You'd think people would listen.

PILGRIM (*Getting his ticket*):   1945.

KEEPER: Miles and miles. Those tracks stretch ahead and the people come. To whisper their claims. It's a confidence.

PILGRIM (*Getting his ticket*):   Round trip.

KEEPER: Years ago everyone was going one way. Philadelphia. Now it's all over. They're taking this place down. They don't want it anymore. Round trip. Round trip. Everyday. The same stretch. Who needs to listen? Back and forth. I think they call it progress. Departing! 1613! New York!

◊ 34

The PILGRIMS *ring the stage with activity. There is a steady flow. Simple. Methodical. Frenzied but dispassionate. One comes up to* KEEPER *for his ticket.*

PILGRIM: Rhodesia.

KEEPER: Zimbabwe.

PILGRIM: Victoria Falls.

KEEPER: Round trip. Definitely.
1918. New Orleans. 1619. England. 1734. 1812. Port-au-Prince.

Into this area strewn with newspapers and trash around a street litter basket, LADY *enters. She speaks to the* PILGRIMS. *They ignore her. They continue their business, then leave, as the drone of destinations goes on.*

KEEPER: Amherst, Massachusetts! Board! 1855! Epistle!

PILGRIM (*Speaking too loud*): Al-ger-i-a. Nine-teen fifty-nine. Please.

LADY: He-not-deaf-he-old. Thank-you.

KEEPER: Lady. I was just here counting the days.

LADY: Don' worry, Keeper. See they go. One behind the next. They don' know where they goin'. 'Tis ass leading hog.

KEEPER: They want to give it all up. Round trip. They don't have to plan. Time was when things were always one way, Lady. One way.

LADY: Tradition. Always your tradition.

KEEPER: 1861! Virginia! Georgia!
Sometimes they forget the old ways.

◊ 35

LADY: A few of their old ways, they does need to forget. Some things got to be new. You gotta keep up with the times.

KEEPER: I keep time, all right, Lady. I keep time.

LADY: The old times?

KEEPER: But not the wrong time.

LADY: Yes, Keeper, you right. Not the wrong time. Not you. You . . .

KEEPER: Here's the book.

A train whizzes by. KEEPER *clicks his watch.*

KEEPER: Time.

KEEPER *leaves.*

LADY *(To herself)*:   Yes, Keeper. That's one thing. You keep good time, for sure. Don' leave. I teasing you, man. Make sport. You see me bags full, so and you think I forget you. . . .

Resting her bags, she takes out a coat hanger. Bending it to new purpose, she sweeps. With rags and newspapers taken from her bags, she dusts.

Home.

Easing herself into her space, she goes about the chores of her day.

Stew again? Rabbit stew. No. Quiche. Ground nut stew. Get your geography together, child.

Picking up and tidying her place, there is peace. She is happy and secure. Laying out some things, she settles in, as the last PILGRIM *leaves and the lights focus on her.*

◊ 36

But look me talk. It's just like I say. Trouble know no rest and I mad with this world today.

Keeper? You out there?

KEEPER (*Offstage*):   Yes, Lady. I'm here.

LADY: You know you me only living friend. All them what's want someting from me. No. No one but you. Got no time. Too much to do.

KEEPER (*Offstage*):   We'll get by, Lady. We will.

She keeps up her work at a steady pace. She's in her world now and all else fades.

LADY: Just yesterday this boy come up to me. Lady. You gotta dime, he say. Well, first up, I wan' know how he come by me name. Young boy callin' me so direct, you know. Lady. Lady. Of all the saints. No "Miss Lady." For "Auntie Lady" I crown he one. But good. Still. "Auntie Lady." Just put a handle to me name. But no. He come so grown. Lady. (*Sucks her teeth*) Chupps! People today don' give respect for no one. Don' respect themselves.

Lady. You gotta dime. What I look like givin' you a dime, I ask he now. Wha'chu wan' it for? Why? Wha'chu goin' do with it? Why?

You just beg me for a dime, so?!

Folks out here beggin'. Regular. Chrysler, they beg. Me, no. I charge for expenses. No charity. I need me coin to stay here so. The people and they needs me. All day long they come, go, see, and stare at me. See if I still here lookin' worse off than them. I got responsibilities.

I no shirk. I take it serious. One a them don' pass, nobody know a ting. Me. I not here? Lord God, come mahnin' and I still not hear the end.

One say I dead. One else say they take me in somewhere. Put me in some "home" somewhere. Never a good word for no one, they got. Chupps. I not them, me dear. I independent.

But I tired now. I tired on the same thing go over year after year. Y'all not tired yet youselves?! I done.

Scares an intruder from her circle.

Don'chu get too close now.
                    (*Scratching*)
They bite. And jump. Jouvé!! Jump up mahnin'. Yes maan. Remember one I had back in '43. Fresh! Finally went back to he wife.
Shoot. Boy come callin' me for a dime like I don' work for what I got.
But, looka here now. I generous. I share what me learn. Everyting what I got.

She pulls out a special piece of bright cloth from her bag.

Here 'tis. I give t'other piece to some but a day gone. Baby hungry. They had to get the information. How else they to get where they goin'?
I know to walk.
Showed some how one go crazy back then in '69. They ain' thanked me yet. Jombie must done got they tongue. 1869 to this very day.

Spreading out the newspapers, settles down to read in "bed," her bags propped up for softness.

No. I tired. I done. No more. I work. I done. Now it's for they do.
                    (*Reading*)
But what this now?

Lights up in the background. STEVE enters his cage. MESSEN-GERS lock him in.

Stephen?

◊ 38

A MESSENGER *slams the door of the cell.*

Now that's someting.

MESSENGER: You must like it here, Biko.

LADY: What you wan' they put you in now for, when I tell you I
tired, I done. I tired. I say I done.

The lights dim slightly on STEVE *as he sits there alone.*

> Steve, you OK? Folk been out here tryin'. But you. Young one. You
> ain' learned yet now, look ye. Keep you that way. We need more
> what knows to forget what they scared of.
> But not now. This time for Lady. Done. All you hear. Mambo
> jambo youself. I no mambo now. No Marinette. I no warrior
> woman today.
> > *(Reading further)*
> But what is this? You no hear me good? I tell you I done, you an-
> swer me so I done.

The lights change slightly. KEEPER *enters and lays out new masks
in the background. Dusting them off, he studies one in particular. A
drum beat starts low.* LADY's *arms thrash the air trying to wave away
memory. A new mood.* KEEPER *leaves.*

> SWISH went the horse's tail. This woman so bright and new. Keep-
> ing away fleas and flies and useless people of all shapes and varie-
> ties.

> SWISH. Keeping away memory unwanted. Not long. How long.
> Not long. Too long. MAMMY!!!

> > *(She is two people now)*
> Mammy, is massa gonna sell us tomorrow?
> > Hush baby, Mama's gon find a way.
> Mammy, is massa gonna sell us tomorrow?
> > Hust baby, Mama's got a dream

◊ 39

Good Lord, and make me a son a leper
Make him with cursèd hand and
Scales on his knees
Make him with broken hand and
Snarled-up knee
Make him of narrowed eye and
Hearty soul
That he will be left alone alive
To live.
Mammy, is massa gonna sell us tomorrow?
Hust baby, Mama's precious, precious baby.

SWISH. Her back so proud.
(*Girlishly*)
Lady. I like my name. Mama said, "You gonna know who you are. You Lady!" Huh. "No one can take it from you." She didn't mean it for no trick none, neither. No, I asked her one day. Say, "Mama, how come not Queen? or Cleopatra or Sheba? or something with some history in it?" "That's something you gotta make for yourself, Lady."
SWISH. Mama? SWISH. Mamaaa? Swish. Swish! SWISH. SWISH! SWISH!!! OHHHHhhhh. Swish.

I'm a conservationist now. Yes. Recycler of broken dreams.

Train and terminal sounds are heard in the background moving away. The lights brighten again as LADY's *original mood is restored.*

No. I just don' like this world today. At all, Steve, not at all.

The MESSENGERS *approach* STEVE's *cage. Entering, one chains* STEVE's *hands behind him and hooks him up to the pole as another stands with rifle ready.*

STEVE: Oh, don't worry with that. I was just about to leave.

MESSENGER: Orders.

STEVE: You flatter me.

◊ 40

MESSENGER: Inspection.

The MESSENGERS *exit.*

LADY: I don' want live this no more neither. People have to change, that's all. 'Fore I old and broke down and these bags wore thin. And look, I near skinny now. Well, close.
Smart boy like that. Life used up for what. 'Tis ignorance and greed. They don' have their own. Ignorance and greed, I say. They just goin' have to change no matter.

Carefully, she puts her home away. She is uneasy now.

And they out there worried so. Scared they goin' lost what they don' know they got.
One sure thing does catch the thief. Give it to he. And watch he *drop!*
No rest for the weary. It's a shame. Move on, now, Lady.

Before she goes, she draws a tied-up cloth from her bag and spreads it out carefully on the floor.

Bones of the dead tell no lie.

Shaking up the bag, she lets the bones scatter on the ground.

If a murdered man falls on his face, no way the murderer's going to get away. If . . .

A MESSENGER *enters, dashing in like there's an emergency.*

MESSENGER: Hey, lady, wha'chu think you're doing there? That's not allowed in these parts.

LADY: You want take me drum. Now this me life.

MESSENGER: Look lady, I'm not . . .

LADY: If! . . . If a murdered man falls on his face. Ainnnn' no way the murderer's to leave this place.

◊ 41

MESSENGER: Say, lady, come on now. You gotta . . .

LADY *finishes packing.*

LADY: Lady. How you come by me name? Where you from? Who
you anyway? Folks callin' you by you first name. Who you now? I
know you daddy? Chupps. Call me so direct. Folks ain' got no
respect. No respect for theyselves, I say.

MESSENGER: Look, lady, I don' know what kinda weird stuff you're
talkin'. Just that you gotta move along now.

The MESSENGERS *usher the* DOCTOR *to* STEVE's *cage and
let him in.* LADY *allows herself to be led away by a* MESSEN-
GER.

LADY: "Lady." How you know me name? I like me name. Mama
said, "You goin' know who you is. You Lady!" Huh. "No one
can take it from ye." She didn't mean it for no trick none, neither.
               (To the MESSENGER*)*
How much money you got? Taxes. You gotta pay. Taxes. You here
causa me. That's right. Call me lawyer! Keeper! Where me book,
Keeper! Call me lawyer. Now.
               (Rambling again)
I ask she one day. Say, Mama? How come . . .

KEEPER *(Offstage)*:   Destination! Destiny!

Act I, Scene 5: CANTICLE

STEVE *is dressed only in torn slacks and is barefoot. He and the*
DOCTOR *have been talking. On the floor between them are a sand-
wich, cigarettes, matches, bottled beer, and the* DOCTOR's *open
satchel.*

DOCTOR: Won't I ever be able to convince you that I am on your side?

STEVE: History is on my side.

DOCTOR: I can contact your wife.

STEVE: She would not understand.

DOCTOR: I speak Xhosa.

STEVE: She speaks English.

DOCTOR: I can take your message.

STEVE: She would have no reason to listen to you.

DOCTOR: But if only you people weren't seething so with violence. Then I could understand it somewhat better. It does take time, you know.

STEVE (*Amused*): What you mean is, we must see to it that you are not hurt. What you mean is that your people may use the force at your command at any time. And we are to be nonviolent. You deliver the kick and tell us how to receive it.
This is not India 1949 and I am not Gandhi. This is not America 1963 and I am not King. This is Africa 1977 and we are the sons and daughters of Nkrumah and Mandela and Senghor and Selassie and Nyerere and Gandhi and King.
We will say nonviolent when we choose to. And it will be for our good, not yours. This is Africa. My father's land.

DOCTOR: Don't preach to me. I am not your crowd.

STEVE: I know.

DOCTOR: This is South Africa. My country. My grandfather's land.

STEVE: Look man, as an African you are an imposter.

DOCTOR: My people came and worked here. This is our home. We built this land and made it what it is. My grandfather died for those mines.

STEVE: And ours because of them. You see, the mistake my grandfather made was to let your people come in at all.

DOCTOR: When the Boers came . . .

STEVE: So much history. So many lies.

DOCTOR: In the 1860s . . .

STEVE: Did it ever occur to you to find out what happened here before that?! I've heard all about your Boers before. You ram it at us every chance in the little time we have for school.

DOCTOR: The English and the Dutch . . .

STEVE: This is Africa. Enough of your history. This is 1977 today. So what are we to do? Here I am rectifying the mistakes of my grandfather and there you are wallowing in the mistakes of yours.

DOCTOR: And if I gave up everything and agreed with you, what would that do?

STEVE: At the very least, it would do something for you.

DOCTOR: And at the most, it would do something for you.

STEVE: Only I can do for me.

DOCTOR: You cannot go it alone, Steve. There are men of goodwill. What of them . . . of us?

STEVE: Until they are men of good acts they have no place. The man who sneaks me something past the guards . . . a cigarette . . . this crust of guilt . . . does not know how deeply I hunger. He does it to massage his own conscience, not to relieve my appetites.

DOCTOR: But you are deliberate! You will not even save yourself.

STEVE: Save myself? Materialism. The best I can do is use myself. Black people are neither saved nor safe.

DOCTOR: Your family. Your boys. What will you leave them?

STEVE: Nothing.
                    (*He smiles*)
So they can be free men.

DOCTOR: My God! At sixty-three would you tell me my life has been a lie?

STEVE: At thirty would you tell me the rest of mine must become one?

DOCTOR (*Shaken*):   But what would you have us do?

STEVE: Your illusion versus my future. Your past for my eternity. That sounds fair. Guard!

DOCTOR (*Pushing contraband to* STEVE): You never give up, do you, Biko?

STEVE (*Pushing it back*):   I hunger. Guard! Messenger!

Hurriedly, the DOCTOR *puts the contraband food back in his bag, concealing it from the approaching* MESSENGER. *The* MESSENGER *looks in on them, rifle ready.*

◊ 45

STEVE (*To the* DOCTOR): Section Six. I'm banned, man. No more than one person with me at a time, you know. Why make a criminal of me now?

(*He laughs*)

DOCTOR (*Examining* STEVE *with a professional air*):   He is strong. His health is good. His bones are getting brittle, though. And his eyes cloud over.

STEVE: I will always see what I must see.

DOCTOR: For not much longer.

STEVE: Then I will be seen.

The DOCTOR *exits, followed by the* MESSENGER.

FATIMAH AFIF

Tanka

Tied-dyed woman wrapped
in Ife Blues—Songhai smiles
murmuring Langston's
words-Monk's melodies-dance O
ver purple passion rainbows

In an infinite
moment our shadows danced by
Ife light bodies
fondled the mangoed sunset
Cherish the fate of Ife

Fayola Kamaria Ama

for "Mamie"

(*poem for my grandmother*)

    awaken a flower/
       petal
    torn from the bulb

    on lands lifted
    by bitter sweat
    of brown/gray hands

    pickin n pickin
      up

    cotton white clouds
    blue with misery

    southern sweet
    chocolate girls
    fine
    warm
    melting when
    sun shines
    tender as
       rain dripping down

    called her "a looker"
    big boned light brown
    black indian hair
    married young to
    a man named allen
    bore for him
    six strong blk seeds

she worked to give
she worked to give
could of/should of
been home
but workin
while neighbors watched
her children over fences
her seeds

seein nights run into years
seein days shut half winkin
spinning years
fillin her blood
with sugar
sweet/unsweet blood
crawled in
like a spider's web
suckin up her body's
strength
takin the life out her foot
draggin like
a broom across the floor

wake flower
golden loooove
let yr spirit bloom
full complete

another harvest
    done come
giving all it could
the soil lays, again,

    ready to be tended. . . .

Johari M. Amini

There Is No Title: Only Echoes

deep along the reaches of me
i remember how you looked that first time
blue jeanned and dashikied in short black boots
clicked and sealed in vacant spaces

the vacant spaces are wide echoes now
pieces of you are the wind
and ultimately i am alone
the fragments of you moving wild like African grasses
wild warm fragments clicked into a hot wind
out of the East

and things caught up with you sometimes
and i withered seeing your tears
and clicked it in to me too
while you went to catch the things
like pieces of the wind

and i was completed in your flood
filling all my far places because
sometimes when you grabbed me up and close
and swung me tight in the music
i would close my eyes to fix the time
into my being

and all the fragments sealed for all my lives
when other pieces of existence fade from me
and you remain the fragments
sealed within touch of my sight
fixed
a clear instant cut from all movement
fixed

◊ 50

and i will have you wherever i go
a blood call
a soft long whistle in the darkness

The Promise

i am warm
great
i am undulating life

my sons are coming home

and they will not remember the cold tribes
the years
far away within the snow
and dying trees

they will not remember
the stripes and the lashes
whip stroking across
the sunless days

they will only know me

Story for the Remainder

sometimes we could feel the impending close
as something about to descend
before we stopped dancing

we were body movements
which kept our minds silent in hunger and misuse
and the deaf dumb and blind were

just ordinary people
living a life of sliding uneasiness
almost
comfortable with their tissues and deodorants
at the base of the volcano

someone said loudly
    "can't we give love without
    stones"
    "can't we sense touches without
    descents into pain and gaping coldness"
    "can't we see and feel the beauty without
    becoming mechanized pleasures to each other"

but not many listened.

much went by without notice
while we spread our selves
to every invention and disease
which became common and expected at all ages.

we exposed our minds
to the embarrassments of idleness
and to releasing the present in smoke drifts
because we didn't want The Responsibility.

and we were encased in our tracks as the times
gathered tightly.

we would take no Understanding
until it became unavoidable

therefore we were surprised
that the journey to our Destination
was not through drifts of contrived and unusual colors.

JOHARI M. AMINI

No. as was revealed,
it was rather in peeling our hesitancy, our delay,
our unwillingness to assert Life.

But now that all has been washed
in the waters of our force
don't let that remembrance escape you.
hold the reflections of the past so
we will never go that way again

The land that bred us is at peace
singing
and has a sweet vibrant smell
it is ripe with the joy of bearing our lives
generous and fertile
in the quick blood of birth
and is not ashamed

we touch one another with sensible fingers
understanding arms
and an attunement to the Divine that we share

our children are wanted treasures
growing in the richness of our own
Creator's sun
alerted with wisdom from our mouths and ways
and none of them have
syphillitic eyes

When we dance now we celebrate
and not decay

Maya Angelou

The Reunion

Nobody could have told me that she'd be out with a black man; out, like going out. But there she was, in 1958, sitting up in the Blue Palm Cafe, when I played the Sunday matinee with Cal Callen's band.

Here's how it was. After we got on the stage, the place was packed, first Cal led us into "D. B. Blues." Of course I know just like everybody else that Cal's got a thing for Lester Young. Maybe because Cal plays the tenor sax, or maybe because he's about as red as Lester Young, or maybe just cause Lester is the Prez. Anybody that's played with Cal knows that the kickoff tune is gotta be "D. B. Blues." So I was ready. We romped.

I'd played with some of those guys, but never all together, but we took off on that tune like we were headed for Birdland in New York City. The audience liked it. Applauded as much as black audiences ever applaud. Black folks act like they are sure that with a little bit of study they could do whatever you're doing on the stage as well as you do it. If not better. So they clap for your luck. Lucky for you that they're not up there to show you where it's really at.

Anyway, after the applause, Cal started to introduce the band. That's his style. Everybody knows that too. After he's through introducing everybody, he's not going to say anything else till the next set, it doesn't matter how many times we play. So he's got a little comedy worked into the introduction patter. He started with Olly, the trumpet man.... "And here we have a real Chicagoan ... by way of Atlanta, Georgia ... bringing soul to Soulville ... Mr. Olly Martin."

He went on. I looked out into the audience. People sitting, not listening, or better, listening with one side of their ears and talking with both sides of their mouths. Some couples were making a little love ... and some whites were there trying hard to act natural ... like they come to the South Side of Chicago every day or maybe like they live there ... then I saw her. Saw Miss Beth Ann Baker, sitting up with her blond self with a big black man ... pretty black man. What? White girls, when they look alike, can look so much alike, I thought maybe it wasn't Beth. I looked again. It was her. I remember too well the turn of her cheek. The sliding way her jaw goes up to her hair. That was her. I might have missed a few notes, I might have in fact missed the whole interlude music.

What was she doing in Chicago? On the South Side. And with a black man? Beth Ann Baker of the Baker Cotton Gin. Miss Cotton Queen Baker of Georgia . . .

Then I heard Cal get round to me. He saved me for the last. Mainly cause I'm female and he can get a little rise out of the audience if he says, as he did say, "And our piano man is a lady. And what a lady. A cooker and a looker. Ladies and Gentlemen, I'd like to introduce to you Miss Philomena Jenkins. Folks call her Meanie." I noticed some applause, but mainly I was watching Beth. She heard my name and she looked right into my eyes. Her blue ones got as big as my black ones. She recognized me, in fact in a second we tipped eyelids at each other. Not winking. Just squinting, to see better. There was something that I couldn't recognize. Something I'd never seen in all those years in Baker, Georgia. Not panic, and it wasn't fear. Whatever was in that face seemed familiar, but before I could really read it, Cal announced our next number. "Round 'bout Midnight."

That used to be my song, for so many reasons. In Baker, the only time I could practice jazz, in the church, was round 'bout midnight. When the best chord changes came to me it was generally round 'bout midnight. When my first lover held me in his arms, it was round 'bout midnight. Usually when it's time to play that tune I dig right in it. But this time, I was too busy thinking about Beth and her family . . . and what she was doing in Chicago, on the South Side, escorted by the grooviest looking cat I'd seen in a long time. I was really trying to figure it out, then Cal's saxophone pushed it's way into my figurings. Forced me to remember "Round 'bout Midnight." Reminded me of the years of loneliness, the doing-without days, the C.M.E. church, and the old ladies with hands like men and the round 'bout midnight dreams of crossing over Jordan. Then I took thirty-two bars. My fingers found the places between the keys where the blues and the truth lay hiding. I dug out the story of a woman without a man, and a man without hope. I tried to wedge myself in and lay down in the groove between B-flat and B-natural. I must of gotten close to it, because the audience brought me out with their clapping. Even Cal said, "Yeah baby, that's it." I nodded to him then to the audience and looked around for Beth.

How did she like them apples? What did she think of little Philomena that used to shake the farts out of her sheets, wash her dirty drawers, pick up after her slovenly mama? What did she think now? Did she know that I was still aching from the hurt Georgia put on me? But Beth was gone. So was her boyfriend.

I had lived with my parents until I was thirteen, in the servants' quarters. A house behind the Baker main house. Daddy was the butler, my mother was the cook, and I went to a segregated school on the other side of town where the other kids called me the Baker Nigger. Momma's nimble fingers were never able to sew away the truth of Beth's hand-me-down and thrown away clothing. I had a lot to say to Beth, and she was gone.

That was a bring-down. I guess what I wanted was to rub her face in "See now, you thought all I would ever be was you and your mama's flunky." And "See now, how folks, even you, pay to listen to me" and "See now, I'm saying something nobody else can say. Not the way I say it, anyway." But her table was empty.

We did the rest of the set. Some of my favorite tunes, "Sophisticated Lady," "Misty," and "Cool Blues." I admit that I never got back into the groove until we did "When Your Lover Has Gone."

After the closing tune, "Lester Leaps In," which Cal set at a tempo like he was trying to catch the last train to Mobile, was over, the audience gave us their usual thank-you, and we were off for a twenty-minute intermission.

Some of the guys went out to turn on and a couple went to tables where they had ladies waiting for them. But I went to the back of the dark smoky bar where even the occasional sunlight from the front door made no difference. My blood was still fluttering in my fingertips, throbbing. If she was listed in the phone directory I would call her. Hello Miss Beth . . . this is Philomena . . . who was your maid, whose whole family worked for you. Or could I say, Hello Beth. Is this Beth? Well, this is Miss Jenkins. I saw you yesterday at the Blue Palm Cafe. I used to know your parents. In fact your mother said my mother was a gem, and my father was a treasure. I used to laugh 'cause your mother drank so much whiskey, but my Momma said, "Judge not, that ye be not judged." Then I found out that your father had three children down in our part of town and they all looked just like you, only prettier. Oh Beth, now . . . now . . . shouldn't have a chip . . . mustn't be bitter . . . She of course would hang up.

Just imagining what I would have said to her cheered me up. I ordered a drink from the bartender and settled back into my reverie. . . . Hello Beth . . . this is a friend from Baker. What were you doing with that black man Sunday? . . .

"Philomena? Remember me?" She stood before me absorbing the light. The drawl was still there. The soft accent rich white girls practice in Georgia to show that they had breeding. I couldn't think of anything to say. Did I remember her? There was no way I could answer the question.

"I asked Willard to wait for me in the car. I wanted to talk to you."

I sipped my drink and looked in the mirror over the bar and wondered what she really wanted. Her reflection wasn't threatening at all.

"I told him that we grew up . . . in the same town."

I was relieved that she hadn't said we grew up together. By the time I was ten, I knew growing up meant going to work. She smiled and I held my drink.

"I'm engaged to Willard and very happy."

I'm proud of my face. It didn't jump up and walk the bar.

She gave a practiced nod to the bartender and ordered a drink. "He teaches high school here on the South Side." Her drink came and she lifted the glass and our eyes met in the mirror. "I met him two years ago in Canada. We are very happy."

Why the hell was she telling me her fairy story? We weren't kin. So she had a black man. Did she think like most whites in mixed marriages that she had done the whole race a favor?

"My parents . . ." her voice became small, whispery. "My parents don't understand. They think I'm with Willard just to spite them. They . . . When's the last time you went home, Mena?" She didn't wait for my answer.

"They hate him. So much, they say they will disown me." Disbelief made her voice strong again. "They said I could never set foot in Baker again." She tried to catch my eyes in the mirror but I looked down at my drink. "I know there's a lot wrong with Baker, but it's my home." The drawl was turning into a whine. "Mother said, now mind you, she

◊ 57

has never laid eyes on Willard, she said, if she had dreamed when I was a baby that I would grow up to marry a nig . . . a black man, she'd have choked me to death on her breast. That's a cruel thing for a mother to say. I told her so."

She bent forward and I shifted to see her expression, but her profile was hidden by the blond hair. "He doesn't understand, and me either. He didn't grow up in the South." I thought, no matter where he grew up, he wasn't white and rich and spoiled. "I just wanted to talk to somebody who knew me. Knew Baker. You know, a person can get lonely. . . . I don't see any of my friends, anymore. Do you understand, Mena? My parents gave me everything."

Well, they owned everything.

"Willard is the first thing I ever got for myself. And I'm not going to give him up."

We faced each other for the first time. She sounded like her mother and looked like a ten-year-old just before a tantrum.

"He's mine. He belongs to me."

The musicians were tuning up on the bandstand. I drained my glass and stood.

"Mena, I really enjoyed seeing you again, and talking about old times. I live in New York, but I come to Chicago every other weekend. Say, will you come to our wedding? We haven't set the date yet. Please come. It's going to be here . . . in a black church . . . somewhere."

"Good-bye Beth. Tell your parents I said go to hell and take you with them, just for company."

I sat down at the piano. She still had everything. Her mother would understand the stubbornness and send her off to Paris or the Moon. Her father couldn't deny that black skin was beautiful. She had money and a wonderful-looking man to play with. If she stopped wanting him she could always walk away. She'd still be white.

The band was halfway into the "D. B. Blues" release before I thought, she had the money, but I had the music. She and her parents had had the power to hurt me when I was young, but look, the stuff in me lifted me up high above them. No matter how bad times became, I would always be the song struggling to be heard.

The piano keys were slippery with tears. I know, I sure as hell wasn't crying for myself.

TONI CADE BAMBARA

Madame Bai and the Taking of Stone Mountain

I

Headachy from the double feature, she tells Tram and Mustafa that she'll take a rain check on dinner. The rest of the household, after all, expect her back by ten o'clock for an English conversation lesson.

"A coffee?" Mustafa suggests. He answers himself with a groan. The only decent cup of coffee to be had in Atlanta is at the house. "Home, then," he shrugs and saunters across the street for a paper.

She views it all as a bit of footage. That is what seeing her neighborhood, the city constantly on the news has done to her perception. Figures moving out of the Rialto into the wind. Man and woman wait on curb. Third figure crossing street. Mustafa's coat, elegantly draped around his shoulders, falls in soft, straight folds, his sleeves swinging like regal robes. From the back he could be her father. All he needs, she's thinking, is a horn case and his beret set a bit more ace deuce.

"Rain check?" Tram gazes at the wintry sky perplexed, wrinkles scarring his broad-boned cheeks. She mumbles an explanation of the figure of speech, standing at the curb hipshot as her mother would. But she does not tap her foot. She can't chance it with the wind beating at her back and her still wobbly from that particular loss. It's a new way to be in the world, she's discovering—unmothered.

"Rain check." Tram nods, dipping his chin down to his arms crossed against his chest, and shoves up his quilted sleeves. He stands against the wind an untippable figure, a pyramid. She shifts her weight to match his stance.

Two young bloods, in defiance of the curfew, shoot out of Luckie Street and race between cars bouncing over the parking lot braker. She takes this in as though through a viewer, widening the lens to incorporate a blind man tapping along the pavement toward them. There is, she decides as Mustafa rejoins them, too lively a curiosity behind the dark glasses. She watches warily as the blind man stops behind the boys inspecting the *kung fu* posters outside the Rialto, his chin stuck out as if to sniff the wind, as if to catch the aromas from the restaurant farther on, as if to smell out his prey. To her list of suspects—Klan, cops, fiend in clerical cloth, little old ladies with poisoned cookies, monsters in Boy Scout gear, young kids in distress used to lure older ones to their death—she now adds blind people.

Mustafa reads the headlines. She does not correct his pronunciation. She's watching the blind man who has hooked his cane in the crook of his arm and is following the boys down Forsyth.

"Oh God," she mutters, bracing herself against her companions and ready to call out a warning. But the boys scoot down a side street toward Central City Park and the blind man continues straight ahead toward Marietta Street. She exhales.

"Yes?" Mustafa is studying her, his eyebrows arched so hard in query, his narrow forehead all but disappears under his beret.

"What?" Tram, hunched and shivery, growls.

She flops her hands around by way of explanation. Her companions exchange a look. Their landlady/friend/English instructor bears watching, the look says. Tram lifts an elbow for her to catch on. Mustafa tucks the paper away and sweeps his coat open. But he doesn't pull his sweater cuffs down. She hesitates. His wrists are deformed. They move up Forsyth, heads ducked, bodies huddled. She's grateful, wedged between the two, for the warmth and support. And grateful too that Mustafa has not offered his latest theory on the missing and murdered children of Atlanta. He doesn't usually talk freely in the streets, reserving his passionate tirades against global fascism for the late-night talk fests in the kitchens, having learned a hard lesson.

They hung him from the barracks ceiling by the wrists. The Israelis whose parents had had them baptized in '36 then sent to the convent school in Mustafa's district to save them from the Nazis. The same convent school Coptic Christians of the district sent their children to save them from the backwardness of Jordanian society. The same district whose faithful evicted the French nuns to save Islam from the infidels. Mustafa, a brash young student, had been relating the take-over of the old convent school by the Israelis, who'd converted it into an army barracks "to save the city from terrorists." Too much irony in too loud a recitation, Mustafa was hustled in for interrogation.

"Whatcha got up your sleeve, Chinaman?"

She cannot believe her ears. Just moments ago they heard that self-same line delivered in badly dubbed stereophonic sound, followed by a whistling knife spun from a tobacco-brown silk sleeve that pinned the speaker's shoulder blade to a beam in the rice shop. Courtesy of Hong Kong Eternal Flame Films, Limited.

"I'm talking to you."

Four white punks in gray, hooded sweatsuits have slipped up along-side and cut them off. They carry what looks like a three-foot grappling hook, something you'd drag the river with. She freezes.

"Whatsa matter?" the leader leers, jiggling the pole. "No speaky de English?" The Confederate flag snaps down at the sharpened end.

Mustafa slides his arm away and quickly rolls his paper into a bat. She fingers the pick comb in one pocket, her key ring in the other. Tram is in a crouch, staring hard at the belt buckle insignia of the big-bellied punk. In the East it would be the reassuring Shorinji *kempo* fig-ure, but in the West the interlocking *z*'s have been corrupted into the swastika. They're jabbing the pole straight at Tram's midsection, the flag snapping like a whip, like teeth.

"Chinky Chinaman no speaky de English." The leader nudges Big Belly with his hobnailed wristband, grinning to his cohorts. "Speak gook then," he prods Tram, no grin.

She does not see the lunge or the spin, only Tram's fists, pulled out of sleeves, striking as he lands. Two of the punks slam hard against the donut shop window. The others stumble between the two newspaper boxes near the curb. Mustafa gets off a few good whacks before his weapon buckles. The clang of the pole against cement propels her. She's leaning hard on the skinniest punk flung against the donut shop window, her pick in his gut, her keys grating across the bridge of his nose. Brothers in the shop have left the counter to rush to the window.

"The cruel and lively Thai boxer legs," Mustafa is announcing to the crowd at the glass, bouncing Big Belly off the *Wall Street Journal* box. She hears glass shatter and half expects to see the donut shop window break away in slow motion, falling. She brings her knee up into the groin as she rams both elbows down hard between collarbones.

Tram's final kick-spin ends with one foot catching the leader on the side of the head, the other foot shoving Big Belly into the street. She and Mustafa rush the two who are scrambling backward over a spatter of glass into the gutter. Brakes screech, tires squeal as the hooded ones race across toward a construction site where the Loews Grand used to be. They leap hurdles of haystacks and sandbags and disappear.

"Well, all right." A brother in seaman's cap and sweater, his body moving in sportscaster replay, retrieves Mustafa's coat and slaps it on. "Welcome to Margaret Mitchell Square," he laughs and hands her her keys.

"That was some set-to," an elderly gent with jelly on his front tooth says, hand raised high to give five but not sure who to give it to. She extends her hand. The brothers size her up—twentyish, redbone, whatcha doin' with these foreign jokers, whatcha story? She knows that look. The gent gives a stingy five as though she, skin-privileged, doesn't need it. And then the two rush back into the warmth of the shop, leaving her with a bad feeling.

Mustafa is brushing off his coat and adjusting the beret. Tram is standing back hard on his heels, the wind plastering his sweater against his chest so that eight separate segments of abdominal muscles lift like bas-relief. He looks like sculpture, she's thinking, the raised scar on his rib cage a length of packing twine, his quilted jacket a packing mat— statuary ready for shipping.

"Let's go home," Tram says squinting when his examination of the construction site shadows fails to produce a sneak attack of rock and rubble.

Once again they hook arms and, huddled, move to the bus stop, saluted by raised coffee mugs and soup spoons.

She hopes the bus will be overheated. Though her companions shelter her from the wind, she is chilled through, brittle, on the brink of cracking. They talk in French, Mustafa recounting each blow in the battle, being droll, inviting her to join in, Tram complaining that breaking bones is not why he studies the arts, not why he's come to Atlanta to await the arrival of the celebrated Madame Bai.

"With these two fingers," he explains, shoving two blunt-nailed fingers near her nose, "I can go home and help heal the wounds of war."

"The first to create the phrase 'What is up the sleeve, Chinaman?' did not meet this *kung fu* fighter," Mustafa chuckles. She ghosts a smile, clamping her jaws tight.

"I'm Vietnamese," Tram says flatly, ignoring the compliment and wagging his two fingers against Mustafa's lapels. "They go in so quick to snatch out disease, no scar tissue forms," he says, snipping off a button.

"Fine hands," Mustafa says, eyebrows arched.

Tram drops the button in Mustafa's palm and shoves his arms up his sleeves once more. "Not Chinese," he adds with a warning grunt. She closes her eyes for a moment, hoping Mustafa will not offer the usual taunts that provoke Tram into a diatribe against Bruce Lee and all things Chinese and launch the rest of the household into endless debate over whether Mao makes it a Gang of Five. Tram leans over to peer for the bus. Mustafa attempts to fit a cigarette into an ivory holder. His hands are shaking, she notices, ruining what might have been an elegant portrait: Jordanian poet, ivory tusk smoldering, coat collar blown against chin. Tobacco shreds down his coat. She looks away and thinks of the figures in Madame Tussaud's, of her mother waxy and spent.

"There will be news on the television," Mustafa says, tossing the broken butt away. "Another child found murdered."

Tram catches her from behind under the armpits before she knows she is falling. Mustafa leads her to the curb waving an oversized hanky. She dumps lunch into the gutter.

II

Madame Bai arrives on a dismal day the week of inauguration. There are two *kung fu* movies playing at the Rialto. There are always two *kung fu* movies playing at the Rialto. The bill is not in honor of the warrior-healer woman revered in *shaolins* and *ashrams* around the globe, honored by masters of the arts, quoted in the reliable texts. The Tai Chi Association silk-screens a batch of T-shirts. But the *yin-yang* figure is not bordered by the trigrams that signal the flag of Korea. Madame's presence in the city is not the occasion for the artwork. Not a line of copy is devoted to Madame's arrival in Atlanta, magnet city for every amateur sleuth, bounty hunter, right-wing provocateur, left-wing adventurer, do-gooder, soothsayer, porno-film maker, scoop journalist, crack shot, crackpot, or cool-out leader not born from the fires of struggle.

The Reagans moving in, Carter moving out, and the hostages coming home from Iran hog the news. The best of medical and psychological help is mobilized for the hostages. Less than little is available for Vietnam vets suffering from shell shock, stress, and Agent Orange genetic tampering. Gifts of things, of cash, of promising jobs await the returnees. But a minister on TV tells people not to send a dime to the parents of Atlanta: "They were getting along without our help before their children got killed. They can get along without our help now." Speeches are made about the hostages, about Carter, about the new President Reagan. Phrases like "not racially motivated" and "no connection between the children's murders and violence in other places" are fed to Atlantans. "The parents are not above suspicion," the FBI poison pen leaks. And as solidarity groups move to mount a movement, "The parents did it," say the authorities.

Yellow ribbons flap from flagpoles, trees, door knockers, wrists in the northeast section of the city. In the southwest green ribbons and black armbands are worn solemnly. The red, white, and blue is waved in *The Thunderbolt* and *Soldier of Fortune,* as articles urge good patriots to beat back the colored hordes rising to take over God's country.

Tram runs a vacuum over the dining room floor, lifting the skirt of the tablecloth pointedly to rout the household from its round-table discussion over the latest National States Rights Party rag. It features faces of African Americans superimposed on apes' bodies. Mustafa, wearing an elaborate headdress of pillowcases and carrying a hammer, goes to tack a sign of welcome on the door for Madame Bai. Panos, at the top of his lungs, sings anti-junta songs and restrings his *oud.* Jean-Paul at the ironing board composes aloud angry op-eds on the refugee situation. Maaza, the Ethiopian film maker, and Madas, the Chilean novelist, fold sheets and discuss a collaborative project built around the visiting Madame with English narration to be supplied by their landlady/English instructor/friend.

She's in the kitchen inching out saffron into the rice and grumbling. The couple from Bahia are mincing peppers and listening.

"Democratic action can be taken too far," she complains. A collective vote was made to postpone lessons—and with it, her salary—until Madame is settled in her studio school. Tram yells over complaints, singing, and hammering to review once more the self-defense system Madame Bai had designed especially for women, a sleight-of-hand technique in which one masters critically quick placement on critical organs while maintaining an ingratiating mien and nonaggressive stance. So quick a placement, it bypasses the notice of the aggressor. So deft a placement, the violent mind is discouraged.

"In days to follow," Mustafa on cue calls from the doorway, "the rogue is coughing blood and urinating red."

"But he continues to think he's tough and won," croons Panos.

"Yeh, yeh," says Maaza, bored.

"All one needs," she mumbles to the Bahians, "is seven years of anatomy and fifteen degrees in one or more arts."

They assemble in the living room to wait like schoolchildren, the house aromatic with rosemary, curry, *ouzo*, and stinking with *nuoc nam* that couldn't be voted down. She is prepared for a light-filled eminence to grace them like song, for an amazon to perform strike-rock-fist on the door, for Madame to pole-vault like dragon fire through the window, or to materialize *ninja*-style in the shadows of the fireplace. Madame Bai arrives like an ordinary person, steps in behind Tram on soft cloth shoes. Bows, sits, eats, fusses with her hair, pinning her grayed topknot with two golden carved fibulae from her grandmother's chest as she explains. With Tram as translator, Madame jokes, converses, and proves herself to be the sagelike wonder he'd promised all along. And by 9 P.M. Madame has stolen away all of her students. A collective decision is made to redistribute the usual thirty dollars a week for room, board, and English lessons into fifteen dollars for her and fifteen dollars for Madame.

"There's such a thing as taking democratic action too far," she complains for months at Madame's studio.

They begin with a roster of thirty—adepts from the Oracle of Maat, instructors from the *tai chi* group near Lonox Plaza, two medicine men and a clan mother from Seminole County in Florida, herbalists from Logos, *shiatsu* therapists and rolfers from the massage school, Fruit of the Nation from the Bankhead mosque, two ex-bodyguards from Mayor Jackson's elite corps, and her erstwhile students of English grammar and conversation. By Easter she is experiencing a bodymind-spirit connection she'd imagined possible only for disciples in the nether mountain ranges of Nepal. Attendance drops off steadily as the weather turns warm, her boarder/students returning to the fold and restoring the good health of her budget. Most of her nights are spent plowing through *Gray's Anatomy* and sticking pins in the red dots of her pressure point chart. Her days are spent working with defense teams, bat squads, and roof watchers. She's made a marshal of the citizen search team for her calm and logical way in the woods.

By late May, when the media converges on Wayne Williams' drive across the Chattahoochee Bridge, complaints are rife at the studio. No mats, no *ka-li* charts to study. No striking bags or apparatus for stretching the legs. No *shurikens,* iron fans, *nunchaku* sticks for practice. Not even an emblem to patch on a sweater, transfer to a shirt, solder on a key ring. Wholesale defection begins in June when headlines around the country announce the fiend has been nabbed. One man charged with two counts of murder, the case hanging literally by a thread, a bit of carpet fiber that changes color as the days advance but no journalist seems to notice. One man, two counts, leaving twenty-six "official" deaths still on the books and an additional thirty-eight or more not being discussed. Eight hundred police are withdrawn from the neighborhoods. One hundred state patrolmen returned to the highways. Roadblocks vanish. Helicopters disappear. Neighborhood security groups disperse. Search teams disband. Safety posters come down. Bumper stickers tatter. Amnesia drifts into the city like fog. "Let the Community Heal Itself," say the sermons. She grunts and continues training. The Medfly in California, a tsetse epidemic in Atlanta, she masters butterfly metamorphosis and requires only five hours of sleep at night.

Madame smiles and wishes the departing students well on their journey. Madame smiles and intensifies training for those that remain. At the studio, at the house, throughout the neighborhood, she is learning to be still as her mother used to counsel, to silence the relentless chatter inside in favor of the small-voiced guide she is experiencing as a warm hand steering at the base of her spine. The cadres of the neighborhood call her Alarm Clock. She keeps the block security tight and keeps watch over the children.

III

They are sitting in a sauna with a name she cannot even pronounce. Nerves frayed, mind seared, muscles screaming for release, she sits beyond endurance till she is the sauna, focused. Madame dismounts from the only cushion in the room and glides to the center of the circle and sits. She looks at Madame's back and traces the carver's journey along the golden fibulae to the points. She senses a summoning, as though her mother had set a space heater down before her, then dragged it slowly away by its cord for her to follow. Madame sending out her power, she concludes, rising to walk round into the light. She sits back on her heels before Madame, palms on her thighs, poised, ready. Madame's face turns from skin to old parchment, an ancient text she's being invited to read.

"One question, daughter." Madame says it in English after a long while. She waits, as if all her life this question has been forming. Not a favor to tax her friendship, nor a task to test commitment, but a question coming together, taking shape, her shape. Daughter. It drives deep within to jimmy open a door long closed, padlocked, boarded over. She leans against the boards, feels the grain of the wood as it swings wide to a brilliant and breezy place she's not visited since the days when she was held dear and cherished simply because she was she and not a pot to mend or dress to hem or chair leg to join.

She smiles at Madame by way of signaling, Let the test begin. Then panic gathers behind the door to shove it to. She gathers the weight of her years into a doorstop. Test. She's heard of disciples who roam the earth unkempt and crazed by a *koan* a master has posed for solution: Where does the dark go when the light is switched on? Why does the arrow never reach the mark despite the illusion of the bowman? The door pushes against her back. She heaves against it, listing. The warm hand at the power base rights her. The door swings wide again.

"Stone Mountain," Madame says finally.

Stone Mountain. A rock to prop a door with. A rock dropped into the pool of the mind. For a moment, she's in a muddle. Rocks rear up out of the ocean. She scrambles across the rock ledge braille-reading the fossils embedded deep within. Stone Mountain. It tumbles down into the waters. She surfaces, crawling across wet rubble in a quarry. Stone. From ledge to peak to cliff she follows the goat trail, shreds of fleece caught on briars and shrubs. She gathers it all within the pouch of her shirt. Mountain. Could it be a Red Army libretto in the repertoire of the Peking Opera? Someone near beats out a tattoo on a knuckle drum. Her mother used to pummel her, knuckles against both temples, when she was too impatient to be still and receptive.

She exhales and lets it flow to her. Stone Mountain. Of course. A mere thirty-minute ride out by U.S. 78. Stone monster carved tribute to the confederacy Mountain. Tourist-trap entrapment of visiting schoolchildren lured under the spell of the enslavers of Africans, killers of Amerinds. Lewdly exposed mammoth granite rock of ages the good ole boys hide in from history. Eight hundred and sixty-five feet high, the guide books say. Five hundred and eighty-three acres. The sacred grove of grand dragons, wizards, greater and lesser demons who crank out crank notes in the name of Robert E. Lee, Jefferson Davis, and Stonewall Jackson riding across the monument on horseback. She smirks.

Madame lifts her brows. Everything above Madame's eyes slides up and back, taking her hair line out of view as though someone is standing behind, tugging at mask and wig, about to reveal the woman as a person she has known always, who has been there all along, just beyond peripheral vision, guiding her through the various rites of passage.

"What is it for, Stone Mountain?" Madame asks with her face in place.

For? To rally the raunchy, Madame, to celebrate the. She clutches the ropes as the scaffolding swings against the side of the mountain scraping her knuckles. For this you summon me? You could have called the Chamber of Commerce, asked any schoolboy at the Peachtree Academy, checked the nearest public li. Balanced, she leans against the cool, damp rock and traces the sculptor's line across hind parts, boot stirrups, folds in the uniforms. For? Any almanac, encyclopedia, atlas could have told you what. Wind and rain have eroded the line of the nose here, a ripple of hair there. An ice pocket just below Stonewall's hand, holding the reins loosely, proves just deep enough to drive the chisel point in. Eighth Wonder of the World, some say, Madame, and. The hammering enlarges a hairline fissure running from the brim of one hat to the forelegs of the first horse. Five sticks of dynamite shoved in just so can bring the whole thing tumbling down. They say, Madame, that staunch materialists who favor symbols over reality can be thoroughly demoralized if. A people's army should focus on.

"Teacher." The word blows through her chest cavity, a breeze amplified in that resonating chamber. The words to be spoken already reverberating around the room, releasing the circle from the sauna. She hears the slap of flesh against wood, a signal, an army awaiting direction.

"Stone Mountain is for taking, Madame."

Amina Baraka

Soweto Song

i come from the womb of Africa
to praise my black diamond
to shine my black gold
to fight my peoples enemies
to stand on my ancestors shoulders
to dance in the hurricane of revolution
       Soweto, Soweto, Soweto,
i come with my hammer & sickle
i come with bullets for my gun
to fire on my enemies
to stab the savages that sucked my breast
to kill the beast that raped my belly
i come painted red in my peoples blood
to dance on the wind of the storm
to help sing freedom songs
       Soweto, Soweto, Soweto,
i come to carve monuments in the image of my people
i come to help hold the flag of freedom
i come to bring my tears to wash your wounds
i come to avenge slavery
i come to claim my blood ties
i come to help free my people
       Soweto, Soweto, Soweto,
i come to hide in your clouds
so i can be in the thunder
i come to work black magic
i come to burn out the eyes of imperialism
i come to chop off its head
i come to carry out my duty
i come to stand with my people
       Soweto, Soweto, Soweto. _ _ _ _ _ _ _

Haiti

black sugar-cane Lady
Papa Doc wa'nt your daddy
he bled your children
chased them from home
bathed in their blood
sucked their breath
made them eat dirt
drank their brain
plucked their hair to make mahogany gifts
Voodoo Woman
Papa Doc wa'nt your daddy
& Baby Doc ain't your son
he steals your spirit
to blind your idols
turns your roots into catholic gods
puts poison in your medicine
sticks knives in your dances
to cut your throats
dark coffee, copper girl
Creole tongue
Toussaint's child
Africa's independent baby
unearth your seeds
spit in Duvalier's mouth
dissect his body
scatter his bones
plow-up your tears
fertilize your weapons
call on on your War Gods
& take your High Ground
to Freedom

◊ 71

I *Wanna Make Freedom*

i want the chains
i want the blood
i want the bones at the bottom of the sea
i want the tribal languages
i want the cut tongues
i want the chopped off limbs
i want the dead babies
i want the broken backs
i want the runaways
i want the lynched
i want the cotton pickers
i want the hog maws & chitterlins
i want the pork chop bones
i want the chicken feathers
i want the yams & the watermelon
i want the sermons
i want the field hollers & the shouts
i want the work songs
i want the blues
i want the rebellions
i want the prisons
i want the drums
i want the banjos
i want the dances
i want the songs
i want the knives & the razor blades
i want the corn whiskey & the gin
i want the craps & the numbers
i want the big hats & the zoot suits
i want Bessie Smith's hair & Billie's flower
i want Pres's pork pie hat & Charlie Parker's sound
i want James P. Johnson & Thelonius Monk
i want Albert Ayler

i want The World Saxophone Quartet
i want the Painters
I want the Poets
i want all the liberation organizations
i want all the conferences & conventions called about freedom
i want to collect them
i want to put them in chronological order
i want to organize them
i want to assault the United States of American
& Super-power contention
so i can stand with the rest of the Third World
against Imperialism

Sortin-Out

she stood there like a Inca statue, African earrings—hanging
from her ears, watching snow fall in the yard—covering
rubbish she should have had the children clean-away
flashes of her life sat in her eyes while her head tried to figure out
how she got here in this house/half full of her
ins & outs of people, places & things
yet there was a part of her unaccounted for
like the pictures & posters from African Liberation Day,
The African Women's Conference, The International Women's
    Conference,
The Day Care Center, The Women's Organizations & what
    seemed like hundreds of
demonstrations & meetings
only Lenin stood across from her pantry with a slogan:
"Long Live The Dictatorship Of The Proletariat"
in three languages
her children would be home soon & there would be no time for
    memories
so she had to jot all of it down on this clipboard right away
& people kept asking her "why don't you write a novel,
since you have had such an interesting & colorful childhood,"

not to mention how a girl pregnant at sixteen, married at seven-
    teen
working in factories wanting to be a movie-star
or at least the mate to the Thin Man
how did she come to his big house, this famous man
& seven children
why wasn't she somewhere working or in school
why did she lose her sense of direction
was it love that led her into this long adventure
that not even she could understand. was this the end
since she never made it to her dreams
was it being born to a fifteen-year-old child
or was it being raised on Howard Street
or was it being raped at fourteen
or having to drop out of high school pregnant
it could have been knowing Franklin
and he introducing her to Charlie Parker, Monk, John Coltrane,
    Miles,
Max Roach & Clifford Brown, Billie Holiday, & Sarah Vaughn
it could have been just Be-Bop that led her
to learn all the lyrics to the songs
& dance to "Green Dolphin Street" & "Parisian Thoroughfare"
but then there was the Jazz Arts Society
& Art Williams on bass, Bill Harris on piano, Jimmie Anderson
    on sax,
& Eddie Gladden on drums & Leo Johnson who we all called
    Jack on sax
& Bob Stewart lookin hip & carryin his sax
it could have been even before that in High School
when she was a painter
& met Van Gogh, Gauguin & Picasso
i mean Rembrandt & them was hip
but they didn't swing like Matisse
though we all know they cool
maybe it was being in a loft in Newark
where lofts as such did not exist
bringing Marion Brown to Newark

more than not it was the Poet, the Monkish One
the famous one, the one she married
the one she stepped into a long complicated sojourn
to end-up standing before this window
& with this clipboard & pen.
one of their sons had a half day
he came in large eyed asking her, "is the heat on yet"
& she answered "yes it is"
he took a drink of water & went upstairs
& she kept writing on the clipboard
tryin not to forget what she was saying
more important what was on her mind
& the snow was still falling/flashes of her life
began to fade away & she wandered
back to the poster the one with Lenin,
that said, "Long Live The Dictatorship Of The Proletariat"
she remembered International Working Women's Day
was just last weekend & she had done nothing
this thought filled her full of shame
& her past seemed less significant
than her present & she did need more from herself
but then she had to sort out her life—like old clothes
they get too small or have too many holes
some things you can keep, others, you throw away
like Abbey Lincoln says, "Throooooow it away
Throoooooooooooooooooow it away
throw it away"

BRENDA CONNOR-BEY

Pretending

i'm playing word games with myself
sitting in this brightly colored
health food restaurant
whisper-like breezes pause at my ears
breathing your name but
i pretend i don't hear them today

turning to look out the window remembering
there were chords of music
beats of drums felt throughout my body
as i walked down the street
limping with cane in hand
the tap of the cane against the pavement
the beat of drums
replacing my heartbeat
the chords of music/your name
crescendoing/combining *its* tune with
the tinkle of silverware hitting
restaurant plates, but
i pretend i do not hear them today

my mind is trying to be foggy now
fighting the whining demons of,
    "ooo baby i miss you" and "yeah,
    yeah, i know you're busy and i'm busy, too,
    but damn, sugar . . ."

there's a part of me/inside
screaming siren screams of,
    "i need you and want you" and,
    "comon baby, let's make the good times roll"

trying not to recall moments spent as
we loved naked in the grasses of
connecticut fields or hear the chorus
of voices as we floated on euphoric
riverbeds of love or
even think about hours spent on
sunday afternoons
tv games and
the smell of special dinners
being cooked

instead/today i close my eyes/my ears
to all the gung ho phrases
for all the causes
turning to the needling selfish
voice inside me
moaning and crying like a baby
and old woman in pain

it says
     i need you man
     i need you to be my friend
     my lover
     my companion

you know
     the light and the dark
     the up and the down
     you be the hard and
     i'll be the soft

no longer can i pretend
a little of you is enough
no longer can there be just
songs of love for you and
songs of peace for me
the music should be mixed

smoothly and very slowly
then there'd be no reason
to pretend
then there'd be no reason
to pretend

Martha

(from oral history series)

when i came to new york
used to work at a factory on twenty-second street
i just prayed for a job
i looked up and
there was a sign in the window saying:

GIRLS NEEDED

that was my signal things would be okay
you know, my momma taught us to hand embroider
crochet, knit and do fine handwork
that's how we made money at home

i learned big machines at that factory
that sew faster than my eyes could blink
(i tell you) place your foot down
that machine shake your whole body
loose if you ain't attached too good

the man i married was big
you see me small and tiny like this
you ask if i don't mind him so big
(you know what i mean?)
but he tell me he like little women
something about bone and skin
him and strength

lord that man was crazy and had
me loving what momma said was wrong
but he could make the nighttime
music happen in the day

one day i bending over the machine
and i get a catch here between my legs
a tight grippin sensation in my back
(i tell you) i stopped that machine
went to the hospital/lost the baby
i ain't even know i carried
my boss wanted to know when
i'd be back to work
(said i worked real good!)

and that big husband of mine
the day i come in from the hospital
dragging my tired bone weary self
(you know i was weak)
he picked me up
carried me to our room
telling me we don't need no children
all we need was this ting here and
we made love so sweet sweet and he
tell me he miss me very much

but look at this ting here now
retire from job
big husband dead thirty years now
they say i can't do nothing
too old
they tell me to relax
enjoy myself
(chips)
i show them my hands
see? my blood still good
why don't you bring me some clothes
you need mending?

◊ 79

The Dancer

(*from* Thoughts of an Everyday Woman)

1.
He wanted her to be with him
didn't want to share her with the public
craving/desiring her voice/her poetic magic
pulling them into her circle
when she danced on stage

He wanted to put her in a box
inside his pocket/to pull her out when he
wanted to see her/listen to her voice
watch the mystical footwork
she brought from her ancestors

It was hard for him to understand
her reluctance to come to him
like he wanted her
    in a white dress
    with bowed head and
    white flowers in her hand
she begged him to understand that
dance was more than movements
on the ground/in the air
it was her life force
something she felt she had to do

2.
A peculiar woman he used to think
the rare kind of flower one could
find hidden in the bush of their small island
she could tell when the stars were about to

pierce the blackened sky above them
when rains were about to be unleased
from overfilled clouds
she knew the cycles of the moon
the rhythms of waves and she
knew how much gregor loved her

but she'd never surrender herself to him
she knew that too

Gregor was a strange man
she'd think while practicing in front of the
wall sized mirror in the room in the
back of her home
that was the only word she could find
to describe the powerfully built black man
she could only love him if
he'd let go of the dream
binding her to him
with rope instead of trust/understanding
Because she had to dance
she had to dance
she had to
she had
she

GWENDOLYN BROOKS

Primer for Blacks

Blackness
is a title,
is a preoccupation,
is a commitment Blacks
are to comprehend—
and in which you are
to perceive your glory.

The conscious shout
of all that is white is
"It's Great to be white."
The conscious shout
of the slack in Black is
"It's Great to be white."
Thus all that is white
has white strength and yours.

The word Black
has geographic power,
pulls everybody in:
Blacks here—
Blacks there—
Blacks wherever they may be.
And remember, you Blacks, what they told you—
remember your Education:
   "one Drop—one Drop
maketh a brand new Black."
         Oh mighty Drop.
_____And because they have given us kindly
so many more of our people

Blackness
stretches over the land.

◊ 82

Blackness—
the Black of it,
the rust-red of it,
the milk and cream of it,
the tan and yellow-tan of it,
the deep-brown middle-brown high-brown of it,
the "olive" and ochre of it—
Blackness
marches on.

The huge, the pungent object of our prime out-ride
is to Comprehend,
to salute and to Love the fact that we are Black,
which *is* our "ultimate Reality,"
which is the lone ground
from which our meaningful metamorphosis,
from which our prosperous staccato,
group or individual, can rise.

Self-shriveled Blacks.
Begin with gaunt and marvelous concession:
YOU are our costume and our fundamental bone.

    All of you—
    you COLORED ones,
    you NEGRO ones,
those of you who proudly cry
    "I'm half INDian"—
    those of you who proudly screech
    "I'VE got the blood of George WASHington in
        MY veins—"

ALL of you—
    you proper Blacks,
you half-Blacks,
you wish-I-weren't Blacks,
Niggeroes and Niggerenes.

You.

◊ 83

To Those Of My Sisters Who Kept Their Naturals

Never to look a hot comb in the teeth.

Sisters!
I love you.
Because you love you.
Because you are erect.
Because you are also bent.
In season, stern, kind.
Crisp, soft—in season.
And you withhold.
And you extend.
And you Step out.
And you go back.
And you extend again.
Your eyes, loud-soft, with crying and
    with smiles,
are older than a million years.
And they are young.
You reach, in season.
You subside, in season.
And ALL
below the richrough righttime of your hair.

You have not bought Blondine.
You have not hailed the hot-comb recently.
You never worshiped Marilyn Monroe.
You say: Farrah's hair is hers.
You have not wanted to be white.
Nor have you testified to adoration of that
    state
with the advertisement of imitation
(*never* successful because the hot-comb is laughing too.)

But oh the rough dark Other music!
the Real,
the Right.
The natural Respect of Self and Seal!
      Sisters!
Your hair is Celebration in the world!

Requiem Before Revival

We still need the essential Black statement of defense and definition. Of course, we are happiest when that statement is not dulled by
assimilationist urges, secret or overt. However, there is in "the souls of
Black Folk"—even when inarticulate and crippled—a yearning toward
Black validation.

To be Black is rich, is subtle, is nourishing and a nutrient in the universe. What could be nourishing about aiming against your nature?

I give whites big credit. They have never tried to be anything but
what they are. They have been and will be everlastingly proud proud
proud to be white. It has never occurred to them that there has been or
ever will be ANYthing better than, nor one zillionth as good as, being
white. They have an overwhelming belief in their validity. Not in their
"virtue," for they are shrewdly capable of a very cold view of *that*. But
their validity they salute with an amazing innocence—yes, a genuine
innocence, the brass of which befuddles most of the rest of us in the
world because we have allowed ourselves to be hypnotized by its shine.

In the throat of the Town Crier throbs the Power.

If you yell long enough and shrilly enough "I'M GREAT!," ultimately you will convince your listeners. Or you will be thrown into the
insane asylum. The scant Caucasian race has escaped the insane asylum and has gone on to *virtually* unquestioned "glory"—has achieved
virtually unchallenged italics.

Swarms of Blacks have not understood the mechanics of the pro-
ceeding, and they trot along to the rear of Pied Piper whites, their
strange gazes fixed on, and worshiping, each switch of the white rear,
their mesmerized mentalities fervently and firmly convinced that there

is nothing better than quaking in that tail's wake. They do not see that the secret of Supremacy success is—you just go ahead and impress yourself on the world whether the world wants you or not. They have not seen some Announcements register just *because* they are iterated and iterated and iterated—the oppressed consciousness finally sinking back and accepting the burden of relentless assault. Though eager to imitate any other property of the white compulsion, much of the Black swarm has refused to imitate the efficacy of Iteration; and the fruit of that Black refusal is chaos, is vertigo, is self-swallow, or self-shrivel and decline.

I continue my old optimism. In spite of all the disappointment and disillusionment and befuddlement out there, I go on believing that the Weak among us will, finally, perceive the impressiveness of our numbers, perceive the quality and legitimacy of our essence, and take sufficient, indicated steps toward definition, clarification.

LUCILLE CLIFTON

for her

(if our grandchild be a girl)

> i wish for her fantastic hands,
> twelve spiky fingers, symbol
> of our tribe. she can do wonders
> with them.
> she can turn personal abracadabra
> remembered through dahomean women born
> wearing extravagant gloves.

my dream about being white

> hey music and
> me
> only white,
> hair a flutter of
> fall leaves
> circling my perfect
> line of a nose,
> no lips,
> no behind, hey
> white me and
> i'm wearing
> white history but
> there's no future in
> those clothes so
> i take them off and
> wake up
> dancing.

morning mirror

my mother her sad eyes worn as bark
faces me in the mirror. my mother
whose only sin was dying, whose only
enemy was time, frowns in the glass.
once again she has surprised me
in an echo of her life but my mother
refuses to be reflected. thelma
whose only strength was love, she
warns away the glint of likeness, she
loosens the woman in the mirror so
thelma lucille can start to wash.

JAYNE CORTEZ

Rape

What was Inez supposed to do for
the man who declared war on her body
the man who carved a combat zone between her breasts
Was she supposed to lick crabs from his hairy ass
kiss every pimple on his butt
blow hot breath on his big toe
draw back the corners of her vagina and
hee haw like a Calif. burro

This being war time for Inez
she stood facing the knife
the insults and
her own smell drying on the penis of
the man who raped her

She stood with a rifle in her hand
doing what a defense department will do in times of war
And when the man started grunting and panting and wobbling
    forward like
a giant hog
She pumped lead into his three hundred pounds of shaking flesh
Sent it flying to the virgin of Guadeloupe
then celebrated day of the dead rapist punk
and just what the fuck else was she supposed to do?

And what was Joanne supposed to do for
the man who declared war on her life
Was she supposed to tongue his encrusted toilet stool lips
suck the numbers off of his tin badge
choke on his clap trap balls
squeeze on his nub of rotten maggots and
sing god bless america thank you for fucking my life away

◇ 89

This being wartime for Joanne
she did what a defense department will do in times of war
and when the piss drinking   shit sniffing guard said
I'm gonna make you wish you were dead black bitch come here
Joanne came down with an ice pick in
the swat freak mother fucker's chest
yes in the fat neck of that racist policeman
Joanne did the dance of the ice picks and once again
from coast to coast
house to house
we celebrated day of the dead rapist punk
and just what the fuck else were we supposed to do

There It Is

My friend
they don't care
if you're an individualist
a leftist   a rightist
a shithead or a snake
They will try to exploit you
absorb you   confine you
disconnect you   isolate you
or kill you

And you will disappear into your own rage
into your own insanity
into your own poverty
into a word a phrase a slogan a cartoon
and then ashes

The ruling class will tell you that
there is no ruling class
as they organize their liberal supporters into
white supremist lynch mobs
organize their children into
ku klux klan gangs

◊ 90

organize their children into
killer cops
organize their propaganda into
a device to ossify us with angel dust
pre-occupy us with western symbols in
african hair styles
inoculate us with hate
institutionalize us with ignorance
hypnotize us with a monotonous sound designed
to make us evade reality and stomp our lives away
And we are programmed to self destruct
to fragment
to get buried under covert intelligence operations of
unintelligent committees impulsed toward death
And there it is
The enemies polishing their penises between
oil wells at the pentagon
the bulldozers leaping into demolition dances
the old folks dying of starvation
the informers wearing out shoes looking for crumbs
the life blood of the earth almost dead in
the greedy mouth of imperialism
And my friend
they don't care
if you're an individualist
a leftist   a rightist
a shithead or a snake

They will spray you with
a virus of legionnaires disease
fill your nostrils with
the swine flu of their arrogance
stuff your body into a tampon of
toxic shock syndrome
try to pump all the resources of the world
into their own veins
and fly off into the wild blue yonder to
pollute another planet

And if we don't fight
if we don't resist
if we don't organize and unify and
get the power to control our own lives
Then we will wear
the exaggerated look of captivity
the stylized look of submission
the bizarre look of suicide
the dehumanized look of fear
and the decomposed look of repression
forever and ever and ever
And there it is

You Know

(For the people who speak the you know language)

You know
   I sure would like to write a blues
you know
   a nice long blues
you know
a good feeling piece to my writing hand
you know
   my hand that can bring two pieces of life
   together in your ear
you know
   one drop of blues   turning a paper clip
   into three wings and a bone into a revolt
you know
   a blues passing up the stereotype symbols
you know
   go into the dark meat of a crocodile
   and pinpoint the process

you know
   into a solo a hundred times
   like the first line of Aretha Franklin
you know
   like Big Mama Thornton
you know
   i sure would like to write a blues
you know
   if i could write me a blues
you know
   a blues that you could all feel at the same time
   on the same level like a Joe Louis punch
you know
   a punch that could break a computer
   into an event like Guinea Bissau
you know
   if i could write me a blues
you know
   a nice long blues
you know
   an up to the minute blues
you know
   a smack dab in the middle of depression blues
you know
   a blues without incidental music
you know
   without spending time being incidental
you know
   if i could write a blues
you know
   a blues without the popular use of the word love
you know
   without running love love love in the ground
you know
   a serious blues
you know
   a significant blues

◊ 93

        you know
            an unsubmissive blues
        you know
            a just because we exist blues
        you know
            a blues
        you know
            a terrible blues about the terrible terrible need
            i have to write the blues
        you know
            if i could write a nice long blues
        you know
            a nice long blues
        you know
            it sure would feel good to my writing hand
        you know
            you know
        you know

Big Fine Woman From Ruleville

(For Fannie Lou Hamer)

        How to weave your web of medicinal flesh into words
        cut the sutures to your circumcised name
        make your deformed leg a symbol of resistance
        Big fine woman from Ruleville
        great time keeper
        and dangerous worker
        I use this hour in my life
        to eat from your spirit
        dance from mouth to mouth with your holler
        hold fingers together in remembrance of your sacrifices
        And I have chosen to wear your riverstone eyes splashed
        with Mississippi blood

    ◊ 94

and your sharecropper shoes braided with your powerful stomp
and now in your riot-stick neck smeared in charcoal burns
and in your sick and tired of being sick and tired look
and in your bones that exhausted the god of whiteness in Sun
     Flower county
I will push forward your precious gift of revolutionary courage
Thanks to the southern knife with terracotta teeth
magnificent ancestor
warrior friend
most beautiful sister
I kiss the mud of this moment

For the Brave Young Students in Soweto

Soweto
when i hear your name
I think about you
like the fifth ward in Houston Texas
one roof of crushed oil drums on the other
two black hunters in buckets of blood
walking into the fire of Sharpeville
into the sweat and stink of gold mines
into your childrens eyes suffering from malnutrition
while pellets of uranium are loaded onto boats
headed for France for Israel for Japan
away from the river so full of skulls
and Robben Island so swollen with warriors
and the townships that used to overflow
with such apathy and dreams
and i think about the old mau mau
grieving in beer halls
and the corrupt black leaders
singing into police whistles
and i think about the assembly line of dead "Hottentots"
and the jugular veins of Allende

◊ 95

and once again how the coffin is divided into dry ink
how the factory moves like a white cane
like a volley of bullets in the head of Lumumba
and death is a death-life held together by shacks
by widows who cry with their nipples pulled out
by men who shake with electrodes on the tongue
and Soweto
when i hear your name and look at you on the reservation
a Xhosa
in the humid wrinkles of Shreveport Louisiana
walking down fannin street
into the bottom hole in the wall of endurance
i smell the odor of our lives together made of tar paper
the memories opening like stomachs in saw mills
the faces growing old in cigarette burns
and i think about the sacrifices made in Capetown
the sisters being mauled by police dogs
while the minister of justice rides
the tall ship of torture
down the hudson river in New York
while vigilantes under zulu mask
strike through the heartland like robots
in military boots with hatchets made of apartheid lips
and Soweto
when i look at this ugliness
and see once again how we're divided and
forced into fighting each other
over a funky job in the sewers of Johannesburg
divided into labor camps
fighting over damaged meat and stale bread in Harlem
divided into factions fighting to keep from fighting
the ferocious men who are shooting
into the heads of our small children

When i look at this ugliness
and think about the Native Americans pushed
into the famine of tribal reserves
think about the concentration camps full of sad Palestinians

◊ 96

and the slave quarters still existing in Miami
the diamond factories still operating in Amsterdam in Belgium
the gold market still functioning on wall street
and the scar tissues around our necks
swelling with tumors of dead leaves
our bodies exploding like whiskey bottles
as the land shrinks into the bones of ancestor "Bushmen"
and i tell you Soweto
when i see you stand up in the middle of all this
stand up to the exotic white racists
in their armored churches
stand up to these landstealers, infant killers, rapists and rats
to see you stand among the pangas the stones
the war clubs the armadillos dying along this roadside
to see you stand with the ocean the desert
the birthright of red cliffs
to see you stand with your brave young warriors
courageous and strong hearted
looking so confident in battle marks coated
in grief and gunmetal tears
to see you stand up to this epidemic of expansion
and flame passbooks into ashes
fling stones into the mouths of computers
to see you stand on the national bank of america
like monumental sculpture made of stained bullets
to see you stand empty handed
your shoulders open to the world
each day young blood falling on the earth
to see you stand in the armed struggle
next to Mozambique, Angola, Namibia, Zimbabwe
Soweto i tell you Soweto
when i see you standing up like this
i think about all the forces in the world
confronted by the terrifying rhythms of young students
by their sacrifices
and the revelation that it won't be long now
before everything
in this world changes

◊ 97

ALEXIS DE VEAUX

...And Then She Said

(for Sara)

question authority.

question:

why should trees or rivers or even
stars
be mega-bombed out of orbit

why should you: or me
or my neighbors across the alley
or the kittens
or the flatbush avenue
traffic
disintegrate

why should children
explode

answer:

the government lies.
these are government words:
acceptable casualties
pre-emptive strike
civil defense
limited nuclear war
survivors
what to do (if)

"come to the rally" I urge my mother "if there's a nuclear war, black
or white, we'll all be killed."

"and that ain't the half of it" she says "if you open your mouth to one
a these teenagers on the bus smoking that shit you liable to end up
with a knife in your gut baby. no respect for your life or nobody else's.
as far as people today care."

'think about this" I say. "we can blow up the world."

"uh huh. you want something to eat?"

> the government lies to the people.
> this is too painful to believe.
> tomorrow may never come.
> this has nothing to do with God.
>
> question authority.
>
> *what kind of fucking world*
> *are we living in*

French Doors: A Vignette

She smelled him right away: the woodsy twang of cologne he wore: the
cigars: his biceps his intentions: Basin's hands was like a woman when
he moved her from Thelma's bed: to the couch in the living room
combination dining room down the hall:

Momma?
Whatchu want baby?
Ice cream.
In the mornin. With some pancakes. I promise.

Even though he was big he was soft carrying Pepper to the faded pais-
ley sofa Thelma was still paying $17.50 a week for. Even though he
was big he was soft. On tiptoes and soft shoe: he carried her. Bundled
into herself neat loose fabric in the dark. How his hands: specific: like a
woman's: rubbed her down with a checkered blanket. And she lay

◊ 99

there. Yards and yards of her self: and the murmur of clothes dropping in Thelma's bedroom: where the magnolia candle she bought burned her allowance away. Listened to him: feel his way along the walls back to Thelma and the dark: of his heat in the railroad flat familiar as the tearing of his zipper. And Thelma: home from the Club/ with him. The once a month date so: she: belly danced in the candlelight.

And closed the French doors. But it was the smell of the house. Certain as a river current which pulled Pepper up the hall: swimming upstream up: against the dark smell of their sex: and stood her: in white cotton draws: at the doorway:

Thelma?
Whatchu want now?
You okay?
Yeah. Go on back to bed.

Stood there: a fertility doll around her mother's neck. With nipples hardly buds on her bare chest: skinny and black: two horns of thick braid perched above her head shimmered: as antennae do: listening: sleep stuck in her eyes: the wood floor was cold: she/ goosebumps all over. And the sixteen rectangular glass panes of the double French door painted apricot shone metallic in the darkened apartment. The child pressed herself against one of them.

Pepper? Pepper?
You sure?   He whispered.
Positive.   Thelma said Pepper?

Stood there: slapped tight against the facets of glass doorknobs and the night latch only the men: only the men closed: unsure/ of their hunger. Unsure of Thelma: with the little blind as a bat girl stiff as a statue: outside her bedroom door.

◊ 100

ALEXIS DE VEAUX

The Woman Who Lives in the Botanical Gardens

is a man. who. sleeping on a hill and a bench among the Chinese maple trees lives there. sleeping in her petticoats of ackee leaf and banana leaf though neither grows in this city: O see: how tall she is the tallest lean: O see: the delicate spread of her branch a thickly muscled arm. how it sways there (quiet) how it dreams of plaintain and rice and the Black Star Line:

O Jah

and the hairless face/the primitive hollow of cheeks taut: with rebellion. black with the dust of upturned earth and the plantings of memory.

O Jah see
O Jah

see: the barest of back/like an island and the hair the long: dangling mats of hair under armpits; the perfumed hair laden with anarchy: hangs from the pit of the arm dangling over the bench.

THE WOMAN WHO LIVES IN THE BOTANICAL GAR-DENS wears underneath her banana ackee leaf petticoat the pants of three generations: her grandfather's her father's: her own. THE WOMAN WHO never comes outside the gates never comes outside the rags around her pine bark hair; the reams of rage: O see, O Jah:

THE WOMAN WHO LIVES IN THE BOTANICAL GAR-DENS/ THE WOMAN WHO LIVES IN THE BOTANICAL GARDENS: is named South Africa. See there how she holds the m-16: how she holds the Gardens hostage. and the bullets in her earlobes: bullets at her breasts: the red green and gold rage. And the necklace of fallopian tube and the egg of children and the bits of blood of hair in the tumors of the homeland: O Jah: O Jah: see her how she: stalks the gates. O Jah/ THE WOMAN WHO THE WOMAN WHO

◊ 101

LIVES: on the squirrels and stray cats of the Garden LIVES. like a guard dog. gums bared. teeth pointed: she snap at the gate:

THERE WILL BE NO   VISITORS
AT THE GARDEN TODAY
OR TOMORROW NEITHER
IN FACT
DON'T COME NO CLOSER:
I REALLY DO MEAN TO SHOOT UP THE MUSEUM
I REALLY DO MEAN TO SHOOT UP THE PARKWAY
I REALLY DO MEAN TO SHOOT UP THE HELICOPTER
SO: DON'T COME NO CLOSER

WHO IS ME??
THIS IS SOUTH AFRICA SPEAKING
BLACK SOUTH AFRICA   BLACK
SOUTH AFRICA
AND I AM TAKING OVAH THIS SHIT
I AM TAKING OVAH.

Y. W. Easton

The Welcome

I saw a screamer this morning
crossin' Broad Street as I
was on my way to Chock Full O'Nuts.
Well, one has crossed the river
                    I thought
                as I bought
a cup of steamin' hot coffee.
                Just like me,
I continued to muse,
New York cost just too much dues.
Even the crazies can't stay
            an' do their street livin'
Penn Station is always packed
an' prowlin' the streets
makes 'em even more nerveracked.
Subway gratin's make a dangerous bed
'cause you just might wake up dead.
Hummpt, I say to myself,
their day is a mighty long night.
Pressure, tension, stress keeps us all uptight.
So they come ascreamin' into the light
of another long day/night.

Some days I want to join them . . .
those times I find it hard to comprehend
the twists and turns my life takes in.
But he makes me feel right at home
the screamer does . . .
He's the only one I've seen
altho' Newark has its own brand of fiend.
Late at night
        when I miss the sight
            of Broadway at Eighty-first,

I recall the screamers at their worst
when they give a burst
to greet the day along Old Broadway;
so thanks for the welcome, brother
    and I hope
        I won't hear another
screamer on Broad Street
'Cause then I'll know
the migration has truly begun
another screamer has gone and swum
             the Hud/son.

Mari Evans

I Am A Black Woman

I am a black woman
the music of my song
some sweet arpeggio of tears
is written in a minor key
and I
can be heard humming in the night
Can be heard
                    humming
in the night

I saw my mate leap screaming to the sea
and I/with these hands/cupped the lifebreath
from my issue in the canebrake
I lost Nat's swinging body in a rain of tears
and heard my son scream all the way from Anzio
for Peace he never knew. . . . I
learned Da Nang and Pork Chop Hill
in anguish
Now my nostrils know the gas
and these trigger tire/d fingers
seek the softness in my warrior's beard

I
am a black woman
tall as a cypress
strong
beyond all definition still
defying place
and time
and circumstance
    assailed
        impervious
            indestructible

◊ 105

Look
   on me and be
renewed

Where Have You Gone

Where have you gone

with your confident
walk with
your crooked smile

why did you leave
me
when you took your
laughter
and departed

are you aware that
with you
went the sun
all light
and what few stars
there were?

where have you gone
with your confident
walk your
crooked smile the
rent money
in one pocket and
my heart
in another . . .

◊ 106

MARI EVANS

Speak the Truth to the People

Speak the truth to the people
Talk sense to the people
Free them with reason
Free them with honesty
Free the people with Love and Courage and Care for their Being
Spare them the fantasy
Fantasy enslaves
A slave is enslaved
Can be enslaved by unwisdom
Can be enslaved by black unwisdom
Can be re-enslaved while in flight from the enemy
Can be enslaved by his brother whom he loves
His brother whom he trusts
His brother with the loud voice
And the unwisdom
Speak the truth to the people
It is not necessary to green the heart
Only to identify the enemy
It is not necessary to blow the mind
Only to free the mind
To identify the enemy is to free the mind
A free mind has no need to scream
A free mind is ready for other things

To BUILD black schools
To BUILD black children
To BUILD black minds
To BUILD black love
To BUILD black impregnability
To BUILD a strong black nation
To BUILD.

◊ 107

Speak the truth to the people.
Spare them the opium of devil-hate.
They need no trips on honky-chants.
Move them instead to a BLACK ONENESS.
A black strength which will defend its own
Needing no cacophony of screams for activation.
A black strength which attacks the laws
exposes the lies disassembles the structure
and ravages the very foundation of evil.

Speak the truth to the people
To identify the enemy is to free the mind
Free the mind of the people
Speak to the mind of the people
Speak Truth.

early in the mornin

early in the mornin
j w brown
whippin' his woman
knockin' her around
said "answer my question
if you please"
(how she goin' to answer
on her knees
groanin' "Buddy, Buddy!
wake up and go
get L C and Mar'gret—he's
hurtin' me so . . .")

Buddy went flyin'
down the stairs in
brown pants over his

underwear but
L C and Margaret wouldn't stir
said: "Buddy we sympathize
with her . . . but from what you say
far as we can see
if she'd answer his question
he'd let her be"

she never did answer
(far as we could hear)
but the sight of that child
in his underwear his
head bent down
shoes untied and all
comin' back alone
down the empty Mall
was sad.
More than I could bear.
Makes you wonder if
anybody cares
anywhere

Lois Elaine Griffith

Prince Harlem

"I'm a rapper
a stoned out trapper.
I've snapped with the best
put my tongue to the test.
I got the moves to cure the blues.
I'm known as Prince on the street
didn't get that way by shuffling my feet
to some hip hop beat.
Let me tell you, baby, life ain't nothing but a cloud
so turn your ass to the sun and take a bow.
I know my way about town
like the back of my hand
up down all around
the slick and the swells
the cool fools
jaded faded ladies with sparkling jewels
and those hard working men with their worn out tools
the hustlers, the whores
and bright eyed kids who want to see it all and more
the old block watchers
the middle aged crotch watchers
even a rich lonely woman
compartmentalized in her apartment cage
who'll pay just for watering her plants
and watching you dance and dance.
I dance for myself.
I go where the moon smiles
and guard my turf keeping a low profile.
Got the wind in my shoes
got the moves to cure blues
call me Prince when you see me on the street
I didn't get that way by shuffling on my feet."

The sweatband on the white straw Panama hat was stained with perspiration. The color changed completely from red to maroon. White sneakers, white socks. Three pieces of dark green polyester on skin. A hand carved walking stick. He stood at the beginning of Avenue A, collecting his thoughts.

The open toed high heeled fucker sticks gave him gyrating ass as it passed, but no sign of recognition came from the face. The red mouth, lips pursed, was ready to be sharp. He felt the need to stop this color in motion.

> "Hey, baby, what's happening?
> I been seeing you pass this way
> watch the wind caress your hips as they sway.
> You look so serious.
> Your perfume makes me delirious.
> Now don't bite off my head . . ."

He held his hand as if shielding his balls when she looked him dead in the eye.

> "What's your name, baby?
> I'm the Prince
> and you're a prize
> that I might like
> some springtime night
> to take a bite of."

She hesitated, not wanting to be cursed for going nameless, but then . . .
"I'm in a hurry. I have to meet someone," she said, walking on.

> "Baby, someday we'll meet
> in the raw of the high noon
> and make talking some sweet gift to the wind.
> Never mind if the sun seems black
> it's still shining and that's a fact.
> Even though the rain falls upwards on your feet
> I'll teach you to talk it backwards to the beat.
> The other way around

◊ 111

when you heard the sound
your swell head found its way from the bathroom to the moon
in the raw of the high noon."

And he laughed.

She stopped and gave him her full faced attention. The red lips moved. "I don't think we'll meet again because I don't have time for games."

"Baby, I ain't no game." She walked away. "You trying to make me a fool, bitch? You think I got time to waste, bitch?" Her perfume fast faded in the air.

"I ain't even gonna let you lick my stick.
You think you're on some transcontinental flight
you think you're moving on to some greater height?
Life ain't nothing but a cloud
got to go with the flow
stay above the crowd.
The pickings are slim.
Girl, it ain't often you meet real men."

On a street filled with garbage he was another piece of discarded debris. The soles of his white sneakers were worn thin from having stood in one place too long. After a while one city street corner looks like another. Trace the cracks from sidewalk to sewer where dreamers' blood has etched a path, seeking return to the river of promise.

Youth becomes soiled on the streets when it's overexposed. Days pass without clean clothes. Rest is a vanishing illusion to real hunters who need shelter only from rain and winter. Solitary creepers are madmen with songs in their heads they learned from sleeping with roaches. Adventure becomes routine. There is an addiction to breathing. Bars, park benches, greasy spoons, the gleam of pinball machines in playground arcades are a preoccupation for people with time to kill. He was a man on the move, on the verge of making that leap to the high life. People there had time to kill but it wasn't desperate time. He watched the sky change evening to night. These were the best hours, when deals were made and chicks got laid.

This forced relocation wasn't such a bad thing after all. He'd made fifty bills today just looking out for a couple of guys who took off an apartment on Seventh Street. The original stakeout man was picked up the night before, selling his ass to an undercover John. Downtown was full of possibilities and he was Prince Harlem, after all. Royalty is royalty anywhere, recognizable even to some white people. Especially women. Women of any color always appreciated him. He did not attribute it to anything as superficial as appearance, but to the mastery of language. He understood how stimulating conversation provokes romance.

It was a cool, breezy night. Spring rain leaves even cheap polyester full of wrinkles. Dave's All Night Eatery on Canal Street was a place to dry off. The woman with the blue streaks in her hair, sitting next to him at the counter, gave him some plastic chains to wear around his neck so he could hear his head move. Here was a bed for the night. He invested in two cups of coffee.

"I know you from somewhere.
You want to meet the street
cop to the beat.
You want to tear yourself apart
open up your heart
just so you can feel
something that's real.
I could tell you about life
about all the struggle and strife
a heart cut by a fast knife
about sugar coated days
about blue songs in May
for shady ladies with captivating ways.
You're not one of those
but you like the manifestation of that sensation.
Don't I know you from somewhere?"

"You got some exclusive right to feel hurt, black man?" She was a tired faced white woman. Her makeup hid how she really looked. It didn't move with her skin.

He took her home and made love to her. It was the least he could do. When he woke up in the light of an airy loft space on Broome

Street, he was angry with himself. The woman had the face of a dog. There was a twenty dollar bill in her purse. He felt he was entitled to it. He didn't want to wake her. It was enough to get him through the day. He wanted a shower so he could face the streets with a fresh look. That should have been the first thing done when he got inside the dog's loft, but she was too horny a bitch to wait and deal with amenities. There'd be other opportunities. He made his own chances. He was not a fool who called luck an excuse for fate.

He was stomping downtown. New York was full of lonely neurotic women of every shape and color, eager for a man like him. He could probably live for years and find a new home every night. Risk was involved: he might get stuck with a bum. Styles these days were raw all over, no indication of financial means.

He never spoke his birth name. He was Prince Harlem, artist, dancer, skater, poetic fashion designing actor in need of a benefactor or at least an agent. He needed a ghost writer to make something of his life story so he could sell this best selling autobiography to Hollywood and make a million dollars in one shot.

The day was too beautiful to be dealing with dogs. He walked to the river so he could think about things. Maybe he could turn over that twenty and make it forty, or maybe he should just chill out and wait for night action. He sat on a bench in Battery Park and watched a tug pulling a garbage barge. A small fast motorboat bounced on the surface of the water. One of these days he'd get himself a boat. He didn't want to put too much energy into that thought, considering right now he didn't even have a place to live.

He was going to swear off black women from now on. That Estelle had no right to treat him the way she did the other night. Locking him out. Throwing his camel's hair coat and genuine hand carved walking stick out the window. He'd spent the best part of two weeks in Tompkins Square Park, carving that cane. The handle got busted in the fall. It was no longer the handsome thing he'd made, but he couldn't leave it there on the street with the coat that landed in a puddle of gasolined water. What a waste. He probably could have sold the coat. He sat watching the river, watching two men walking along. One of them wore a loud red and blue Hawaiian shirt under wide lapelled pinstripes. He could have sold the coat to this guy. It looked like his style.

What did that Estelle know anyway. Even with two years of college she still had to go on welfare with that kid of hers. He didn't like that kid. It was better this way. He wouldn't go back to her roach motel. Asylums are places for people with no place else to go. He'd been discharged a long time ago. So he had no history? How did she think he got to be the way he was? Many called, few chosen. It's a spiraled road that leads to the lunatic fringe. There was a state certified card in his pocket to prove it. He sat laughing and watching the river. How long does it take to make history?

He would chill out for now. Tonight would bring on all the action he would need. He stretched out his long legs and settled the Panama hat down over his eyes. This was the life. If there were no tomorrows, the warmth of this spring sunshine would be happiness enough. Bad thoughts tend to soften the brain, drive you insane. He walked up to Canal Street, then across to West Broadway. This was the main strip through Soho. Maybe he could find someone with an afterhours club and convince them to hire him as a D.J. He knew all the hit tunes by name. No. He didn't want to spend eight hours a night penned up in a D.J. booth. You never get to meet people that way. How the hell was he supposed to make his contacts and sell his life story, his history, to the movies? He was Prince Harlem and right now he was making a royal visit to the lower provinces, increasing his knowledge of foreign ways. How far away is the dark that reveals the stars? How many steps are there between day and night?

He stood on the corner of Sixth Avenue and Third Street watching the players on the asphalt basketball court. Run you maggots, run, he laughed. The world was a bigger place than any square marked off in yellow lines could define. There were other ways to sweat. A young woman in a short white skirt stopped her skating to check out the men playing ball. He sniffed gold in the wheels.

> "You into skate shock
> not games of beat the clock.
> Young and free
> you make the time to be all you can be.
> You into skate shock
> and everything that rolls and rocks.

◊ 115

You got the heat to burn
the body to turn the lock on any man's screws.
Can I be in skate shock with you?
You look like you got something on the cap
life don't give no handouts to those who nap.
Can you read and write?
How fast can you type?
You could be my agent.
Don't give me a look like you just had an accident.
Listen, this is no con.
You want to write my life story, baby?
It's more far out than you could get off being crazy."

She laughed. "How'd you learn to rhyme on time?"

"Your head and your mouth go at the same pace
spit out the words into outer space
let it fly, let it go fast
lay back, relax and have a blast.
Life ain't nothing but a cloud
sail with the wind, stay above the crowd."

She shook her California curls as if testing the vibrations in the air.
"You're right on, man. Go with the flow, got to be free." Turning
away from the games in play she skated towards the park, almost
stumbling over a big crack in the sidewalk halfway down the block.

"Who's a clown!
Go ahead bitch, break your ass, fall down!"

She didn't respond to his voice. Nets are for fish who want to be
caught. He followed her and watched her talking with a Rasta man
near the fountain. Where did that nappy headed nigger get off rapping
to such a cute little booty. He laughed to himself. He didn't know her
and he was jealous. It was a business transaction anyway. Everybody
knew how good Jamaican *ganja* was these days. If he had a stake, he'd
be out there hustling too.

"Ness got finesse. Loose joints, good bags here, man."

Ness was a black man with light brown eyes that peered out from
under the fringe of his dreadlocks.

"Ness got the best here for less."

"I'll get a dime, bro."

He figured with this investment, along with a bottle of oregano from the deli, he could roll some joints and sell them loose. The oldest scam on the street, if the white papers didn't make a trail back to your feet. Thirty, maybe forty dollars while he waited for dark. No sense wasting time daydreaming. He sat under a tree near the bathrooms in Washington Square Park. It took about an hour to roll up his stake. He'd be out of everyone's way before they'd finger the dude pulling cheap tricks. He had to laugh to himself as he sold six for five to a frail looking scholarly type. That kind gets high on cigarettes and says it's groovy stuff.

The man with the traveling piano was playing a jazz sonata under the arch. White echo tunnel of music called out to the dark.

"This is shit, man. You sold me shit. I look like some kind of fool to you, man? Don't you walk away from me. I'm talking to you, polyester Jackson. You burned me. I don't like being burned."

The young man stood with bare arms in the chill of late afternoon. His eyes were wide open. A spark might catch his reeking breath on fire. He was ready to break the back of anyone who said he staggered.

"Why don't you chill out, bro, and get your hand out of my face before I start taking you seriously."

"You better take me serious. I don't like being burned."

Echo tunnel of music called to the drum for heartbeat at dusk. Nocturne for traveling piano and conga drums. There was a brown skinned girl in a red skirt dancing with a baby. The sun was setting on the skyline.

Prince Harlem searched the pockets of his suit jacket. He needed the mirror surfaced sunglasses to reflect the night lights in the park that appeared as floating white balloons.

"Look, Romeo . . ." The young man standing in front of him wore a T-shirt that was tight fitting over a muscular torso tensed and strained. LOVER ROMEO was written across the chest in big white letters.

"Look, Romeo, get out of my face before I take this knife I got here in my pocket and put it to your throat." Behind the glasses Prince Harlem could watch the man and catch the night embracing the skyline. Evening came on in red.

"I ain't finished with you yet, black boy. I ain't gonna eat your shit."

◊ 117

Romeo put his hand on the arm of the polyester suit that tried to walk away.

> "The name is Prince Harlem.
> You better keep them hands to yourself, white boy.
> I'm a man of the street
> don't take to jive ass turkeys
> trying to cop a plea or stop my beat.
> Now what you choose to eat
> is your own special treat."

He'd never needed to carry a weapon. His sharp edged tongue had cut him out of tighter spots than this. Straitjackets were light action. The time that crazy jealous Wilson came looking for him with his boy and a piece. You've got to make it over the first heat. He'd had to run it down to them about dope and women.

> You find what makes them high
> you cross your fingers and tell them lies.
> All in all the price you pay for a woman's love
> ain't worth the time it took
> to get the broad to spread her legs and play.

Yeah, he'd been fast on the case, pointed out a few things about that faithless hussy, a doper too. Wilson should have known. The poor old guy never really wanted to use the gun. It turned out to be a twist of friendly persuasion.

"Don't give me no smart assed talk, nigger, 'cause you ain't shit and I'm ready to cream you here and now."

Prince Harlem had to remove his mirrored glasses to see if the crazy light shining in the boy's eyes was the real thing. It matched the steely glint of the switchblade the kid had flicked open and was now holding in his hand.

In the business of doing business, push turned to shove in an effort to knock the knife out of a young man's hand. The blade entered the throat, stopped the spit that held the words to move clouds across one more heart in the dark of the park.

Next day the local media were full of a story about mental cases given out-patient status, living in welfare hotels, allowed to roam the city streets unchecked. Victims and perpetrators of senseless violence. One such, Bernard Williams, was slain in Washington Square Park. Police suspected he was involved in a racially motivated incident, precipitated by one Romeo Valentino, who objected to the niggers' playing incendiary music on their drums. Such instruments were, henceforth, prohibited in the park, and a nine o'clock curfew was to be strictly enforced.

Nikki Grimes

Fragments: Mousetrap

i crawl to his door
peek through dilating iris
i blink
unaccustomed darkness
watch out for hazards
say the eyes
there are few comers
those that enter
trip
i feel my way
first one question,
then another
sometimes the answers come
a neatly rigged bucket
image full
words spill atop my head
sometimes, a slickness underfoot
i slide lay sprawled
ache from the suddenness
once, like dust swilled in sunbeam
i grab, grasp grope for
then sigh
often, they don't come at all
the answers
i pace the halls of his thought
find them meticulously
bare
the closets neatly packed
tightly locked
the key upon my chain
mistaken in its grooves
then i stare

heave a sigh
and leave
no good byes
just a crawling through
the tiny space
back out into the
what?
all alone
with him beside me where
even his silence is
unshared—

Definition

Love is not the only face
a poem wears
a poem can be shaped to cry
know rage and tear,
can stomp or twirl mixed rhythms,
a poem is a veto,
a short straw for the war,
a monument to martyr,
or tribute to scarred knee'd
straight back'd Black women
a poem is
an act
or more
No less

The Takers

I
they come
to knead my flesh
brown bread

◊ 121

i rise to the occasion
praying that this time
(O holy day!)
morning won't find me
kneaded
and needing
still

II
they bring no flowers
no candy
only hot blood
and pain

III
he came
with silver plated word
honey'd gesture
removing his pants
"what did you say your name was?"
he asked
i pointed to the door
"lies only tinkle in the night"
i said
"in the morning,
they become inharmonious clang"
"now you're acting like a nigger"
he said
i wished for a blade
wanting to gash his ears,
they served him not at all

IV
i'm tired
i know what you want from my life
the question is
what do you propose
to bring
to it?

◊ 122

V
first,
take me to dinner
let me eat
before i'm made a meal of

VI
we made love
prologue to deeper rivers
(wasn't that the way it went?)
but the flow was cut
by invisible dam
of your design
and you were gone
bandit!
without discovering me,
my favorite color,
the special pain i had
that needed to be kissed away

VII
i want flowers
bring me fresh bouquet
or loneliness,
sweet, bitter rose

i need no takers
to leave me half empty
i'd rather be alone
half full

VÉRTÀMÀÈ SMART-GRÒSVÈNÒR

Skillet Blond

Nòté: in thè deltàs, swàmps, and òther sultry placés of the southland if you àsk how à néwbòrn bàby looks and théy téll yòu "it's skillet blònd," that means the child is dark-skinned wìth Africàn fèaturés.

You're a kid and you believe everything they tell you. They are grown and grown folks know everything.

They tell you miz mamie got a big belly cause she swallowed a watermelon seed. You know it's the truth cause if you swallow a grape pit you get appendicitis. You do ponder on it a while cause they said that lightning dont strike in the same place twice. But you figure maybe watermelon seeds do and besides miz mamie must be kinda dumb cause this is not the first time she has swallowed a watermelon seed.

You hold all the truths they tell you as self evident. Why question you will reap what you sow, still waters run deep, the fruit dont fall far from the tree, always wear clean underwear when you go out so if something happen and you have to go to the hospital people wont think colored folks are dirty.

They are forever commenting on how you look. What they say hurts your feelings. Specially when they tell you that you are entirely too dark to wear red. Red is your favorite color. You feel like crying when they predict that you will never be able to wear lipstick.

"How come she always grinnin and showin her teeth, look like a african with them big liver lips."

"Aint it the truth, she'll never be able to wear lipstick. They dont make lipstick for two-toned lips."

"Umm dont that bottom pink lip look like a monkeys behind?"

It's all you can do to hold it in and not cry.

"Nose flat as a aunt jemina pancake and not nough hair in the kitchen to even think bout curlin."

"Aint it the truth, look at them nappy edges."

You dont cry cause the last time you cried they laughed so hard you dont think you could stand it again. They took it for a stage joke.

"Tsk tsk do you believe it? She ought to be shame of herself."

"A big black gal like that actin tenderhearted."

"Aint it the truth, she ought to be shame."

You aint shame of crying but you shame of being a freak. You are eleven years old and almost six feet tall. Your mama buys all your clothes a size too large to "get the length."

When you go to the movies they always want you to pay the full fare. You explain that you are tall for your age. They say bring your birth certificate. You explain that you were born in the country down south and dont have a birth certificate. They say pay the full fare.

You shame of being taller than anybody in your class. Every class you go in you have to stand at the end of the line.

You hear the ones in the front discussing your romantic future.

"She go have a hard time gettin a boyfriend."

"Aint it the truth, she go have a hard time gittin a boyfriend cause boys have to be taller than girls and anyhow boys dont chase behind flat-nosed two-toned liver-lipped long-legged girls with nappy edges in the kitchen."

When the boys chant the blacker the berry the sweeter the juice and the albino says "yeah, but i aint looking for wine that sweet" you know it's the truth.

You dont cry cause they say everthing changes. They say every dog has its day and good dogs have two.

So you wait. You know when you grow up you can wear as much red as you please when you please if you please. When you grow up your size, the size and color of your lips, how much hair you have, and the shape of your nose wont matter.

Things like that dont matter to grown people.

And then you grow up and it's devastating to discover that it's another seed that makes a big belly, still waters can be shallow, you dont always reap what you sow, folks who think colored people are dirty dont care if they—the colored people—wear clean drawers or not.

You are undone when you find out people havent stopped talking bout nappy edges, they still believe the blacker the berry the sweeter the juice but very few people like sweet wine, they do make lipstick for two-toned lips and lightning will strike in the same place twice. Thrice if you get in its way.

◊ 125

It is unsettling to be grown. All the things you thought would change are frozen myths. All the truths you held as self evident are shattered lies.

You feel like crying.

You read a poem by Gylan Kain and you know it's you.

> *Insulation pain glass woman. Your lips run red with*
> *the blood of disenchantment.*
> *I look into your face as I would into a mirror,*
> *but things fall apart and you are so much shattered*
> *glass.*
> *Black Satin*
> *Amazon*
> *Fire Engine Cry Baby*

You feel like crying but now you speak French so you shrug your shoulders and sigh *le plus ca change le plus c'est le meme.*

Now you are a writer and you decide to write not cry. You will write from the heart on how it feels to be a skillet blond woman. A Myth.

You can explore the curious way folks have of talking out of both sides of their mouths about myths: if she protests she is a ball-busting matriarchal bitch. If she keeps quiet she is a handkerchief head aunt jemina mammy bitch.

You could speak on how weary a myth can get carrying the weight of the race on her back. You can remind the people that her back is made of mahogany *skin* not wood.

You can tell stories that will show the more things change the more they are the same.

STORY #1

Two myths entered a florist shop on Manhattan's Upper West Side. Contributing a dollar apiece—the last for both of them—they bought one lovely yellow tea rose.

They were on their way to visit a friend who loved tea roses. She was in a deep blue funk and had invited them over for wine and a pot of greens. Nothing like a coupla skillet blond chicks sitting round talkin, sippin wine, eating greens and admirin a yellow tea rose to chase the blues away.

As they were leaving the shop the florist allowed "This is a surprise!" "Why?" asked the first myth with a dangerous tone in her voice that only another myth would recognize as dangerous. "Well" said the florist "the colored girls who come in here usually like a flashier flower." Looking him dead in the eye she demanded that he tell her "Just what the fuck is a flashy flower!" Before he could answer the second myth grabbed the first myth's arm and led her out before she started acting like a myth. Sapphire.

STORY #2

At a gallery opening in the big apple a young myth sitting on her mother's lap was so amused by the avant-garde pictures that she rocked with laughter, accidentally hitting her mother in the mouth.

The mother went to the hospital emergency room where they acted like they were expecting her. It was Saturday evening.

The intern informed her that she needed to see a surgeon and get stitches. After the typical long emergency room wait the surgeon, an Anglo woman, examined the mother's mouth.

Placing a butterfly bandage on the wound she told the intern "Normally in cases like this i would recommend stitches but since her lips are so big and thick it wont make any difference."

Honestly, when you think about it, think about what people think about black women, think about the *myth* of black women, its enough to make you wanna pull a Sojourner on them, take out your titties and shout "Aint I a woman? Aint I feminine?"

But you dont. If you did they would probably say "My my my arent you strong to do that!" Like they do when you talk about how hard it is to raise children alone. "I dont see how you do it" they say. "You must be strong."

They dont understand that's just it. You strong but you aint *strong*. You come from people who were truly strong but you scared that you aint made of what they was made of and it frightens you. You afraid that you wont be able to carry on in the tradition.

They say the Lord dont put no more on you than you can bear but you think maybe the *Lord* was busy and gave your case to somebody else.

When you get the assignment to go to Chicago to talk to a group of

Black feminists you think hot digity do dodo. You done growed up to be a writer skillet blond gal. Go head with you bad self. Right on the money. Write from the myth's mouth. It will make a difference.

You check in the hotel feeling good but nervous because there arent any other women guests checking in. You think you know what they think. The myth is with you.

When the bellman escorts you to your room and gives you a spiel about the terrific hotel pubs, bars, etc., you hardly listen because you have decided that you wont hardly be going to the bar alone.

In your room you realize that thinking about what people think about is driving you crazy.

The first step in fighting a myth is to rid one's self of the myth. You cant go to the pub alone. You are writing alone. You're on assignment alone. You decide that people who have a problem with women, skillet blonds, brunettes, redheads, drinking in bars alone are backward. If you want a drink when you want a drink in the bar have one if you please. Fuck a myth. Advance.

However before you get the chance to advance to the pub a male writer friend invites you over to fill you in on the furor *For Colored Girls Who Have Considered Suicide When the Rainbow Is Enough* is causing.

You are not surprised because black women talking their lives always causes waves. You are surprised to hear that some black men picketed the theater.

Your friend has given you explicit instructions on how to get to his house, lessen the taxi driver think you are a tourist.

It doesnt make a difference though because after you give the driver the instructions and he says "that's right off Champlain, aint it?" you say "i dont know" and he knows that you dont.

Chicago is at its winter wonderland best. The wind chill factor is twenty below and the snow is thigh deep.

Riding along you observe how clean and organized chicago snow is, unlike the dirty dog pooh slush of the apple.

You mention this to the driver. .

"Chicago streets are so clean, one can walk after a snowstorm."

"You like to walk?" the driver asks.

With great enthusiasm you tell him "Like, i love walking the streets."

The ride is long and bumpy, to which you say "Now, that's New York, potholes we got."

"Potholes, potholes" says the driver "please spell potholes. I hear that word all the time but I dont know how to spell it. I'm from Poland only a few years and some Americans words I dont know." You spell potholes and go back to thinking about *For Colored Girls . . .* controversy. The taxi driver cuts into your thoughts and forever you wish you hadnt said "Beg your pardon sir?"

"I said" he repeated "the life of a hooker must be rough, huh? Walking the streets all the time?"

A hooker? Walking the streets? With a sinking heart you realize that he thought because you a woman, a myth, got in at a hotel was going to visit a "him," "loved walking the streets," you were a hooker!

But you a poet and a writer. You can get taxis in front of hotels, go to bars and pubs, walk the streets and love without being a hooker. This is the decade of the woman! you feel like shouting, but you dont because you know the stereotype, the myth has gotten to him as soon as he got here from Poland. Maybe before he left. Isnt there a joke about the immigrant who was in this country and after forty years could only speak one word of English. Nigger.

But you're a poet and a writer. They always said that you are what you think you are. So, you want to ask the driver how he could think/say such a thing, but you dont. You aint no writer, no poet. You is what *they* think you are. A myth. A stereotype. A nigger woman. A hooker. You think he could at least called you a singer. But it dont much matter what myth he had in mind. A singing hooker or a hooker who sings.

It doesnt matter because from the six-foot wall of defense that you'd put up, the tears break loose and you weep. Black satin Amazon fire engine crybaby. You wept for your mama, your grandmama, your aunts, your sisters, your cousins, and your daughters. For hookers. Singers. Flashy flowers. And for the long-legged skillet blond girl in the red dress with the thick two-toned lips and nappy edges in her kitchen. You wept for the myths that make us weep.

Well so jesus, Ms Crusader, Ms Liberator, Ms Changer face-to-face with a no spelling sexist racist and the only thing you can do is cry. WEEP because there aint nothing you can do, you aint nothing but a myth. You're nobody's dream. Weep mammy, mother earth, weep

◊ 129

Sapphire, cry your heart out you ball-busting Caldonia castrating bitch. Cry till your strong matriarchal heart breaks.

Your rage is overwhelming.

You remember the story one of your aunts told. As a young girl the insurance man who came weekly to collect the burial money would put his hand under her dress and fondle her. Finally she told her mother who said "Hush child, I will take care of it but under no circumstances whatsoever are you to tell you father about it or you will git him kilt." She meant that the father would want to "take up" for her and the white folks would kill him.

You know if you get out the cab and tell your friend what happened he will want to "take up" for you and you could get him "kilt" so you wept harder, wept with the pain of understanding. And with a sigh of resignation, you figure since it couldnt hurt worse, you might as well act in concert with the myth.

When you got out the cab you pay the driver with exact change. He lows with that intimidating tone that taxi drivers use "What no tip?"

In perfect stereotypical, Sapphire skillet blond mythical style you say "What's this a Polish joke? A tip! Tip my black ass you white muthafucka!"

A month later in the apple you attend a feminist meeting and you tell the story. One of the sisters, a white professional woman, really got angry at you. She said you shoulda laughed at the driver. She said that you should have considered the source and shrugged it off. She said you were bigger than that. She said "I'm surprised at you, a strong Black woman acting like a Jewish princess."

SAFIYA HENDERSON

Portrait of a woman artist

here I sit
like a bird
in the wilderness,
a bird in the wilderness,
a bird in the wilderness,
here I sit like a bird
in the wilderness
waiting for my dessert.

paintbrush, colors, dishes, sex,
no.

sex, dishes, mop floor, lestoil, ajax, dance, paintbrush,
colors.
no.

relatives and friends to talk to, children, school meetings,
trains to ride, buses to wait for, grocery lines, con edison
lines, phone bill lines, welfare lines, poetry, paintbrush,
dance, sculpt.
no.

clean the house, kill roaches, find a new roach killing
spray, kill all the fucking roaches, wash clothes, dried
shit in everyone's underwear, mop, brillopads, broom,
sponge, wax, defrost refrigerator, someone is crying,
frying pan hot, dinner burned, face in mirror gone, poem,
where the hell is that poem, novel, I had a novel somewhere,
in with the dirty clothes, everything is in with the dirty
clothes, sculpt, music, dance.
no.

◊ 131

child gets sick—heal child.
man gets sick—heal man.
child grows—leaves.
man grows—leaves.
paintbrush bristles disintegrate.
no.

man in jail, cry for man, work to free man, work to free self.
poet.

hospitals and schools closing, stretch body across the
roof of hospital, school, dare anyone to touch your hospital,
school, your paintbrush, poetry, music, dance, sculpt.
no.

your sex.

be more lady like bitch.
be more caring.
dinner on table, shine on floor, face, nails, teeth.
wear something sexy.
comb your hair.
watch t.v.
smell like a rose.
yes be more like a rose.
bitch.

thorns in my dance, my sculpting, poem, lestoil, in my mama's
pancakes, my granma's cornbread, a million thorns in my ass.
no painting.

work for a living.
sell yourself, your colors, your music.
no singing.

get married, live with one man, become a nun, a nurse,
everyone loves a nurse, everyone can see that you care

if you nurse, no one sees or cares if you care with a
mop, sponge, furniture polish, starch, routine, mundane,
dance, poet, paint, sculpt.
no.

take it to the bridge.
take it all to the bridge.
lestoil, ajax, brillo, pine, ivory snow, burnt eggs, tampax,
diaphragm, phone bill, razors for the wrist, poetry, colors,
dishes.
no dancing.
take it all to the bridge baby, sweet, good cooking mama,
take it right to the fucking edge and jump.
one less stain.
one less line.
one less bundle of dirty clothes.
take it to the edge, girl, that's all you got left to
do, you've done everything.

no.
no jumping.

the children are sleeping.
the man is sleeping.
there's nothing else left for you to do.

no.
no jumping.
dance pretty lady, poet, paint, sing, sculpt, raise your
children, get married if you want to, kiss many men if
you want to, poet pretty lady.

fight like Josina Machal.
no jump, drown in lestoil.

no fight precious woman like Zora Neale Hurston.
no easier to chew brillo, fake orgasms, watch t.v.

no fight woman like June Jordan.
no slash wrist.

no fight good much needed person like Fannie Lou, Sojourner,
Harriet, Billie, Pat, Jo-Ann, Assata, Mama, Granma, Francis,
Monifa, Cheryl, Milicent.

be militant.

spread your legs, your arms, let your hair go bad and
dance, poet, sing, sculpt, paint, fight.

it's alright woman.
it's alright woman.
it's alright woman.
it's alright woman.

harlem/soweto

zimbabwe
and we
are one

there is no separation

one stone hammered
by foreign hands
my sons have your physique
muscles pulled
taut
over of ice
and steel

here my wrist
there your hand

◊ 134

fingers knotted
around one stick

you say bantusans
we say harlem
you say soweto
we say watts
you sweat coal
we burn steel
you're locked on lands
we're locked indoors

my body smells of your nights
lips cracked with your hurt
one bruised back
no broken spirits

we are woven
inseparable as sky
with one sun
    one moon
    one tongue
    rolled to spit
    in one
    eye . . .

letter to my father . . . a solidarity long overdue

i remember sunshine
and summers by rivers
friends and grandma
hooking crabs
your eyes sharp
young blades of grass glowing

◊ 135

like me, mama and the boys
in the springtime of your smile

i remember early morning kisses
bed tucks
when your childhood fables
were nearly real
your head tall amid clouds and skyscrapers
for all torchers to see
for all swordsmen to challenge
sweet

torso firm
promises certain
palms asked no questions

i remember
and the moons, father
all the moons were bright

but something happened
the sky broke
and the torchers' armies
smashed your promises
between half-opened doors
and a faceless silence
that ignored your worth

the grass began to decay
and you pawned your sword
for a pat on the back
a barstool
and a derelict's smile
sad . . .

as me, mama and the boys
were young

SAFIYA HENDERSON

as the years began to swell
and fester
and winter set in the corner
of our lives

and the moons father,
the moons were so bright . . .

but when leaves fell
covering laughter
we didn't love much
never meeting eyes
your hands became hard
and square against our smiles
amber/green bottles
lined the bedroom floor
as you slept alone
with sweat and
loose bowels

and me, mama and the boys
not knowing why your thirty-eight years
of wishes wept
before they were born
watched you

watched you
as you stumbled thru doors
in mid-nights
with burnt smells
spitting dreams

we watched
wishing to console
stop the glasses from filling
the memories from staining

◊ 137

and the moons
father, the moons from fading!

night encircled sun
mama cried for children
mama cried for man
and then we left

stripped the walls
of stares
packed our lives in bent boxes
leaving the amber/green bottles
and you
cracking . . .

we left
traveled south
mother and children
running from misery to misery
trying to separate our wanting days
from your wanting nights

mama's tears became stone
cold and threatening
your memory like ice
we didn't look back
not even
a call

but i remembered
saved your smile
and painted my bedroom wall
took your courage and shined it for all to see
hung a moon in your memory
and hung that moon in my eyes

for you see daddy
we, me, mama and the boys
were young then
our limbs still bending
my sights knew only afternoons

but now thru winters
and columns of promises destroyed
i've lived to know you
father,
a man chiseling out a space
in times and towns
where saints
and good men are refused
entry

seen your dreams
roll down my cheek
and settle on my cold empty floor
your wishes snap and split in my mirror
and good intentions drowned
by the darkness of day
and the wasted luster of night
seen the insanity of narrow spaces
and father i've
grown
inward

seeing life stopping and running
and stopping again
like a frail heart
like a thought with fear

i've danced the solitaires
dance
kicking shadows
trying to resettle the seasons

i've seen you father
now fifty
me twenty-five

amber/green bottles
sometimes lining my bathroom floor
i sometimes alone
with sweat and loose bowels

i see you
me twenty-five
you fifty
but daddy how did you stand all these years
how did you hold back
the rain

father father father
bear your witnesses
and tell me
for this bourbon
is flat
and does
talk . . .

Akua Lezli Hope

Lament

my contraceptive history
pregnant with pain
the breech birth of clashing cultures

forced cervical dilation
snake steel rods
insidious contraint and rape

sometimes i bear mulattoes
strangers to my skin
strongwilled aliens
strangers to my heart

i remove rods
to early brand or slay them
each choice conceives anguish
capitulation harkens suffering
rebellion beckons despair
        upon my womb
        upon my womb

        upon my womb
i swear silent oaths
razortoothed and lockjawed
my raised clenched hand
a hammer melting in-
to silent throbs

hardened
against plow and chord
thick heads and slow behinds

◊ 141

what milk have i
that neither nourishes
or binds

goat don't bring sheep
what jumby ate
my children's souls
these veiled miscreants
Third World beaus and belles
who outright reject
or play Love's caricature.

August

for Baron

    i am anxious for answers
    this night after
    back to self singular, no
    nervous laughter
    or sighs break against fan's
    whirr and gargle.

    watchfully tender and giddy
    lust. yr eyes bound me
    tighter than fevered caress,
    locked closer than legs
    deeper to core than rod divining,
    found water faster.

    lips more equal than mine
    their burning succulence
    their fleshy suppleness
    their opulent articulations

◊ 142

speak to me and soon
before again night enters
aimless   to sling
its sweaty suit across me.

1.

my mother is an indictment
i am fettered by the genes
limited before beginning
        i cry against her
        that she was not more
        than second generation running
        from that tropic tongue
        too chastised to be fast
        too whipped to be hip
                not bold enough to embrace
                heatrhythms wilderness
                ackeeplaintain mornings
                spice nights of peas n rice
                the lingolilt of her people
                persisting after backs dry
                and green ripen
                like banana like guava
                like mango comesome
                gingerbeer burn in mouth
little blackgirl runningfasthard breathless
beyond sweat her braids loosening in flight
running (monkee monkee monkee chaser)
hurled wordspears falling short
of flailing black legs monkee chaser
tribe silver on her arm marking her
as sure as cheekscars monkeechaser she stop
hard turns shescared shefight flailing arms
of fear fight strong with fear fatigue shefight

shestrong shechange shebecome
yankeegirl accentless
Harlemcool and homegrownsweet
she nocookhot this second generation
she no jibe-jive with elders
in accented imitation no
she run fast nocook
she run fast she run fast
slicing off edges cutting her mythical tail
    collecting menstrual blood
    offerings for the melting pot
    idol of her parents new religion
        multistoried monstrosity with fools
        gold pasties on witches marquee
        beautiful at the distance/unbridgeable gap
        why-o why-o why-o she can't crossover?
my mother is an indictment
i am fettered by the genes
directed before beginning
    i cry *for* her
    this is not capitulating blood
    that run fast through my vein
i am the twice born
i take back her tail
to bury it in heartsoil
like placenta by tree and water it
i celebrate saving distance
embrace difference as identity as key
i cook yam say yes ma'am
i deeplisten to grayhairs
before memory flees
of Harlem as home
of being free . . .

my mother is an indictment
i cry for her
i take back her tail.

Mariah Britton Howard

reports

there is a woman
with a mountain
of stones
   she didn't
throw.
everyday, one two
five were placed
gently.
      bitter-
ness, she learned to
lay away,
nurse & night
& toil,
she gave them
rest on the steep
the race trouble
    supermarkets
& landlords have
incline near
the door.
lately though
            i hear
reports of
broken glass.

a using

i see
her sit
every noon
except winter's

maybe
monday is a
long drink
it swallows her
weeks' yearning
for the tall
field, that
summer, he
led her to
damp earth
where love
sprouted
a gentle green
thing cupped
by hope in
young brown
hands

the years of
waiting show
on her wrists'
turning the knob
each time
sound was
his footsteps

now
by the river
she talks into
the wind, hoping
the air will
find him near
an open door

i hear
her warn
passersby

◊ 146

"ya can't use somethin'
ya never met"

startled, they hurry

solution #9
"to touch you"

want to
really touch you
become
a stroke filled
with care
since being
born
want to
touch you

want to part
your nappy hair
and clear some
confusion
the world don't change
cause people die
it change cause they
live and touch
COME!
let me touch
you and you
find me the same

yes, i do
want to percuss
lay a solo on you
a valiant

◊ 147

palm for them
paintings that
scream from
your fingertips
set the design
for shimmering
cities and clay
for your hands

heard Brown say
"When you touch me
I can't stand it. . . .
I break out in a cold
sweat." he dared us
dared us to come
near

my grandma wants to
my momma wants too
my baby wants too
to to to touch your
arms, dreams
ideas, mareish
cross, your seein'
eyes

bunions and knees
the promises that
bent you, the scar
on your cheek
from turnin' so long
the way you toss
before mornin'
my holler at this
plight
the cotton in your
clothes

MARIAH BRITTON HOWARD

moisture
your lips

let me touch you
        get to know
my name

blame is a
fantasy stuffed
with voids
is one of a
billion words

i want to touch
you
round the arch
of who
we
am.

LATEIFA-RAMONA LAHLEET HYMAN

Paraphernalia for a Suicide: a revelation of life

(for myself and Sonia Sanchez)

The mother sat on
the curve of her bed
pitched pennies to woodworks
she spoke:

"What is this sound that
shatters the copper as
I throw it against your womb.

The daughter lifts her head,
"I have not the nuance to be called woman," she said.

As they spoke, rain rose
to claim the sky. The mother
looked into the daughter's face.

"Have I not taught you
that women are not judged by the
men they encounter nights.
To be woman means you
have felt earth."

"Yes, this is true," the daughter replied,

But,
"a woman who has not smelled her womb
falters in the midst of audiences.
She greets, I am a lonely
asylum: I cannot be amid crowds so

◊ 150

long ago she thinks of dying,
of becoming the collage of a cement canvass,
of stepping from the roof."

The mother shook her head like
summer shaking into fall.

"Daughter," she echoed,
"suicide is not a death praised by rivers."

And the daughter stretches
on her sheetless mattress.
She feels, she is a reason
to cry, but tears she has been
taught are for rain.

So, she vibrates storms, lightning:
the thunder becomes grave.
She writes,

"Mother,
teach me to harness wind for
you are the herbal fiber
that churns crocodile eyes
and every time I think of
dying, I hear your prayers
bulging from my sides."

ADRIENNE INGRUM

Loomit

On May 18, 1980, Mount St. Helens erupted, tearing 1300 feet from its summit—reducing its elevation from 9677 to less than 8400 feet—and ripping out its entire north side. The mountain is young, still in its conebuilding stage and will eventually regain and, Lord willing, exceed its former elevation. The mountain was called Loomit by the Klickitat people, native to northwest America, and audaciously renamed by a British explorer. This is an untitled story of the eruption.

I

There is no solitude
like the death of a sinner.
Among the clutter on this smoldering slope
two shoes
peculiarly worn
lie singed beneath a cot.

The digits on my arm
form and reform.

Tilson's bones lie charred
upon this grid where he had lain
fantasizing that the seismic wave
rippling through the mountain
was a corpulent woman
coming beneath him.

There is not a sign of resistance.
The skull, which splinters
as I whisk away the ash,
is face down, not skyward.
Was he ignoring the jets of light
the premenstrual display,
fired by this pubescent Cascade?

Though the survivors were reluctant to go
even as ash rained like dry snow,
three toothless whorers after gold,
a gnarled, arthritic cattlerustler,
a speechless, crusty ogre,
a leathery Klickitat woman
whose gray hair was half yellowed
and whose yellow teeth were half green,
a pair of hardy, long-forgotten New Yorkers,
and their cublike toddler—
these cliffdwellers had come by ones and threes
in reverent terror to Helen's foot.
Relief workers had cheered
and forced masks upon them
and more than one reclusive soul had fled
to the siblings—Hood or Rainier or Adams—
who have matured beyond their dysmenorrheic sister.

But here is Tilson
known to the town below
only as a P.O. Box
and a queer mountain nigger.

I have questioned the townees.
All concur that She gave warning.
"Ah fust mistook it for a eclipse."
"Me, I were looking for the Horseman,
the strange way the darkness come about."
"Something in y'eyes and y'throat tol ya . . ."
"Everybody knowed it fo she relly got to bleedin
yup, the Loomit bleeded fire,
I say ol squaw bleed *some fire*."

I have what I came for—
the facts, the quotes, the faces.
I did not come with camera, pen and pad
to climb and sink in warm ash
or to sift bones and scorched belongings,

but I have uncovered
more than news.
The rangers approach and herd me
like a graverobber, from these ruins.
I take only his name
and a mental picture of a man
who reached a mountaintop.

II
El Salvador erupts
Zimbabwe quiets
Reagan is nominated, elected,
turned loose on the poor,
shot
Astronauts stall, shuttle, land
and since affairs of man and state
precede those of God and Nature
in the press,
I lay aside John Tilson's story.
In the middle of a feature on taxes
(and mine still needing to be paid)
an Edna Smith calls:
"Was it anything left
from that mane name in the paper,
John Tilson?"

"Huh?"

"I say what did you find
of that mane John Tilson
from the vulcainna?"

"Find?"
"Yeah."

"His bones."
"Beside bones," she demands.

III

I have been a guest
in enough kitchenettes
where the weary, reborn
sit among their potted plants
with Jesus, King and JFK.
No—one does *not* get old being no fool.
No—I have *not* heard every lesson, chiding, secret.
No—no loneliness compares
to evenings
of virtuous, elderly women.
But my digital conscience complains—
there is no news here.

I pout over papery butter cookies
and plain Tetley tea. A journalist
cannot *be* courteous.
I have no time
to listen to you reminisce.
You, who have slit your oxfords
to accommodate your bunions,
are page "C16."
Taxes will be "A" next week . . .
. . . The Taxing Task of IRS . . .
Tell it to a songwriter!
Every niggerwoman of voting age
has been abandoned.

"I caint see how outdoors
take a holt so on some mens.
Do the colored worsern
cause he caint git no deed.
That why John rather die
up in that ol vulcainna."

"Was he moved off land
down South . . . ?"

◊ 155

"John Tilson never been south
of Sheepshead Bay.[1]
John and his daddy and granddaddy,
both Brecklam Tilsons,
been silvermens in Greenwich Village.
When we took up Harlem John moved on up.
My sweet fool aint know a calf from a hoe.
Only country thang that mane known was me.
John was just tetched.
Ya know how a moon do some peoples—
ya know how it get em moon streck?
Well John was earth streck.

"Uh mm. Didnt have no more sense
n buy some ol rocky soil
caint nuthin grow.
Aint nobody else buy but JT.
Al em crackas rounere squattin,
but JT take all he had
to git a deed."

The mini-recorder cannot digest her silence.
I will hear as static
what is really inner violence
mitigated by grace.
This dark, heavy, animalistic decor
is now that forest of thigh-high trees
where Tilson lies, like remains
of an offering.
Those and he were humbled in grandeur.
These and she in mediocrity.
But both sites reek
of their consummate failure
to share fates.

[1] Sheepshead Bay—south end of Brooklyn, N.Y.

"We useta walk up Seventh Avenue—
nobody couldnt tetch us in those days
John wit the business, me wit the lodge—
n John would ast somethin odd, say
'Baby, why our folk live so close to concrete?'
I'd say, 'I dont know John.' And I didnt.
Didnt matter to me.
But it stirred him up.
Those canfires, like they made wit
plywood, planks and floorboards,
he say they was richwuls.
And sometime that mane
stand in the way of the shop
polishing and just watchin people
gut n scale they fish
in the street
the jacklegs preach
womans lean on cars
mens lean on lampposts
cotin n lyin.
He get bothered and ast me again
'Baby, why the Race livin so close to concrete?'
"I couldnt tell him today
cepn they like it."

Again, I have what I need—
these cassettes which make jazz
in the purse at my hip.
I have an old posed sepia tone.
But I will not attempt John Tilson's story.

I am watched, "hey babied"
accosted to buy goods.
I pick my way
past pet shit, throw-away architecture
and the peel of human idleness,
but that same preference he abhorred
for this half-fallow urban valley,

for these funky, beguiling, littered streets
is my informed choice
and I must align my aesthetics
with my reality.

These defiant ailanthus
have always and too well shaded me,
these fire escapes been the seat
of too many fulfilled longings,
these pyramid rooves tempered me,
and these cosmically patterned lights
so subtly kindled me
that I have far less compassion for Tilson
than had he remained in a burning tenement.
I turn into my street,
weighing John Tilson's lust for Helen,
which though purer than Harlem
was no less merciless,
against Edna Smith's frigidity
to the brute that wastes in a man
without a terrestrial fantasy.

What is holy and infinite
seems neither to be grass
nor cement
but the acts of love
which hallow them.

Friday the 13th Candlelight March

The awning of funeral homes
along Harlem's broad avenues, yawn
as we rebury Atlanta's young.

We have no alms to send,
no more lies of Northern refuge to mail home,
no spare offspring of our own;

Newspaper clippings are all we have
and use of these streets,
who have great memories of processions.

So we, mostly manless and very childful
women, have gathered to course mothers' grief
down Lenox Avenue and 135th Street.

Having hurried to fry our porgies, we
have come out of our cabinets with fire
and stand protesting this license to *bear* lives
we are not empowered to *protect.*

We are here like village women
reconnoitering at the well
preparing for tomorrow's thirst.

We compare height, manners and age
of our children, Auntie Somebody commands
a pilferer to get from behind her,
And we and the kids laugh, as he obeys.
We ignore the nocounts being interviewed
and frugally snuff out our candles.

A rascal on a dangerously cracked lamppost
sees the parade———
and *it is something!*

Toddlers on shoulders of tall, broad men,
teenagers—proud to be big brothers and sisters—
escorting a preschooler on each hand,

◊ 159

Archbacked women-with-child,
permissive grands, taxed uncles, overprotective aunts,
one glowing, chanting, filial display!

Our children cannot be contained.
They draw us to the very curb,
insist they won't be wax-burned,

And beg us again to join in.
Cautious central-Harlem mothers,
we remain on the sidewalk

Clasping their hoods and collarbones,
nagging them to be careful with those candles,
feeling momentarily important, and being intoxicated
by the swell of families and smoke.

Only as Mrs. Bell makes her dirgeful steps
up to the podium do we queue the crowd—
like stragglers joining a Creole funeral
after the music stops.

Anthony Carter, age 9, stabbed.
Charles Stevens, 12, suffocated.
Clifford Jones, 13, strangled.

Edward Smith Hope, found July 1979, shotgunned.
Alfred James Evans, cause undetermined—*evidence*
eaten by wild dogs and rotted by summer heat

Milton Harvey, her baby Yusuf Bell, Jeffrey Lamar Mathis,
Eric Middlebrooks, respectively undetermined,
strangled, still missing, bludgeoned then stabbed.

Christopher Richardson—never reached the swimming pool
Aaron Wyche, said to be afraid of heights,
tossed from a railroad bridge.

Earl Lee Terrell and Darron Glass, both 10, gone.
Four nameless killed when Bowen House boiler exploded
and one fortnight later Aaron Jackson suffocated.

The girls: Angel Lanier, 12—found tied to a tree
her panties stuffed in her mouth. LaTonya Wilson, 8—
stolen from her home, "dead *only*" they said.

Lubie Geter, 14, has disappeared.
Two other teens found dead are suspected
of prostitution and thievery, thus not counted . . .

Our children hear and have stopped
whining. "But *whose*
blue 'n white car was it?" the quickest asks.

"What make was it?" my son pipes in.
"Yeah, they coulda painted it by now," says another.
We shush them, unable to provide answers
we ourselves have not demanded.

The throng applauds the mourner,
and we take careful, silent inventory, leading
these precious stones-around-our-necks home.

Rashidah Ismaili

Murderous Intent with a Deadly Weapon

Cold and shiny
long and hard
metallic phallus
dangling under
armpits and crotches
fingered by an
unresolved statement;
the poetry of
impotent masculinity
rubs against human flesh.

Justice is held in check
blinded by the steel glint
under storm helmets
and blocked by vests
impenetrable . . . .
the enforcers of holy writ
come out on cue and
applause echoes the trail
of spent sperm shot from
synthetic genitalia.

They masturbate with a
deadly weapon.
Their minds are aimed
with murderous intent.
In their nets they drag
the guilty and oppressed;
justice is a dungeon cell.
Men have given in to the
nonentity of human beings
not dogs but still not men.

In the strip mining
bombs detonated blows
sanity to bits and pieces.
The prisoned poet whose
song is denied by pencil
and by word of mouth
secretes his thoughts
inside his bowels
where alien light has
not yet learned to
penetrate.

In the depths of hallowed holes
where orgies take place
in equal doses the young and aged
wrong and right lay down upon
a bed of nails and stroke the
deadly arm of justice

The poet is lying cold and silent.
The streets are void and hushed
computed voices and timed rhythms
echo holy writs and orders.
It is the hour of bewitching
and broomsticks wait in corners.
A witch shall rise to sweep the skies
and dust will cloud our eyes.
The poet lies cold and silent.
His hands are numb and his hands
head is still. The phallus softens
and its sensual dropping mix
with sighs and blood. Penetrated
non-virgins bleeding—an epitaph
to the silent dispensing of the
impartiality of law and justice
for all.

◊ 163

Dialogue

There is reason for disrespect.
Self negating does not fall from
a merciful sky but rather drops
a lethal bomb—blotting out all.

I know where rain comes from;
and, babies do not birth from
tree trunks, fairies are not
hidden behind my eyelids when
shut up sleep tight.

Rainbows are not a clear-cut path
to fortune's end and Papa Noel is
an eunuch.

I will not bow to someone's aunt
save mine. She is not holy because
of her resemblance to a child I
never knew.

The kingdom I seek is enstooled
in the golden yield of black earth
tunnel, and, your member is too short,
you should have stayed home.

Revolution is not a dinner party—
where diners come to eat dressed in
black and white. Its battleground
are not stately mansions, a country club
where only select members are allowed.
Weaponry has nothing in common with
heirloom cutlery passed down. If I

have only one life to live, let me
live it now.

There is a circle in a circle;
it spreads its wheels like a leaf
caught in a whirlpool. If you do
not listen, how can you hear—change
is slow and comes unannounced. If I
have to scream, you might not understand
my need to be silent and sure.

Behind a veil of purdah, in a basket woven by hand—
neath layer upon layer of intellectuality, the Simbas
are hid. A complex of handshakes, a myriad of plans,
and, quaking beneath their ponderances an Empire of old
in thunderous death gives way.

Who are these new bloods; these young ones with
questions for answers and tongues for dreams?
Revolution a plot, is buried in a washerwoman's pot.
She boils calalu and coos, ferments mavi and palm
wine, making a haven for new days and, dreadlocks
a fashion!

I too have seen the promised land, and, the
grass only looks green. The hand that tills soil
still remains a sun black bone hoe. And I still
dream. I yet have hope! In the storefronts and
bayous; slums and favellas, a tin town is a tin
town—and white is not always right. But black
false prophets proliferate and somewhere, in between
sandwiched betwixt truth and death, a compromise is
made. The gain may not be to my liking and treaties
have histories of times when humanity did tear and
turn their backs on bits of paper hastily penned,
a term for bills of lading.

Struggle of Class

Struggle of class
etched across the richness
of my flesh—
This color of wealth
the seeker's quest
is ruined upon rocks of hostility
and thrown amongst
the shoals of foreign waters.
Piranhas are excited
by my monthly menstrual cycle—

Blood flow easy
make lines of distinction less clear.
May I see the lines of demarcation
Warfare is smooth in paucity of
pigment/ making contradictory
statements. The assignment of
colorlessness
is washed upon white beaches
of Brittany.

My class is colored
and covered in
gold earthen yields
bowls of diamonds
spoons of silver
and yet
on cold and snow-capped mountains
You sit in tempered rooms
counting pennies and dimes
marks and yens; francs and dollars.
While I am without/ you are within.

◊ 166

RASHIDAH ISMAILI

The struggle goes on and on.
I must call a new accountant
to balance the books and
compose a new ledger for
checks/cheques and balances.

MAE JACKSON

For The Count

bring out the glasses of crystal
one for you
and one for me
and as you pour the wine
i will reflect on times gone by
and lovers spent against this backdrop of un-real
i will try to leave
more silently than i came

call out the spirits to join us in this
one last drink
a tribute to us and the way we were last week
and the week before
tell the spirits to dress themselves in bright colors
this is a tribute to our last night together
and
tell me
how shall i toast you,
should i say
to love
to life
to us when we were in total darkness and
our bodies/two-toned blended in some strange manner
and all that was present
was romance
at its best

light all the candles
let the humming
the chanting begin
let us dance and move in a circle
and when it has been broken
let there be only smiles for what we had

say that i appeared
because
someone wished it
and you are not to blame
and i will
more than likely
say the same

A POEM FOR ALL THE MENS IN THE WORLD

Just
Look
At me
A typical black woman
Unwed
And unloved

There is nothing new
Unique
Or different
About me
Just an every day grass root sweet street talking black
Woman
Alone
With her child

On Learning

You have taught me how to dress without
awakening the whole world
i
have

◊ 169

learned to tiptoe quietly
out
of
love filled nights
into
tomorrow's daily routine
and,
you have taught me to smile
half days because
whole days are not up for grabs
and
i
want to
thank you, baby
for teaching me how to leave
gracefully,
without stirring the neighbors,
or kicking your cat

My Last Feeling This Way Poem

there are some poems that you just don't want to write
they are usually the
"gone away"
"why did you have to leave me this way?" poems
poems that ask questions
to which
there may be no answers to
but,
you are a poet and it's your job
and so you go about it the exact same way anyone else would
go about their job,
you do it,
you write the poem that you really don't want to write
not because you can make pain beautiful or noble—

it never is,
you write it
because
you can understand it

there are some poems that people give to you,
like,
someone gave me this poem,
a poem of five years,
a tall poem—at times
a small poem—at times,
a poem of hope,
a poem of dis-appointment
a poem that said, in five long years
he had never learned
to trust me,
a
painful poem
but
a poem nonetheless,
and he has got a right to feel this way,
and I have got a right to write this angry poem that asks,
"why did you stay so long?"
and he had a right to find someone else,
someone who would be in agreement with him,
someone who would not argue back,
and I have a right to write this poem about being
a rebellious black woman,
and I have got the right to say,
"I want something real in my life"

there are some poems that people give to you,
like,
someone gave me this poem,
a poem of five long years,
a poem that stood beside you while you stood trial and was
convicted,

◊ 171

a poem that heard the words,
"you are guilty," and did not cry,
a strong poem,
a woman's poem,
a poem that took it as far as it could go and stayed
more out of loyalty
than love,
because I am a poet
I have to write this poem,
because I am a lover of men and women and children
and truth,
this is why I write the poem

there are some poems that people give to you that you just
don't want to write
but,
you do so,
not because you can write wrong or write right,
but,
because it is so necessary for the artist to give it away
I have
long ago,
been/is
a people's poet
been the kind of poet who has lived just about every line
I have written
joy,
and
pain,
have put my life right out there in print and dared anybody to
laugh at it,
because I am a serious poet/ woman

there are some poems that people give to you,
and you want to say,
"thanks, but, no thanks."

◊ 172

MAE JACKSON

still,
they give it to you, anyway,
and you accept
because
You are gracious (in an old-fashioned way)
And I have got a right to write this poem

GAYL JONES

Ensinança

I

He was a man who did not like to be much in evidence. He would disappear if given half the opportunity. But he had a malady that kept him visible—conspicuous hairy nevus. The top of him was all black, the bottom was all white. His navel divided him into night and day.

The women he knew were either too surprised or too afraid. He learned that surprise and fear were the same.

His mother, an innkeeper in Olinda, said he had had the "thing" happen to him because he had betrayed his destiny, his gift from heaven.

"You were born to be a healer, a *curandero*."

But he was a man of modern times and modern possibilities, an engineering student in Rio.

"Men make their destiny," he said.

"I'll call you Heaven's Punishment then, Ensinadelo, not Ensinança, because He gave you the special gift of making men and women whole again, and you've traded it for pottage."

"I want to build bridges and skyscrapers," he said.

"In the old days it was what *He wants*."

The woman rubbed her eyes with her brown knuckles.

"You can't work against heaven. No. And look what heaven's given you. Its own evidences, that you can't lift one finger against. Go design your bridges, half-one-half-other. Only heaven can make you whole again."

"Perhaps heaven has made me whole already," he said.

"You were meant to be a *curandero*. To poke a shoulder and make it well. To turn a head and make it better. To make a dumb man talk. To draw the pain from knuckles. To make them whole. To stop a cough. To mend a knee. To see where the devil's hiding and draw him out! Eh, you've betrayed your destiny."

There is no convincing her. They seem opposing spirits. But doesn't

◊ 174

he carry two worlds? He hides one part of himself in denim, the other in white cotton shirts.

II

Ensinança met a woman staying at his mother's boarding house. They were not strangers long.

The sky opened. The world changed from trouble to kisses. She was not afraid or surprised when she discovered him.

"You are the first woman," he said. "Why don't you fear me? Why do you look at me as if you've always seen me, as if I've always been? Why do you look at me as if I'm possible?"

She didn't answer. They sat in cane chairs. They kissed each other. They kissed the sun. They ate oranges and coconuts. They touched fingertips. They played games. They lifted each other up. They named and renamed each other.

"Why don't you think I'm a monster?" he persisted.

"If you are a monster, you are the loveliest monster," she said.

She welcomed him into her arms again. She kissed his forehead. She kissed his moustache. She kissed his stomach where his landscape changed.

"Are you happy?"

"Yes."

"You were not surprised or afraid?"

"No."

III

"Tell me what you believe," he asks.

She only kisses him.

"Can I survive with kisses?" he asks. "Tell me what you believe."

She plays with his armpits. She kisses his elbows. She won't answer.

"Are you superstitious? Do you believe in destiny?" he asks.

The woman laughs at him and chews an olive.

"Shall I tell you my destiny?" he asks.

She smiles.

"If it's a gift from heaven," she says, "you should take it."

"Who have you been talking to?" His look is intense and fierce.

She lights a cigarette. She sits in a turquoise chair.

◊ 175

He calls her a dishonest woman, the worst kind.

"I am a little," she says.

She kisses the nape of his neck.

"What are you here for?" he asks.

She opens her mouth, and there's oil on her tongue. He flies to the center of her.

IV

In the daytime, he designs with steel and stone. At night, he rebuilds flesh and spirit.

Sometimes he dreams of a peregrine woman neither afraid nor surprised at his differentness, the landscapes above and below his navel, who herself could draw light from darkness, darkness from light.

"I came to ask you, where's the devil hiding?" a client asks.

He drives the devil out in a hurry. He makes them wonder what manner of man he is.

Anasa Jordan

Sweet Otis Suite

Charcoals
and blues poured from you.

Broad lips kissed pregnant
melodies that lingered there;
we listened to rhythms of
your suite,
      Otis.

Sweet Otis,
you be liftin us higher
than the last time
your sun drenched blues toasted we;
slippin us into deeper shades
of charcoal
that go to midnight blue
in ray of full moon.

Full Otis,
you be spillin over into us
fillin those open places
with parts of pain that
always give way to joy.

Sweet, joyful Otis Suite—
screaming through air
swooping down to scoop up
dreams from the bay.
Squeeze memories from those dreams
and we be flyin, too,
Otis.
Sing a suite, sweet baby, sing

◊ 177

June Jordan

ON THE REAL WORLD: Meditation #1

5 shirts
2 blouses
3 pairs of jeans and the iron's on hot
for cotton:
I press the steam trigger to begin
with the section underneath the collar
from the inside out.
Then the sleeves. Starting with the cuffs.
Now the collar wrong way before it's right.
I'm not doing so good.
Around where the sleeve joins the shoulder looks
funny.
My hand stops startled.
New like a baby there's a howling on the rise.
I switch the shirt so that the iron reaches
the front panel easily.
That howling like a long walk by the Red
Brigades for twenty years between improbable
Chinese ravines with watercolor trees
poked into a spot as graceful as clouds
missing deliberate from a revolutionary landscape printed in Japan
ebbs then returns a louder howling cold
as the long walk towards the watery
limits of the whole earth blasted by the air
become tumescent in a lonely place
inhabited by the deaf or the invisible
but querulously looming victims of such speed
in spoken pain the louder howling large
as the original canvas containing that landscape
printed in Japan almost overloaded as the howling loses
even its small voice while I
bite my lips and lower my head

◊ 180

hard into the ferocity of that sound
dwarfing me into someone almost immaterial
as now I smell fire
and look down all the way to the shirt
pocket
skyblue and slightly burned

Blue Ribbons for the Baby Girl

In memory of fifteen year old Veronica Vaughn
Dedicated to Savannah Thulani Eloise Shange Binion
Born November 2, 1980

> When the bell rings or you hear the knocking at the door
> Tell the bell to go to hell and show the door there's more
> important things you have to do than meeting
> with the enemy
>
> There's the coffee to be made and the flowers
> to arrange and the bookshelves still to raid for power
> that will last like turkey sandwiches and
> sweet anemones
>
> There's somebody swell on the phone and next
> somebody in your bed and love and sex
> come through the breathing body faster
> than disaster
>
> Don't run. Running does not dance.
> Don't die. Dying is a poor romance.
> Don't forget the party. And please set up the date
> so the killers will come late.
>
> If you set up the date
> The killers will arrive too late.

◊ 181

A Last Dialog on the Left

Dedicated to Barbara Masakela

Whereas the outrageous violation of human rights
under that racist regime persists—

(He's gonna recommend regular rights
for women so finally we can vote/own land/
look you in the eye the moment that
the revolution—)

and duly recognizing the need to punitively
isolate the perpetrators of such heinous
acts against—

(Wow! Maybe The People's Army will beat the shit
out of rapists and lock up the fathers
who fuck with child support—)

all humanity. I therefore move—

(Or maybe he's about to take a turn typing
up the minutes from the meetings)

for an international boycott of Diana Ross
who will lend credibility to these enemies
unless she cancels—

(Christ A'mighty! You mean the coming out and upside
down sister of the mirror on the wall? Oh Brother.
That'll be hard.)

Poem Towards a Final Solution

In a press conference this afternoon the Secretary
of Space Development confirmed earlier reports
of a comprehensive plan nearing completion
in his Office.

Scheduled to meet with the President later
this week, Mr. Samuel B. Fierce the Third
jokingly termed the forthcoming package of proposals
"A Doozie."

The following represents a news team summary
of his remarks:

His Office will issue findings of a joint survey
of all National Parks conducted in cooperation with
the Department of the Interior in an effort to delimit
unnecessary vegetation.

His Office will recommend installation of nuclear
reactors inside low-growth residential areas of American
cities in order to encourage voluntary citizen relocation at estimated savings to the Federal Government
of more than two billion dollars, yearly.

At the same time, Mr. Fierce suggested that he will recommend
quick phasing out of federal programs for land reclamation
described by the Secretary at one particularly light-hearted
moment during the press conference as "Neanderthal nostalgia
for the little flowers that grow."

In addition, the Secretary indicated he will call
for the computation of food stamps as income so that,

for example, a legitimate Welfare recipient in Mississippi
will have exactly eight dollars a month as disposable cash.

Finally, Mr. Fierce alluded to a companion proposal
that will raise the rent for subsidized housing by twenty percent.

These various initiatives can be trusted to contribute
significantly to the President's economic goals and to
the development of more space, coast to coast. They
will furthermore establish the Office of Space Development
as an increasingly powerful factor in budget-conscious
policymaking.

An unidentified reporter then queried the Secretary as to
whether this plan could fairly be translated as take
down the trees, tear-up the earth, evacuate the urban poor,
and let the people hang, generally speaking.

Mr. Fierce dismissed the question as a clear-cut attempt
at misleading and alarmist language deliberately obtuse
to the main objective of economic recovery for the nation.

Pending official release of his recommendations to
the President, the Secretary refused to comment on the snow
falling on the stones of the cities everywhere.

Abbey Lincoln (Aminata Moseka)

I am the Weaver

I am the weaver.
I knit and sew and twine and braid and
plait and twist and turn and
zig zag and compose and
create and make things be . . . .
See, makin' it is the magic word for me,
I am the weaver . . . and knead
and press and paste and mass and
make dough and bread.

I am a kneader of a mud wall construction . . .
and bring into being, into form by shaping
and putting parts and ingredients together,
and build, construct, fabricate, fashion,
devise and formulate
ways of doing things,
and cause and bring about and produce
and prepare for use.

I am the weaver and make the beds in which people lie.

I establish
and make a rule
that only members could attend
to get and acquire
and make money . . .
and do and perform
or make a quick movement.

I am the weaver
and succeed in becoming the lover of tricks,

and take with a card and name the trump and
shuffle the cards
in a game . . .
to get a score.
I am the weaver.

To cause something to be
I start to do something.
To go, to proceed, to tend, extend,
to point, to behave in a particular manner,
and make bold,
make steady,
make ready and
make fast.

I increase in depth and volume
and rise and accumulate
as does the tide,
the sea,
water in a ship.

I am widely and variously used
in idiomatic phrases
many of which use the key word—make—
faces,
make fun make
eyes,
make good and make sure.

I am the weaver,
the act and process of making,
the way in which something appears,
is made,
style,
build, construction, type, sort, brand,
the disposition, character
and nature,
the weaver,
the maker.

◊ 186

ABBEY LINCOLN (AMINATA MOSEKA)

On Being High

On the edge of his tongue, it was the one word
he dared not speak,
Father to Mother . . . . Young in adultness,
going to and from school, it was spewed out windows
of cars to me, thusly; "Want a ride?" . . . .
Cruising the neighborhoods I was calling home.
A leer in a face,
forcing my head a little higher
in the air.

On a date, I thought, with somebody I thought I knew,
bursting with blooming love songs,
I was raped . . . . While terror ran rampant
in a tearful face, the lawful sheriff,
investigating, questioned him first . . . .
Then, securing me alone to talk, leered and said
I oughta drop the case.
Unsure of rights, I sent my head on higher
and dropped the case.

Stagewise, a piano-player, after being refused a meal
in Salt Lake City, punched me to the floor
after hurling, "hincty Bitch!"
I worked on crutches for two weeks
while a nightclub owner leered . . . . The air was getting thinner.

In Honolulu, the sound was so blatant I became finally deaf . . .
getting higher.
In Hollywood, managers said I was a beautiful bitch
and oughta make a lotta money. I was on my way, . . .
getting higher . . . .
Press agents reported of my bitchyness
and in the thinness of the air, I saw you . . . .

◊ 187

Then, somebody you said you knew
screamed "Bitch."

When I ran to you for cover,
you,
in your fear,
gave me the just deserts
a man gives a bitch.

Locked by now into bitchness,
I began to see dimly
because of blooming love songs
where things can lead
when people labor
under the bitch theory.

I finally heard "Bitch!"

I am high

In The Middle

I am
in the mean
hot
cold
warm
red
purple
blue
high
deep
low
middle

◊ 188

ABBEY LINCOLN (AMINATA MOSEKA)

A Name Change

It's the day of never
I am bloodied
beat
and bowing.
Here,
in pretty chambers
smoking
fuming
plump and fine
unresigned
envious
and envied
Aminata
who are you?
and Moseka too . . . ?
Abbey's blue
The pain comes and goes
stabbing my soul,
flagellating, debilitating,
crushing wings
desirous of flight.

Still waiting for a sign
of structure.
Structureless,
struck
with consternation,
still wondering
what in hell
is going on about me.

Clouds gather
and then disperse.

◊ 189

I am the sun,
warm, shining,
something hot,
yet
there is a chill in the air.
Cold to hot,
cool to warm,
clear to cloudy.
And I wonder
at the sceptic
lurking in entrance ways.
The child scurries for cover.

Feeling all accomplished
sometimes.
Anger choking,
pressing, squeezing,
captive
of my own webbing,
singing, screaming
to release it,
this charge
that sees me in queer attendance,
skillfully being
above myself
in principal,
but in feeling,
feeling put off, and upon.
Moseka, see me through.
Hell is here, too.

AUDRE LORDE

NEED: A Chorale of Black Women's Voices

For Patricia Cowan and Bobbie Jean Graham and the hundreds of other mangled Black Women whose nightmares inform my words[1]

tattle tale tit
your tongue will be slit
and every little boy in town
shall have a little bit.

—nursery rhyme

I.

I:
This woman is Black
so her blood is shed into silence
this woman is Black
so her death falls to earth
like the drippings of birds
to be washed away with silence and rain.

P.C:
For a long time after the baby came
I didn't go out at all
and it got to be really lonely.
Then Bubba started asking about his father
I wanted to connect with the blood again
thought maybe I'd meet somebody
and we could move on together
help make the dream real.

[1] Patricia Cowan, 21, bludgeoned to death in Detroit, 1978. Bobbie Jean Graham, 34, beaten to death in Boston, 1979. One of twelve Black Women murdered within a three-month period in that city.

An ad in the paper said
"Black actress needed
to audition in a play by Black playwright."
I was anxious to get back to work
thought this might be a good place to start
so on the way home from school with Bubba
I answered the ad.
He put a hammer through my head.

B.J.G:
If you are hit in the middle of your body
by a ten-ton truck
your caved-in chest bears the mark of a tire
and your liver pops
like a rubber ball.
If you are knocked down by boulders
from a poorly graded hill
your dying is stamped by the rockprint
upon your crushed body
by the impersonal weight of it all
while life drips out through your liver
smashed by the mindless stone.
When your boyfriend methodically beats you to death
in the alley behind your apartment
and the neighbors pull down their window shades
because they don't want to get involved
the police call it a crime of passion
not a crime of hatred
but I still died
of a lacerated liver
and a man's heel
imprinted upon my chest.

I:
Dead Black women haunt the black maled streets
paying the cities' secret and familiar tithe of blood
burn blood beat blood cut blood

seven-year-old child rape victim blood blood
of a sodomized grandmother blood blood
on the hands of my brother blood
and his blood clotting in the teeth of strangers
as women we were meant to bleed
but not this useless blood
my blood each month a memorial
to my unspoken sisters falling
like red drops to the asphalt
I am not satisfied to bleed
as a quiet symbol for no one's redemption
why is it our blood
that keeps these cities fertile?

I do not even know all their names.
My sisters' deaths are not noteworthy
nor threatening enough to decorate the evening news
not important enough to be fossilized
between the right-to-life pickets
and the San Francisco riots for gay liberation
blood blood of my sisters fallen in this bloody war
with no names no medals no exchange of prisoners
no packages from home
no time off for good behavior
no victories no victors

B.J.G:
Only us
kept afraid to walk out into moonlight
lest we touch our power
only us
kept afraid to speak out
lest our tongues be slit
for the witches we are
our chests crushed
by the foot of a brawny acquaintance
and a ruptured liver bleeding life onto the stones.

◊ 193

ALL:
And how many other deaths
do we live through daily
pretending
we are alive?

II.

P.C:
What terror embossed my face onto your hatred
what ancient and unchallenged enemy
took on my flesh within your eyes
came armed against you
with laughter and a hopeful art
my hair catching the sunlight
my small son eager to see his mother at work?
Now my blood stiffens in the cracks
of your fingers raised to wipe
a half-smile from your lips.
In this picture of you
the face of a white policeman
bends
over my bleeding son
decaying into my brother
who stalked me with a singing hammer.

B.J.G:
And what do you need me for, brother,
to move for you, feel for you, die for you?
You have a grave need for me
but your eyes are thirsty for vengeance
dressed in the easiest blood
and I am closest.

P.C:
When you opened my head with your hammer
did the boogie stop in your brain

the beat go on
the terror run out of you like curdled fury
a half-smile upon your lips?
And did your manhood lay in my skull like a netted fish
or did it spill out like blood
like impotent fury off the tips of your fingers
as your sledgehammer clove my bone to let the light out
did you touch it as it flew away?

ALL:
Borrowed hymns veil the misplaced hatred
saying you need me you need me you need me
like a broken drum
calling me black goddess black hope black strength
black mother
you touch me
and I die in the alleys of Boston
with a stomach stomped through the small of my back
a hammered-in skull in Detroit
a ceremonial knife through my grandmother's used vagina
my burned body hacked to convenience in a vacant lot
I lie in midnight blood like a rebel city
bombed into false submission
and our enemies still sit in power
and judgment
over us all.

P.C:
I need you.
was there no place left
to plant your hammer
spend anger rest horror
no other place to dig for your manhood
except in my woman's brain?

B.J.G:
Do you need me submitting to terror at nightfall
to chop into bits and stuff warm into plastic bags

◊ 195

near the neck of the Harlem River
and they found me there
swollen with your need
do you need me to rape in my seventh year
till blood breaks the corners of my child's mouth
and you explain I was being seductive

ALL:
Do you need me to print on our children
the destruction our enemies imprint upon you
like a Mack truck or an avalanche
destroying us both
carrying home their hatred
you are re-learning my value
in an enemy coin.

III.

I:
I am wary of need
that tastes like destruction.
I am wary of need that tastes like destruction.
Whoever learns to love me
from the mouth of my enemies
walks the edge of my world
like a phantom in a crimson cloak
and the dreambooks speak of money
but my eyes say death.

The simplest part of this poem
is the truth in each one of us
to which it is speaking.
How much of this truth can I bear to see
and still live
unblinded?
How much of this pain
can I use?

AUDRE LORDE

ALL:
"We cannot live without our lives."
"We cannot live without our lives."[2]

---

[2] "We cannot live without our lives" from a poem by Barbara Deming.

◊ 197

ESTHER LOUISE

enough

i ask no more than
you're willing to give
or if the need isn't
in you, it doesn't matter.
i can't stop your moving
without cutting short
what's left of my life
(an hourglass grown fat
with sand at the bottom).
we are tugboats, hosting
a ghost whose pleasure
is our command (one pilot
to a vehicle, no passengers
in the rear). please,
please, understand clearly:
we are not keepers;
no need for zoos.
get off your knees and
don't apologize.
no wrong has been done.
you are outside of me.
that is, we are outside
each other. that is,
we are passing vessels
in a go slow. that is,
time stepped in, slowed
us down just long enough
to touch and that is
enough.

ESTHER LOUISE

it's all in the name

in the last question
i ask, the answer
will not be different.
a same somehow, a laid
low reckoning of who
resides in me. for eons,
i have sat in the same
position without thought.
i'm the third corner
of a triangle; an unwilling
participant in an unholy
struggle; like most veterans,
i can't answer the call
of my name and be honest
in reply. we are a race
of limps, tripping over
each other, trying to escape.
some say, i must check out rumors
of flight. they say,
it is all in the wrist;
there are ways to maneuver
in air. the trick is
getting off the floor;
freeing your arms for
ascension to where real
thought lives and self
is a friend you can call
by your name and be
honest in reply.

◊ 199

running to gone

perhaps, i snapped
shut my mouth too late.
found declarations and
continuums of yesterday
without a voice (which
seems less profound
in our common knowledge).
how could there be a
promise for anytime
of future, without
commitment to the sum
of our past?
in shutting my mouth,
i learned to rise off
pillows of benign comfort.
without leaving any imprint,
i can embrace a malignant
posture with a new love;
a new defiance.
i can sing without lyrics;
be melody without structure;
no longer depend on form
or its labels.
i have stepped out of
presence into absence;
left vague morning memories
on dried sheets of plasma,
and a message reading:
"yesterday, i was running;
today, i am gone."

for us

for us who sometimes fly in dreams,
speaking a dialect of eye language.
sustain thought, a reflective neck
caught in the curve of time. a road,
not starting nor stopping. who is
witness to the whole? i know you
don't always remember when it's
me in the morning with the sun and
the purple. knocking, knocking,
knocking. me in the morning, saying
prayers for the flyers who remain
in dreams speaking, speaking eye.

tokens for "t"

when tokens were thirty cents and
telephone bills seventy-five units,
a lady from school gave me your number.
said, you might be helpful with this
newly acquired craft i use. just saying
how expensive my habit of talking has become.
with inflation and years of practice,
i no longer have use of tokens, but the
telephone is still very dear and talk is
not cheap anymore. i ask the man with
the dog in the window: what is it?
a man teaching craft without touch?
a man speaking lower than whispers

◊ 201

without touch? the man with the dog answers:
"he is a ghost. he has no flesh."
i persist. the voice has a source.
there must be flesh. talk is not cheap
anymore. i could use tokens again.

Paule Marshall

Barbados

Dawn, like the night which had preceded it, came from the sea. In a white mist tumbling like spume over the fishing boats leaving the island and the hunched, ghost shapes of the fishermen. In a white, wet wind breathing over the villages scattered amid the tall canes. The cabbage palms roused, their high headdresses solemnly saluting the wind, and along the white beach which ringed the island the casuarina trees began their moaning—a sound of women lamenting their dead within a cave.

The wind, smarting of the sea, threaded a wet skein through Mr. Watford's five hundred dwarf coconut trees and around his house at the edge of the grove. The house, Colonial American in design, seemed created by the mist—as if out of the dawn's formlessness had come, magically, the solid stone walls, the blind, broad windows and the portico of fat columns which embraced the main story. When the mist cleared, the house remained—pure, proud, a pristine white—disdaining the crude wooden houses in the village outside its high gate.

It was not the dawn settling around his house which awakened Mr. Watford, but the call of his Barbary doves from their hutch in the yard. And it was more the feel of that sound than the sound itself. His hands had retained, from the many times a day he held the doves, the feel of their throats swelling with that murmurous, mournful note. He lay abed now, his hands—as cracked and callused as a cane cutter's—filled with the sound, and against the white sheet which flowed out to the white walls he appeared profoundly alone, yet secure in loneliness, contained. His face was fleshless and severe, his black skin sucked deep into the hollow of his jaw, while under a high brow, which was like a bastion raised against the world, his eyes were indrawn and pure. It was as if during all his seventy years, Mr. Watford had permitted nothing to sight which could have affected him.

He stood up, and his body, muscular but stripped of flesh, appeared to be absolved from time, still young. Yet each clenched gesture of his arms, of his lean shank as he dressed in a faded shirt and work pants,

◊ 203

each vigilant, snapping motion of his head betrayed tension. Ruthlessly he spurred his body to perform like a younger man's. Savagely he denied the accumulated fatigue of the years. Only sometimes when he paused in his grove of coconut trees during the day, his eyes tearing and the breath torn from his lungs, did it seem that if he could find a place hidden from the world and himself he would give way to exhaustion and weep from weariness.

Dressed, he strode through the house, his step tense, his rough hand touching the furniture from Grand Rapids which crowded each room. For some reason, Mr. Watford had never completed the house. Everywhere the walls were raw and unpainted, the furniture unarranged. In the drawing room with its coffered ceiling, he stood before his favorite piece, an old mantel clock which eked out the time. Reluctantly it whirred five and Mr. Watford nodded. His day had begun.

It was no different from all the days which made up the five years since his return to Barbados. Downstairs in the unfinished kitchen, he prepared his morning tea—tea with canned milk and fried bakes—and ate standing at the stove while lizards skittered over the unplastered walls. Then, belching and snuffling the way a child would, he put on a pith helmet, secured his pants legs with bicycle clasps and stepped into the yard. There he fed the doves, holding them so that their sound poured into his hands and laughing gently—but the laugh gave way to an irritable grunt as he saw the mongoose tracks under the hutch. He set the trap again.

The first heat had swept the island like a huge tidal wave when Mr. Watford, with that tense, headlong stride, entered the grove. He had planted the dwarf coconut trees because of their quick yield and because, with their stunted trunks, they always appeared young. Now as he worked, rearranging the complex of pipes which irrigated the land, stripping off the dead leaves, the trees were like cool, moving presences; the stiletto fronds wove a protective dome above him and slowly, as the day soared toward noon, his mind filled with the slivers of sunlight through the trees and the feel of earth in his hands, as it might have been filled with thoughts.

Except for a meal at noon, he remained in the grove until dusk surged up from the sea; then returning to the house, he bathed and dressed in a medical doctor's white uniform, turned on the lights in the parlor and opened the tall doors to the portico. Then the old women of the village on their way to church, the last hawkers caroling, "Fish, flying fish, a penny, my lady," the roistering saga-boys lugging their heavy steel drums to the crossroads where they would rehearse under the street lamps—all passing could glimpse Mr. Watford, stiff in his white uniform and with his head bent heavily over a Boston newspaper. The papers reached him weeks late but he read them anyway, giving a little savage chuckle at the thought that beyond his world that other world went its senseless way. As he read, the night sounds of the village welled into a joyous chorale against the sea's muffled cadence and the hollow, haunting music of the steel band. Soon the moths, lured in by the light, fought to die on the lamp, the beetles crashed drunkenly against the walls and the night—like a woman offering herself to him—became fragrant with the night-blooming cactus.

Even in America Mr. Watford had spent his evenings this way. Coming home from the hospital, where he worked in the boiler room, he would dress in his white uniform and read in the basement of the large rooming house he owned. He had lived closeted like this, detached, because America—despite the money and property he had slowly accumulated—had meant nothing to him. Each morning, walking to the hospital along the rutted Boston streets, through the smoky dawn light, he had known—although it had never been a thought—that his allegiance, his place, lay elsewhere. Neither had the few acquaintances he had made mattered. Nor the women he had occasionally kept as a younger man. After the first month their bodies would grow coarse to his hand and he would begin edging away. . . . So that he had felt no regret when, the year before his retirement, he resigned his job, liquidated his properties and, his fifty-year exile over, returned home.

The clock doled out eight and Mr. Watford folded the newspaper and brushed the burnt moths from the lamp base. His lips still shaped the last words he had read as he moved through the rooms, fastening the windows against the night air, which he had dreaded even as a boy. Something palpable but unseen was always, he believed, crouched in the night's dim recess, waiting to snare him. . . . Once in bed in his sealed room, Mr. Watford fell asleep quickly.

The next day was no different except that Mr. Goodman, the local shopkeeper, sent the boy for coconuts to sell at the racetrack and then came that evening to pay for them and to herald—although Mr. Watford did not know this—the coming of the girl.

That morning, taking his tea, Mr. Watford heard the careful tap of the mule's hoofs and looking out saw the wagon jolting through the dawn and the boy, still lax with sleep, swaying on the seat. He was perhaps eighteen and the muscles packed tightly beneath his lustrous black skin gave him a brooding strength. He came and stood outside the back door, his hands and lowered head performing the small, subtle rites of deference.

Mr. Watford's pleasure was full, for the gestures were those given only to a white man in his time. Yet the boy always nettled him. He sensed a natural arrogance like a pinpoint of light within his dark stare. The boy's stance exhumed a memory buried under the years. He remembered, staring at him, the time when he had worked as a yard boy for a white family, and had had to assume the same respectful pose while their flat, raw, Barbadian voices assailed him with orders. He remembered the muscles in his neck straining as he nodded deeply and a taste like alum on his tongue as he repeated the "Yes, please," as in a litany. But because of their whiteness and wealth, he had never dared hate them. Instead his rancor, like a boomerang, had rebounded, glancing past him to strike all the dark ones like himself, even his mother with her spindled arms and her stomach sagging with a child who was, invariably, dead at birth. He had been the only one of ten to live, the only one to escape. But he had never lost the sense of being pursued by the same dread presence which had claimed them. He had never lost the fear that if he lived too fully he would tire and death would quickly close the gap. His only defense had been a cautious life and work. He had been almost broken by work at the age of twenty when his parents died, leaving him enough money for the passage to America. Gladly had he fled the island. But nothing had mattered after his flight.

The boy's foot stirred the dust. He murmured, "Please, sir, Mr. Watford, Mr. Goodman at the shop send me to pick the coconut."

Mr. Watford's head snapped up. A caustic word flared, but died as he noticed a political button pinned to the boy's patched shirt with "Vote for the Barbados People's Party" printed boldly on it, and below that the motto of the party: "The Old Shall Pass." At this ludicrous touch (for what could this boy, with his splayed and shigoed feet and blunted mind, understand about politics?) he became suddenly nervous, angry. The button and its motto seemed, somehow, directed at him. He said roughly, "Well, come then. You can't pick any coconuts standing there looking foolish!"—and he led the way to the grove.

The coconuts, he knew, would sell well at the booths in the center of the track, where the poor were penned in like cattle. As the heat thickened and the betting grew desperate, they would clamor: "Man, how you selling the water coconuts?" and hacking off the tops they would pour rum into the water within the hollow centers, then tilt the coconuts to their heads so that the rum-sweetened water skimmed their tongues and trickled bright down their dark chins. Mr. Watford had stood among them at the track as a young man, as poor as they were, but proud. And he had always found something unutterably graceful and free in their gestures, something which had roused contradictory feelings in him: admiration, but just as strong, impatience at their easy ways, and shame. . . .

That night, as he sat in his white uniform reading, he heard Mr. Goodman's heavy step and went out and stood at the head of the stairs in a formal, proprietary pose. Mr. Goodman's face floated up into the light—the loose folds of flesh, the skin slick with sweat as if oiled, the eyes scribbled with veins and mottled, bold—as if each blemish there was a sin he proudly displayed or a scar which proved he had met life head-on. His body, unlike Mr. Watford's, was corpulent and, with the trousers caught up around his full crotch, openly concupiscent. He owned the one shop in the village which gave credit and a booth which sold coconuts at the race track, kept a wife and two outside women, drank a rum with each customer at his bar, regularly caned his fourteen children, who still followed him everywhere (even now they were waiting for him in the darkness beyond Mr. Watford's gate) and bet heavily at the races, and when he lost gave a loud hacking laugh which squeezed his body like a pain and left him gasping.

The laugh clutched him now as he flung his pendulous flesh into a chair and wheezed, "Watford, how? Man, I near lose house, shop, shirt and all at race today. I tell you, they got some horses from Trinidad in this meet that's making ours look like they running backwards.

◊ 207

Be Jese, I wouldn't bet on a Bajan horse tomorrow if Christ heself was to give me the top. Those bitches might look good but they's nothing 'pon a track."

Mr. Watford, his back straight as the pillar he leaned against, his eyes unstained, his gaunt face planed by contempt, gave Mr. Goodman his cold, measured smile, thinking that the man would be dead soon, bloated with rice and rum—and somehow this made his own life more certain.

Sputtering with his amiable laughter, Mr. Goodman paid for the coconuts, but instead of leaving then as he usually did, he lingered, his eyes probing for a glimpse inside the house. Mr. Watford waited, his head snapping warily; then, impatient, he started toward the door and Mr. Goodman said, "I tell you, your coconut trees bearing fast enough even for dwarfs. You's lucky, man."

Ordinarily Mr. Watford would have waved both the man and his remark aside, but repelled more than usual tonight by Mr. Goodman's gross form and immodest laugh, he said—glad of the cold edge his slight American accent gave the words—"What luck got to do with it? I does care the trees properly and they bear, that's all. Luck! People, especially this bunch around here, is always looking to luck when the only answer is a little brains and plenty of hard work. . . ." Suddenly remembering the boy that morning and the political button, he added in loud disgust, "Look that half-foolish boy you does send here to pick the coconuts. Instead of him learning a trade and going to England where he might find work he's walking about with a political button. He and all in politics now! But that's the way with these down here. They'll do some of everything but work. They don't want work!" He gestured violently, almost dancing in anger. "They too busy spreeing."

The chair creaked as Mr. Goodman sketched a pained and gentle denial. "No, man," he said, "you wrong. Things is different to before. I mean to say, the young people nowadays is different to how we was. They not just sitting back and taking things no more. They not so frighten for the white people as we was. No, man. Now take that said same boy, for an example. I don't say he don't like a spree, but he's serious, you see him there. He's a member of this new Barbados People's Party. He wants to see his own color running the government. He wants to be able to make a living right here in Barbados instead of going to any cold England. And he's right!" Mr. Goodman paused at a vehement pitch, then shrugged heavily. "What the young people must do, nuh? They got to look to something . . ."

"Look to work!" And Mr. Watford thrust out a hand so that the horned knuckles caught the light.

"Yes, that's true—and it's up to we that got little something to give them work," Mr. Goodman said, and a sadness filtered among the dissipations in his eyes. "I mean to say we that got little something got to help out. In a manner of speaking, we's responsible . . ."

"Responsible!" The word circled Mr. Watford's head like a gnat and he wanted to reach up and haul it down, to squash it underfoot.

Mr. Goodman spread his hands; his breathing rumbled with a sigh. "Yes, in a manner of speaking. That's why, Watford man, you got to provide little work for some poor person down in here. Hire a servant at least! 'Cause I gon tell you something . . ." And he hitched forward his chair, his voice dropped to a wheeze. "People talking. Here you come back rich from big America and build a swell house and plant 'nough coconut trees and you still cleaning and cooking and thing like some woman. Man, it don't look good!" His face screwed in emphasis and he sat back. "Now, there's this girl, the daughter of a friend that just dead, and she need work bad enough. But I wouldn't like to see she working for these white people 'cause you know how those men will take advantage of she. And she'd make a good servant, man. Quiet and quick so, and nothing a-tall to feed and she can sleep anywhere about the place. And she don't have no boys always around her either. . . ." Still talking, Mr. Goodman eased from his chair and reached the stairs with surprising agility. "You need a servant," he whispered, leaning close to Mr. Watford as he passed. "It don't look good, man, people talking. I gon send she."

Mr. Watford was overcome by nausea. Not only from Mr. Goodman's smell—a stench of salt fish, rum and sweat—but from an outrage which was like a sediment in his stomach. For a long time he stood there almost kecking from disgust, until his clock struck eight, reminding him of the sanctuary within—and suddenly his cold laugh dismissed Mr. Goodman and his proposal. Hurrying in, he locked the doors and windows against the night air and, still laughing, he slept.

The next day, coming from the grove to prepare his noon meal, he saw her. She was standing in his driveway, her bare feet like strong dark roots amid the jagged stones, her face tilted toward the sun—and she might have been standing there always waiting for him. She seemed of the sun, of the earth. The folktale of creation might have been true with her: that along a riverbank a god had scooped up the earth—rich and black and warmed by the sun—and molded her poised head with its tufted braids and then with a whimsical touch crowned it with a sober brown felt hat which should have been worn by some stout English matron in a London suburb, had sculptured the passionless face and drawn a screen of gossamer across her eyes to hide the void behind. Beneath her bodice her small breasts were smooth at the crest. Below her waist, her hips branched wide, the place prepared for its load of life. But it was the bold and sensual strength of her legs which completely unstrung Mr. Watford. He wanted to grab a hoe and drive her off.

"What it 'tis you want?" he called sharply.

"Mr. Goodman send me."

"Send you for what?" His voice was shrill in the glare.

She moved. Holding a caved-in valise and a pair of white sandals, her head weaving slightly as though she bore a pail of water there or a tray of mangoes, she glided over the stones as if they were smooth ground. Her bland expression did not change, but her eyes, meeting his, held a vague trust. Pausing a few feet away, she curtsied deeply. "I's the new servant."

Only Mr. Watford's cold laugh saved him from anger. As always it raised him to a height where everything below appeared senseless and insignificant—especially his people, whom the girl embodied. From this height, he could even be charitable. And thinking suddenly of how she had waited in the brutal sun since morning without taking shelter under the nearby tamarind tree, he said, not unkindly, "Well, girl, go back and tell Mr. Goodman for me that I don't need no servant."

"I can't go back."

"How you mean can't?" His head gave its angry snap.

"I'll get lashes," she said simply. "My mother say I must work the day and then if you don't wish me, I can come back. But I's not to leave till night falling, if not I get lashes."

He was shaken by her dispassion. So much so that his head dropped

◊ 210

from its disdaining angle and his hands twitched with helplessness. Despite anything he might say or do, her fear of the whipping would keep her there until nightfall, the valise and shoes in hand. He felt his day with its order and quiet rhythms threatened by her intrusion—and suddenly waving her off as if she were an evil visitation, he hurried into the kitchen to prepare his meal.

But he paused, confused, in front of the stove, knowing that he could not cook and leave her hungry at the door, nor could he cook and serve her as though he were the servant.

"Yes, please."

They said nothing more. She entered the room with a firm step and an air almost of familiarity, placed her valise and shoes in a corner and went directly to the larder. For a time Mr. Watford stood by, his muscles flexing with anger and his eyes bounding ahead of her every move, until, feeling foolish and frighteningly useless, he went out to feed his doves.

The meal was quickly done and as he ate he heard the dry slap of her feet behind him—a pleasant sound—and then silence. When he glanced back she was squatting in the doorway, the sunlight aslant the absurd hat and her face bent to a bowl she held in one palm. She ate slowly, thoughtfully, as if fixing the taste of each spoonful in her mind.

It was then that he decided to let her work the day and at nightfall to pay her a dollar and dismiss her. His decision held when he returned later from the grove and found tea awaiting him, and then through the supper she prepared. Afterward, dressed in his white uniform, he patiently waited out the day's end on the portico, his face setting into a grim mold. Then just as dusk etched the first dark line between the sea and sky, he took out a dollar and went downstairs.

She was not in the kitchen, but the table was set for his morning tea. Muttering at her persistence, he charged down the corridor, which ran the length of the basement, flinging open the doors to the damp, empty rooms on either side, and sending the lizards and the shadows long entrenched there scuttling to safety.

He found her in the small slanted room under the stoop, asleep on an old cot he kept there, her suitcase turned down beside the bed, and the shoes, dress and the ridiculous hat piled on top. A loose nightshift muted the outline of her body and hid her legs, so that she appeared

◊ 211

suddenly defenseless, innocent, with a child's trust in her curled hand and in her deep breathing. Standing in the doorway, with his own breathing snarled and his eyes averted, Mr. Watford felt like an intruder. She had claimed the room. Quivering with frustration, he slowly turned away, vowing that in the morning he would shove the dollar at her and lead her like a cow out of his house. . . .

Dawn brought rain and a hot wind which set the leaves rattling and swiping at the air like distraught arms. Dressing in the dawn darkness, Mr. Watford again armed himself with the dollar and, with his shoulders at an uncompromising set, plunged downstairs. He descended into the warm smell of bakes and this smell, along with the thought that she had been up before him, made his hand knot with exasperation on the banister. The knot tightened as he saw her, dust swirling at her feet as she swept the corridor, her face bent solemn to the task. Shutting her out with a lifted hand, he shouted, "Don't bother sweeping. Here's a dollar. G'long back."

The broom paused and although she did not raise her head, he sensed her groping through the shadowy maze of her mind toward his voice. Behind the dollar which he waved in her face, her eyes slowly cleared. And, surprisingly, they held no fear. Only anticipation and a tenuous trust. It was as if she expected him to say something kind.

"G'long back!" His angry cry was a plea.

Like a small, starved flame, her trust and expectancy died and she said, almost with reproof, "The rain falling."

To confirm this, the wind set the rain stinging across the windows and he could say nothing, even though the words sputtered at his lips. It was useless. There was nothing inside her to comprehend that she was not wanted. His shoulders sagged under the weight of her ignorance, and with a futile gesture he swung away, the dollar hanging from his hand like a small sword gone limp.

She became as fixed and familiar a part of the house as the stones— and as silent. He paid her five dollar a week, gave her Mondays off and in the evenings, after a time, even allowed her to sit in the alcove off the parlor, while he read with his back to her, taking no more notice of her than he did the moths on the lamp.

But once, after many silent evenings together, he detected a sound apart from the night murmurs of the sea and village and the metallic tuning of the steel band, a low, almost inhuman cry of loneliness which chilled him. Frightened, he turned to find her leaning hesitantly toward him, her eyes dark with urgency, and her face tight with bewilderment and a growing anger. He started, not understanding, and her arm lifted to stay him. Eagerly she bent closer. But as she uttered the low cry again, as her fingers described her wish to talk, he jerked around, afraid that she would be foolish enough to speak and that once she did they would be brought close. He would be forced then to acknowledge something about her which he refused to grant; above all, he would be called upon to share a little of himself. Quickly he returned to his newspaper, rustling it to settle the air, and after a time he felt her slowly, bitterly, return to her silence. . . .

Like sand poured in a careful measure from the hand, the weeks flowed down to August and on the first Monday, August bank holiday, Mr. Watford awoke to the sound of the excursion buses leaving the village for the annual outing, their backfire pelleting the dawn calm and the ancient motors protesting the overcrowding. Lying there, listening, he saw with disturbing clarity his mother dressed for an excursion—the white headtie wound above her dark face and her head poised like a dancer's under the heavy outing basket of food. That set of her head had haunted his years, reappearing in the girl as she walked toward him the first day. Aching with the memory, yet annoyed with himself for remembering, he went downstairs.

The girl had already left for the excursion, and although it was her day off, he felt vaguely betrayed by her eagerness to leave him. Somehow it suggested ingratitude. It was as if his doves were suddenly to refuse him their song or his trees their fruit, despite the care he gave them. Some vital past which shaped the simple mosaic of his life seemed suddenly missing. An alien silence curled like coal gas throughout the house. To escape it he remained in the grove all day and, upon his return to the house, dressed with more care than usual, putting on a fresh, starched uniform, and solemnly brushing his hair until it lay in a smooth bush above his brow. Leaning close to the mirror, but avoiding his eyes, he cleaned the white rheum at their corners, and afterward pried loose the dirt under his nails.

Unable to read his papers, he went out on the portico to escape the unnatural silence in the house, and stood with his hands clenched on the balustrade and his taut body straining forward. After a long wait he heard the buses return and voices in gay shreds upon the wind. Slowly his hands relaxed, as did his shoulders under the white uniform; for the first time that day his breathing was regular. She would soon come.

But she did not come and dusk bloomed into night, with a fragrant heat and a full moon which made the leaves glint as though touched with frost. The steel band at the crossroads began the lilting songs of sadness and seduction, and suddenly—like shades roused by the night and the music—images of the girl flitted before Mr. Watford's eyes. He saw her lost amid the carousings in the village, despoiled; he imagined someone like Mr. Goodman clasping her lewdly or tumbling her in the canebrake. His hand rose, trembling, to rid the air of her; he tried to summon his cold laugh. But, somehow, he could not dismiss her as he had always done with everyone else. Instead, he wanted to punish and protect her, to find and lead her back to the house.

As he leaned there, trying not to give way to the desire to go and find her, his fist striking the balustrade to deny his longing, he saw them. The girl first, with the moonlight like a silver patina on her skin, then the boy whom Mr. Goodman sent for the coconuts, whose easy strength and the political button—"The Old Order Shall Pass"—had always mocked and challenged Mr. Watford. They were joined in a tender battle: the boy in a sport shirt riotous with color was reaching for the girl as he leaped and spun, weightless, to the music, while she fended him off with a gesture which was lovely in its promise of surrender. Her protests were little scattered bursts: "But, man, why don't you stop, nuh . . . ? But, you know, you getting on like a real-real idiot. . . ."

Each time she chided him he leaped higher and landed closer, until finally he eluded her arm and caught her by the waist. Boldly he pressed a leg between her tightly closed legs until they opened under his pressure. Their bodies cleaved into one whirling form and while he sang she laughed like a wanton, with her hat cocked over her ear. Dancing, the stones moiling underfoot, they claimed the night. More than the night. The steel band played for them alone. The trees were their frivolous companions, swaying as they swayed. The moon rode the sky because of them.

Mr. Watford, hidden by a dense shadow, felt the tendons which strung him together suddenly go limp; above all, an obscure belief which, like rare china, he had stored on a high shelf in his mind began to tilt. He sensed the familiar specter which hovered in the night reaching out to embrace him, just as the two in the yard were embracing. Utterly unstrung, incapable of either speech or action, he stumbled into the house, only to meet there an accusing silence from the clock, which had missed its eight o'clock winding, and his newspapers lying like ruined leaves over the floor.

He lay in bed in the white uniform, waiting for sleep to rescue him, his hands seeking the comforting sound of his doves. But sleep eluded him and instead of the doves, their throats tremulous with sound, his scarred hands filled with the shape of a woman he had once kept: her skin, which had been almost bruising in its softness; the buttocks and breasts spread under his hands to inspire both cruelty and tenderness. His hands closed to softly crush those forms, and the searing thrust of passion, which he had not felt for years, stabbed his dry groin. He imagined the two outside, their passion at a pitch by now, lying together behind the tamarind tree, or perhaps—and he sat up sharply—they had been bold enough to bring their lust into the house. Did he not smell their taint on the air? Restored suddenly, he rushed downstairs. As he reached the corridor, a thread of light beckoned him from her room and he dashed furiously toward it, rehearsing the angry words which would jar their bodies apart. He neared the door, glimpsed her through the small opening, and his step faltered; the words collapsed.

She was seated alone on the cot, tenderly holding the absurd felt hat in her lap, one leg tucked under her while the other trailed down. A white sandal, its strap broken, dangled from the foot and gently knocked the floor as she absently swung her leg. Her dress was twisted around her body—and pinned to the bodice, so that it gathered the cloth between her small breasts, was the political button the boy always wore. She was dreamily fingering it, her mouth shaped by a gentle, ironic smile and her eyes strangely acute and critical. What had transpired on the cot had not only, it seemed, twisted the dress around her, tumbled her hat and broken her sandal, but had also defined her and brought the blurred forms of life into focus for her. There was a woman's force in her aspect now, a tragic knowing and acceptance in her bent head, a hint about her of Cassandra watching the future wheel before her eyes.

◊ 215

Before those eyes which looked to another world, Mr. Watford's anger and strength failed him and he held to the wall for support. Unreasonably, he felt that he should assume some hushed and reverent pose, to bow as she had the day she had come. If he had known their names, he would have pleaded forgiveness for the sins he had committed against her and the others all his life, against himself. If he could have borne the thought, he would have confessed that it had been love, terrible in its demand, which he had always fled. And that love had been the reason for his return. If he had been honest, he would have whispered—his head bent and a hand shading his eyes—that unlike Mr. Goodman (whom he suddenly envied for his full life) and the boy with his political button (to whom he had lost the girl), he had not been willing to bear the weight of his own responsibility. . . . But all Mr. Watford could admit, clinging there to the wall, was, simply, that he wanted to live—and that the girl held life within her as surely as she held the hat in her hands. If he could prove himself better than the boy, he could win it. Only then, he dimly knew, would he shake off the pursuer which had given him no rest since birth. Hopefully, he staggered forward, his step cautious and contrite, his hands, quivering along the wall.

She did not see or hear him as he pushed the door wider. And for some time he stood there, his shoulders hunched in humility, his skin stripped away to reveal each flaw, his whole self offered in one outstretched hand. Still unaware of him, she swung her leg, and the dangling shoe struck a derisive note. Then, just as he had turned away that evening in the parlor when she had uttered her low call, she turned away now, refusing him.

Mr. Watford's body went slack and then stiffened ominously. He knew that he would have to wrest from her the strength needed to sustain him. Slamming the door, he cried, his voice cracked and strangled, "What you and him was doing in here? Tell me! I'll not have you bringing nastiness round here. Tell me!"

She did not start. Perhaps she had been aware of him all along and had expected his outburst. Or perhaps his demented eye and the desperation rising from him like a musk filled her with pity instead of fear. Whatever, her benign smile held and her eyes remained abstracted until his hand reached out to fling her back on the cot. Then, frowning, she stood up, wobbling a little on the broken shoe and holding the political button as if it was a new power which would steady and protect her. With a cruel flick of her arm she struck aside his hand and, in a voice as cruel, halted him. "But you best move and don't come holding on to me, you nasty, pissy old man. That's all you is, despite yuh big house and fancy furnitures and yuh newspapers from America. You ain't people, Mr. Watford, you ain't people!" And with a look and a lift of her head which made her condemnation final, she placed the hat atop her braids, and turning aside picked up the valise which had always lain, packed, beside the cot—as if even on the first day she had known that this night would come and had been prepared against it. . . .

Mr. Watford did not see her leave, for a pain squeezed his heart dry and the driven blood was a bright, blinding cataract over his eyes. But his inner eye was suddenly clear. For the first time it gazed mutely upon the waste and pretense which had spanned his years. Flung there against the door by the girl's small blow, his body slowly crumpled under the weariness he had long denied. He sensed that dark but unsubstantial figure which roamed the nights searching for him wind him in its chill embrace. He struggled against it, his hands clutching the air with the spastic eloquence of a drowning man. He moaned—and the anguished sound reached beyond the room to fill the house. It escaped to the yard and his doves swelled their throats, moaning with him.

MALKIA M'BUZI

Lament

(for Nina Simone)

>   This sun touched Benin
>   blew away shackles
>   with the wind of her howl
>
>   She was a full chorus of royal song
>
>   till they raped the uterus of her mouth
>   drew blood from her breast
>   cut the dance from her hands
>   & the clap from her heel
>   her face became a Jung circle
>   of punctured anger
>   peering out of laser eyes
>   a rug mouth of needles
>   sand tongue of tunes
>   deflated lips of deaf songs
>   we watch the nose weep
>   while we sit in an ocean of
>   excrement fanning.
>   Who will drag the waters,
>   resurrect the drowned rain?
>   Who will raise Nina from the mud,
>
>   Replace her crown?

MALKIA M'BUZI

Tree Women Quest for Sun . . .

(for the women of Namibia)

Tree women quest for sun thru
threaded rains in this
space of paradox,
dance the joyful dance
thru drenched coals and
solicit peace with
iron breastbones.
lower extremities are full.
worlds are contained
where people are grown
and gourds carried.

in this place of absurdity
women of covered space
polish stone & shatter myths
with hands that lay
across earth.
they protract struggle, disguise
their waiting well
as the done things
squat limbs & scorch eyes.

women of mahogany spines
in this place of parallels
freedom stomp,
interrupt plié;[1]
break line of tutu[2]

[1] In ballet, bending the knees with the knees widespread, the feet turned outwards.
[2] A very short skirt, used in ballet, that stands out like an umbrella from the waist to the hip.

◊ 219

with hip force.
move to wood aged rhythms
thru blood.
become stick that beats
monster to ground.

in a place of fertile earth
and barren mouths
women of covered spaces
pull life from midst
of dead things that
are washed in free rains
and fed from their high places.

in this country of
long horrors and tall promise
tree women of whole space
mold a new nation
with oak fingers from
charred memory stone.

Rosemari Mealy

A Love Poem to an African Freedom Fighter

Our victories at this time
    seem so minute
    compared to the length of time
    they have held the
        yoke around our necks

Proclaiming our victories at this
    time, seem so minute
    compared to what they
        have stolen at our expense

Centuries of false victories have
    they declared
In your country and mine
        So . . .
If we claim our victories
    together/we emerge
      United
    against them . . . thus
    our victories are many
    exposing their
      racism
      bigotry
      hatred
      lies and greed
sentencing them, using
    their own definitions of "crime"
now so vividly painted
    upon the walls
        of
    Soweto

◊ 221

For all the world to see
    while Boston echoed
    The Parallel in my country.
That is why
    A love poem to an
    African Freedom Fighter
      becomes a symbol—
   it's a writer expressing
    another form of
    victory!!

untitled

    Spring comes slowly—
       after
stormy winters and
    deep snows

    Freedom comes quickly—
       after
bitter battles/death
    destruction/pain
new battles—
    reborn . . .

How are we to know
that our freedom spring
is yet to come

Amidst all of this . . .
    silently
      we
      wait

New Chapters for Our History

Take this rose and share with me
for just a few moments
I want to take you on an imaginary voyage
across the sea . . .
  The scenarios are real
  in this interpretation
  The attempt is to expose
  the bourgeoisie and their distorted accounts of history
  Oh, how they have misled you and me.
Pretend that you are speaking to water and if you listen
closely, rippling waves will articulate the ugliness of our
country's history.

First Africa:
  After a stormy voyage, we shall land there now/as accounts
      read:
  The colonizers rejoiced when they set foot upon its shores—
So much wealth did they plunder
so many women did they rape
and ships plentifully were they loaded
with cargos not of gold
but Black flesh was it laden
ten million or more died at sea/
the Atlantic's wealth must boast of floors/
of Black bones decayed now ivory fossils.
Ten million or more, died at sea
referenced as the Middle Passage in liberal history.
  No cannons were shot into the air
  to ceremoniously close the book of death—
  No.markers designate my ancestors' graves
  so what! ten million Blacks.

◊ 223

Back and forth, back and forth, the ships they did sail,
   to America
   the RED People's land
   where they too met a similar fate

   To America
   built not in honesty
   but on the sweat and blood
   of women and men—laboring in chains

   To America
   built not in honesty
   destroying the dignity of women—
   Black sisters breast-fed the mouths
   of those when grown
   would bid upon her at the auction block
   as they did the planters' corn . . .
Take this rose and share with me
an imaginary voyage across the sea.
From Africa, southward too,
the ships did sail/
   to Cuba
   Jamaica
   Venezuela
   Barbados
   Puerto Rico
   Guyana
   Brazil
Portugal, the Dutch, Spain, Britain and France
carved up the world, according to plan.
And up North, America grew!!
Black slaves labored
shackled and chained
while persecuted whites
indentured to masters
toiled and worked
barren lands.

◊ 224

History moved FORWARD
and there was struggle/
   Revolts/
   Black men, women, children
   All fought!!
Wars were declared
slaves were set free/
only to be entrapped
   in promises, rendered to those
   living in bourgeois democratic societies.
History moved FORWARD
machines were invented
industry developed
the rich, they grew richer
while racism ran rampant . . .
A new voice of reaction emerged
   the Klu Klux Klan
   reminiscent of the Middle Passage
   All over again . . .
   This time, death
   hung from trees
   Black men castrated
   Black women raped
   Black people fought back
And issues were debated . . .
   Conventions were held
   organizations were formed . . .
And some decided to leave America, convinced
this country's decadence
could not be reformed/
   to be born Black
   the desire to die free/what was the solution?
   back to Africa was
   the cry of men like
   Marcus Garvey—
   Back to Africa, the home of
   our ancestry!!

◊ 225

Then, there were those who said no—
  Why should we leave?
  we built it
  we fought in their wars
  it's as much ours as it is of theirs
  So they too organized
  to defend themselves.
  They taught each other,
  built schools and colleges,
  worked farms/
  their strength symbolic
  of an emerging nation
  Black women always in the forefront of this
  struggle for identity and liberation
Now, take this rose, and rest with me
while I listen to the narration of my ancestry—
  In the rest of the world
  the oppressed began to fight back
  forcing in Africa
  the colonialist to flee!
  In Latin America/
  peasants rose up
  demanding that they too
  be set free . . .
  In Asia and Europe
  and in Russia, too
  the peasants and workers
  championed something new!
  the October Revolution ignited the fuse . . .
  The October Revolution was seen as the solution
  It became the decisive beacon
  shining brightly, a herald to the world
  the first socialist state a new order—
  that workers could control their own destiny, in life, their own
    fate.
  This inspired all workers,
  that indeed there was a solution, it held hope for the future
  for unborn generations.

And the children of the Black slave
led the Americans in this fight.
    Dubois, the great Black internationalist
    organized the first congress of Pan Africanist
    solidifying the links
    with our sisters and brothers
    on that vibrant continent ...

    The idea of one Africa to unite—
    from the West Indies to the
    Americas—its people subjected to
    the same dominance—the myth of the
    dark continent, can now be cast
    aside/we are now awakened to those
            lies/lies/lies

And now, my rose, its petals flutter in the wind,
as if life oozes, even though
it's held by this broken stem—
but the voyage is yet to end/
on each continent, the blood of my ancestors
is strongly infused
Death/and those who survived the Middle Passage
destined our struggle, international
in its character—
Take this rose and share with me, the task of
passing on to our children
the essence of our history ...
We Black mothers especially—
must teach our young to answer
the call for solidarity/remembering our foremothers who
died in chains
and about the unsung heroines most recently—
Remember Birmingham in '63? when
four Black children died in flames
we must be taught to remember their names:
    Cynthia
    Denise

◊ 227

Carol and Addie May
Give them an atlas so that
they may know, where in '78
hundreds of Black children were shot down in Soweto.
Teach them the songs of Vietnam
write them stories about Madam Binh
that Lolita is in prison because
she wanted to stress the plight of her
people living in a colony—
that Josina led her people in Mozambique
and Allende was murdered by American big business/now
fascism reigns in Chile.
　　Teach our children about
Lucrecia, Irene, Teresa and Engracia who
died for freedom in their country of Angola/that
Amilicar came from Guinea-Bissau—that
Amman was a Palestine sister, her
movement is called Al Fatah
That Emiliano Zapata was a Mexican warrior/who led his people
　　against
annexation and the creation of a border.
That the memories of Cassinga where 1,000 men, women and
　　mostly children
massacred/refugees from Namibia will never be forgotten
　and when the likes of Ian Smith are toppled
　We salute the heroic guerillas of SWAPO.
　South Africa will be next, destroying the ideology of racial
　supremacy
Take this rose and share with me, the glorious gains made by that
little island—shining so brightly in the Americas—Cuba may you
always remain FREE!
Where women lead struggles in every area—and children are the
　　only
privileged class in that society . . .
And now I leave this rose that you have shared with me/
it's a symbol of hope/
its color, a reminder of the pain and struggle in the voyage to
　　freedom.

We have sailed together upon an imaginary voyage—it has taken
　　you
through many epochs in our history . . . it has presented the in-
　　ternational cause—legitimizing the international links of
　　why we echo loudly
the necessity of solidarity . . .
　　It has stated in simple tones/the Afro American's status
　　throughout the reign of the wrong privileged class
　　and why as Black women on this day—we must state
　　emphatically a very natural message of solidarity.
　　We want to reflect hope on this voyage
　　Our children symbolize that intent like
　　the strength of the roses stem.
From Africa, to Latin America, to Asia, to Europe, that Afro
　　America's
message is that we can struggle to win, despite the stakes that we
　　are
up against, that we can struggle to win as implicit from Angola,
　　to
Cuba, to Mozambique, to Guinea-Bissau,
　　　　　　　　And most importantly
　　　　　Our children will fulfill this task in future history.

LOUISE MERIWETHER

A Man Called Jethro

It was almost midnight, the time Jethro used to quit the late shift
and head for home. He hung his heels on the rung of the barstool and
swallowed a mouthful of sour mash in the place he had picked, the
closest black joint to the college only minutes away. He was in the
neighboring town, a little burg off the Hudson River, in a tavern on
the wrong side of the tracks, he thought with contempt, although it
wasn't a bucket of blood but a neat little bar. Checkered red table-
cloths. Fading red linoleum. Homey. A hangout. Folks kept dropping
in for a quick one and remaining to add to the steady hum of chatter,
men mostly, wearing rough work clothes to match their rough-hewn
faces, and a few wine-flabby women.

Jethro gulped down his drink and avoided looking at himself in the
bar mirror, avoided his bleary eyes and day-old beard and what loomed
behind him. He shifted his weight and the gun in his jacket bumped
against his thigh. Damn. The letters in one pocket, his son's thirty-
eight in the other, he had to be crazy. Why had he crammed both letters into his pocket, knives that they were trying to cut off his balls?
"Sonofabitch," he muttered.

Al, the bartender, poised in front of him, asked, "You talking to me,
man?" Jethro shook his head. " 'Cause if you was," Al said with the
stingiest smile, "call me Mister Sonofabitch." Al's bald head resembled a speckled brown egg and he was lean but muscular, with biceps
that rippled as he flicked a damp rag at a moist spot on the bar.

In his plaid mackintosh and visor cap Jethro looked like a lumber-
jack. He was of medium height but powerfully built and his broad
black face boasted the strong nose of a hawk without the hook. "I'm
fifty-four and still in my prime," he said explaining, and sucked in his
gut to prove it. His jutting outthrust chin dared contradiction.

"Is that a fact?" the bartender said, noncommittal, and Jethro
changed gears, peered around as if interested.

"How long this joint been here?"

"Six years?"

"I never noticed it before. I useta work at the college and passed by here sometime." He hadn't been boozing then like a lush.

Al appeared skeptical. "You a teacher?"

"Naw. I was a maintenance man at the college. Give me another shot. A double."

With a swift, deft motion the bartender refilled the glass from a row of bottles in front of the mirror. "Yeah," he said, "a coupla them guys that work there drift in here sometime."

Jethro strained to sound casual. "Any of them here now?"

"No." Al moved down the bar to wait on a woman and Jethro called after him. "Well, let me know if somebody drops in. I'd like to say hello." He would like to blow their goddamn heads off.

He had seen them. A few months ago he had returned to the campus. Its fieldstone buildings resembled manor houses and he had stalked around spying on the maintenance crew in the locker room. It was a private wealthy college on acres of rolling ground in a beautiful wooded area. Woodrow Hall was on a rise, the back of it sloping down a steep incline screened from the road by a thick forsythia hedge, and he had crouched there peering through the basement window. Six of them were in the locker room changing clothes, speaking broken English, all of them of some swarthy mixture that had rendered them almost but not quite white. A bunch of damn foreigners and he had wondered why he was sneaking around when he hadn't done anything wrong. "*I aint done nothing wrong, I aint give them cause,*" he had told Rosa *when she had snatched the letter out of his hand to read it herself.* Rosa. Rosa. Blood on her lip. Oh, my God.

Jethro felt a presence standing next to him at the bar, or rather he smelled the stink of decay. A walking bag of bones with a rope tied around his middle leaned over him, spat fetid fumes into his face, and whispered, "My main man, let me have the loan of a quarter, brother." His breath promised vomit and as he stood there his head dropped into a nod.

Jethro inched away in disgust. This nigger was already dead and he despised addicts.

"Alex," the bartender yelled, "I done told you, stay outta here."

"Man, don't get an attitude."

"If I gotta come around this bar and put you out I'm gonna split

◊ 231

open your head." He made a threatening move and the addict staggered toward the door, pausing for a moment to bum a cigarette from a lady who also gave him a light.

Jethro studied this plump yellow woman seated at the far end of the bar. She swung around on her stool and stared into the contents of her glass, her concentration deadly, as though wishing she could dive head first into her drink and disappear. Trouble. She was obviously in trouble. Like his Rosa. He was her double trouble man. He compared them pound for pound, this sallow woman whose flesh sagged and Rosa, his wife, the mother of his sons, still slender, still beautiful. He loved the square lines of her dark face with its high cheekbones and the long slash of her mouth and her wild tangled hair. She had surprisingly heavy, low-swung breasts, surprising because she was a small-boned woman. "I'm still in my prime," he liked to tease and laughing she would touch him into hardness.

Jethro squirmed on the stool and the letters stabbed him again, reminded him where he was and why. A bunch of damn refugees. Foreigners. Like Andy who he had worked with years ago, a foreigner too but somehow that had been different. Andy was West Indian, from Barbados, and the other colored workers on campus had called him highfalutin. Jethro wondered now how Andy would have responded to the letters, to Mr. Seabury, fast-talking blue-back Andy who had chosen solitude. The little runt. He had refused Jethro's invitation to a dance once, which had bugged him. "They can grab me green card anytime and deport me arse," Andy had said. "For going to a little social to raise money for the church?" Jethro asked and Andy came clean. "I tell you straight out," he said. "You colored born here, it's like you all in a war with them with your white folks. A war with no end, man. You born in it, mixed up with them in a cutthroat way, and you gine die in it. It's that kinda t'ing, so count me out." Jethro was perplexed. "What you talking, man? I aint at war with nobody." "Good. So don't involve me. I come to this country to work, work, that's all. The cold and snow shiver me carcass but it's work I here for, any little t'ing. I lookin' for a second job now and tell you plain as a woman's tits, I dancin' no dance." They worked together another year and although Jethro admired the ferocious little man he never again asked Andy to share even a beer.

He would share a drink now with the sallow woman who had been nice to the junkie. "Bartender," Jethro called, "another double and see what the lady is drinking." He laid a bill on the bar, the remainder of the rent money Rosa had given him last week. In an attempt to ignore that nasty fact he turned to the man sitting next to him and asked for a match. He inhaled deeply, not tasting the smoke as he was no longer tasting his whiskey. Desperately he said to the match giver, "So what's happening, man?"

"You know that woman?" The man indicated the lady Jethro had treated to a drink. She raised it in a salute of thanks.

"No," Jethro said.

"She's stashed out here each and every night," the man informed him. "That's what's wrong with kids today. They momma's too busy wearing pants and trying to act like a man instead of staying home and raising them right. It confuses them. 'Specially a boy. He looks at his momma in her ass-tight jeans and his father with his hair long and wearing jewelry and the kid don't know whether to stand up and pee with his pecker or squat on the toilet stool."

Rosa didn't wear jeans but white nylon pants and a smock to her beauty shop. Jethro said anyhow, "You so right."

The man asked him, "You work around here? Don't think I've seen you in here before."

He had a pockmarked face like a punk Jethro had once heaved through a plate glass window in a sudden rage for patting his oldest son's butt. Then Jethro had taken his son home and whipped that same butt for being in the streets instead of in school. His rage was always there, dammed up beneath the surface, rising to high tide when he whipped his boys, threatening to kill them if they didn't straighten up. They never did to his satisfaction. His oldest two couldn't find jobs and enlisted in the army with Rosa crying, "That's why I raised them? They think that's the only job my sons fit for?" And him yelling, "It'll make a man of them," and Petey, the youngest, saying, "They already men." Petey with his bushy natural and pinched nostrils. Petey who he had bailed out of jail and loaned money to, and yet his son considered him a stumbling block to progress and the beauty of black power. "What power?" Jethro demanded. "Them poems you write? What kinda occupation is that for a grown man?" And Petey, who lived in

Harlem with a welfare mother, said, "I am a visionary, the voice of the people, the people's poet." "Yeah," Jethro said, "well, don't shoot them all," referring to one of Petey's early poems about a young fellow who killed his mother, who wasn't revolutionary enough. The tide. Dammed up. So kill your own godforsaken mother.

"No, I don't work around here," Jethro told the pockmarked man. "Hey, what's your name?"

"Edward."

"Mine's Jethro. Jethro Bowen." He was suddenly drunk and reeling and pulled the letters out of his pocket. "I'm a working man," he said. "All my life I done worked. Since I was twelve, understand? Nobody can say I'm a shiftless nigger." He held a letter up. "This one came first. Sixteen years, man. I worked for them sixteen years. You got it? Four more and I woulda had a pension. Abercrombie Hall. That was my last shift. Cleaning up Abercrombie Hall."

Edward said, "Yeah, well, you been lucky. And that senile cowboy in the White House doing away with three hundred thousand CETA jobs. My kid just got axed. Now what the hell is my boy gonna do?"

Rosa had snatched the letter out of his hand with all the fury in her small body. "I aint give them cause," he said and she asked, "You sure?" Her question was automatic, born from generations of taking on the burden, trying not to stir up the wrath of white folks. It was the unformed question he had asked himself and for one clear moment he hated her.

Edward sipped his beer morosely. "Check out that shit in Miami," he said. "No jobs and the police shooting to kill and then lying as usual. Those black veterans down there got ammo, though, and know how to use it."

Rosa had looked up from the letter and said, "They crazy," aligned with him at last, her black eyes fierce. "I aint give them cause," he repeated and she said, "Call them up and chew them out. But maybe it's a mistake, hon."

"It was not a mistake," Jethro told Edward and read him the letter. It clearly stated that his services were no longer required at their exclusive college and gave him two weeks notice. "Me. Their main flunky. I took care of the boiler. Changed the dormitory locks. Cleaned out the toilets. My last stint was in Abercrombie Hall and I was always polite, entering their back doors with my hat in my hand." *My* school, he had been fond of saying. *Our* students. Like he was a damn part of them. Petey had been right. He was a stumbling block to progress. He looked at Edward. "Man, four more years I coulda got a pension."

The entire maintenance crew, most of them black, had been jettisoned and an agency hired, operated by one Kenneth Seabury, who had signed a contract with the college to perform all of the maintenance work at a saving. Some of the faculty were outraged; some of the students cried foul and circulated petitions. The men who had been fired were recruited by Seabury to work at the college at a lower hourly rate.

"A loss in pay? After sixteen years?" Jethro had spat out the words so forcefully he scattered saliva on Mr. Seabury, seated behind his neat little desk in his neat little office. The man's sandy hair and eyebrows made him appear anemic, too anemic to push a broom himself. "You can either work for me," Kenneth Seabury said, "or find another job. This is a clear-cut case of free enterprise."

Another job. The maintenance union belched fire and brimstone, suggested their dismissed crew hold out until the matter was decided by a labor mediator. Another job. "You operated a cat during the war but not since then? We need an experienced man." He drove a taxi until the accident and then he couldn't be insured. Another job. "Sorry, no openings. Try us again in three months." His unemployment checks ran out. Rosa said, "Don't worry, hon, we'll manage," and fried hair double time in her beauty parlor. At night they held on to the tangible and clung to each other, made love with desperation. At times they just lay there wrapped in each other's arms.

"Can I buy you a taste?" Edward asked.

"Thanks. Sour mash." Jethro waited until his drink had been replenished then said, "Six, seven months later this second letter came from the mediator."

"Might as well be the goddamn Depression all over again," Edward complained.

"So I said to Rosa, okay, they ruled in favor of Seabury so that's out. I'm going back to Manhattan and lug meat. She tell me I'm crazy, that I aint a young man no more. I tell her I can do it again."

Jethro saw himself shivering in the snow. Up and down the street in front of the ugly wholesale meat plants knots of men huddled around open fires burning in trash cans. He stretched out his hands to the flames. The heat licked his face while his backside froze from the bite of the wind blowing in from the ice floes in the Hudson River. "This cold's a bitch," a young man next to him who was built like a fullback muttered. "Hope the damn trucks come soon." "Four o'clock," Jethro said, the voice of experience. He had worked as a lugger for more than twelve years after the war, Rosa complaining that his body wasn't some kinda machine that couldn't wear out. So he had quit, found the job at the college, and besides they paid meat luggers by the day, casual labor, no sick leave, no workmen's comp for your pulled groin, your broken hand, your sprained back. But they paid good. Pick up your cash in the morning on your way out. "They pay good," the young man said, "but I'm thinking of taking a union job. Less per hour but you got security. Know what I mean?" Yeah, he knew.

"Jesus Christ, why you men build your goddamn fire right in the driveway? Move that can. A truck's coming." I'm still in my prime, Rosa, still in my prime. He sucked in his gut, which froze to his spine in the refrigerated truck. He eased the quartered two-hundred-pound steer off the hook, stumbled out of the truck, hung the meat on the overhead rail, watched it roll into the plant. Inside the truck again, back to the rail, his lungs bursting. His blood turned to ice, his muscles to stone. "A hard day's work aint never killed a body," he recalled Andy saying once and he had replied, "I thought you said your grand-father died building the Panama Canal." Andy had the last word. "Man, he died with the fever."

"You got a fever," Rosa said and rubbed Jethro's chest with cam-phor ice. "What you trying to prove? That you know how to kill yourself?" Four weeks. He had been a lugger for only four lousy weeks. "Pneumonia," the doctor said and slammed his behind into a hospital bed.

The bar had become crowded. Edward, toying with his drink, said, "But then again, it's always been a depression here for us."

Al, the bartender, paused in front of Jethro. "Some of those dudes that work at the college are over there." He pointed to a corner table.

Jethro turned around quickly. His breath rattled out of his chest with a grunt, threatened to cave in his ribs. Men were standing behind him two and three deep, obscuring his view. Two waitresses had come on duty, wearing red checkered aprons. "Coming through," one of them yelled. She teetered on skinny legs balancing a tray of drinks. A path opened. Jethro craned his neck, half stood up, and then he saw them, four or five swarthy types like those he had spied on at the college, and sitting among them like a fly in a dirty bottle of milk was a grinning black man.

Jethro eased himself back onto his stool. He couldn't touch her because of them, couldn't hold her or be held, couldn't plunge into the sweetness of her flesh. Rosa. *Blood trickled from her mouth onto her coat.* He threw back his head and encountered his face in the mirror. I'm dying, he thought, and closed his eyes. For months guilt had clawed at his insides until he was all raw nerves, until he couldn't accuse himself anymore and live. Nigger, you aint good for nothing. It was only a job, he kept reminding himself, but a man was a man because he bent his back and worked. Taking a deep breath he blinked and was surprised to discover himself standing at the table with no recall of threading his way through the crowd, still holding his drink in his hand. He swayed drunkenly, grabbed the back of a chair to steady himself.

"Y'all work at the college?"

A chap with gray eyes and a walrus moustache said something foreign, guttural, and a thin fellow murmured through stained teeth, "*Qu'a t'il dit? Ze college? Qui. Qui.*"

They were all drinking beer, counting their pennies, Jethro thought, and their collective thriftiness also wounded him. "Don't any of you bastards speak English?"

"Man, why you come charging here so to cuss we out?" The accent staggered Jethro as did the strangely familiar blue-black face frowning at him sternly.

"Andy? You Andy Brathwaite?" Jethro asked.

"Who dis Andy?" The man glanced around the table. "You all know me to be Andy? I is Sylvestre."

"He was a fella from Barbados I useta work with. At the college. You sound just like him." But Andy had been smaller. A runt.

Sylvestre's eyes twinkled. "All o' we is one." This seemed to tickle him and he broke into a boisterous laugh, took a gulp of beer and almost choked. "I is from Barbados too, and these friends here from all over." He waved his arms grandly. "Cuba, India and . . . But why you interrupt we, man?"

"I had a job at the college. Then you all come."

"Sit down," Sylvestre said.

Jethro squeezed in between him and the East Indian, put his glass down. On the other side of the table, Gray Eyes stared at him with suspicion.

"Man, on me wee island, people does have to leave," Sylvestre said. "Here I work in the kitchen, help out the cook."

"Green card say work," a chap with greasy hair falling into his eyes muttered. "No work, zzz . . ." he passed his hand like a knife across his throat.

"College good," another man said. "Money good. I kees dis ground."

The fog in Jethro's head grew thicker, clouded his vision. He drained his glass, felt the room spinning. "You aint tied up in it the way I am," he said. "It aint just the money, the pension. It's me and them. We go back a long piece together. A long way." Suddenly it seemed longer than sixteen years, more like a lifetime and beyond. "You unnerstand," he pleaded. "We mixed up in it together. You foreigners aint in it like me." His gaze settled on Sylvestre, who was drumming his hand impatiently on the table. Jethro's voice was broken, sad. "Why you aint come to the dance with me, Andy? Why you hang out with these guys?"

"Why you call me out my name, man? Aint I tell you straight off I is Sylvestre?"

"And you were late tonight." The waitress was moving among them, emptying ashtrays. "Another round of beer? How come you guys was so late tonight?"

Sylvestre smiled. "We wait on him." He pointed to the East Indian, who looked pleased. "A toilet flooded in Abercrombie Hall," Sylvestre continued, "and he fixed it. We aint want shit floatin' freely down the hall."

With a roar Jethro jumped up, overturning the table, and yelled over the sound of breaking glass and scuffling feet, "Abercrombie. My job." He heard the scrape of chairs and a voice moan the nigger's crazy and in the darkness the East Indian's face closed in and receded, made him feel for the cold steel, jerk the pistol out of his pocket, and a voice screamed oh shit but he couldn't find the brown face drifting away in the distance and voices shouting and the bright lights in his head shooting off sparks that turned purple and filled the horizon, changed to green then razor blue, and the roaring in his ears said throw some water in his face why niggers drink what can't hold they likker? His arms were pinned to his side and he was numb so he said, "Leggo."

Al said, "You all right now?"

He nodded and the bartender released him. Jethro looked into the embarrassed faces staring at him, looked in vain.

Al said, "I told those dudes to split 'cause I don't want my place shot up. You got some gripe with them, settle it elsewhere."

He escorted him to the door and Jethro stumbled outside into the night. The moon rode high in the sky, casting a pale cold light on the little frame houses. The trees were mourning shadows. "I'm dying," Jethro told them, "dying." It demanded retribution and he stumbled upon it a few blocks away from the bar sitting on the curb. Alex, the junkie. In a nod. Practically falling into the gutter. The rope around his waist seemed to be all that held his body together. Nausea rose in Jethro's chest, fueled his anger, and he kicked the man. "Get up."

The addict jerked like a puppet. "Go away."

Cursing, Jethro bent down and hauled the man to his feet, dragged him across the pavement. His visor cap fell off and Jethro stuffed it into his pocket. The streets were deserted and the occasional cars driving by speeded up at the sight of the two men careening drunkenly between the houses. In an alley Jethro dropped his burden on top of a wooden crate.

"Hey, man. Why you drag me back here?"

Jethro pulled the gun out of his pocket. "You already dead and I'm gonna make it official."

Alex's spine straightened, jerked by an invisible hand. He stared directly at his tormentor. "Go ahead, man," he said calmly, "shoot me."

Jethro could have cried. His arm fell to his side. Heavily he crashed down to the crate, almost falling on top of the junkie. "Go ahead, shoot me," Rosa had said, her mouth split open. He felt cold, already in his grave, and buttoned up his mackintosh. "I promised myself never to hit a woman again," he babbled to Alex, whose head was drooping. "Only once before I done that. I was a young man, full of the crap you hear in the streets. The studs bragging about putting they foot up their old lady's ass. And me and my woman argued about some man who liked her and I hit her. Broke her jaw. We busted up then and I swore never again. Never. Curse her, call her a whore, but don't hit no lady. I never did again until tonight." He slapped Alex's face. "Wake up."

"Man, shoot me if you gonna but I aint no damn punching bag."

"Rosa came home complaining how tired she was, how hard she's worked, and that made me mad. She's working. She's tired. So what does that make me? We argue all the time now. I find myself hollering junk I can't believe myself. Complaining the house aint clean. That she aint clean. The food aint cooked the way I like it. And she screams, 'Cook it yourself.' She hollers a lot too and that's excuse enough for me to slam outta the house, stay away till she's asleep 'cause I can't deal with her no more. She pays the bills, gives me pocket change, and for months I aint been able to touch her. Aint that cold? And if she touches me I move or get outta the bed and naturally that makes her mad. So she says tonight, 'You paid the rent?' I say, 'No.' She's sitting on the bed taking off her stockings, looking kinda drained and hollow. She say, 'Dammit, you didn't mess up the rent money.' I lie. 'Every dime of it.' She so mad she's crying, pulling her stockings back on and yelling that she'll work to keep a roof over our heads but not to supply my bad habits. And where's the money coming from to pay the rent? 'You sleep all day and booze all night. Aint that enough,' she say. 'Why you trying to drive me outta my mind, too?' She put her coat back on, still yapping, and heads for the door. I spin her around. 'Where you think you going?' She yell, 'None of your damn business and you pull this trick one more time I'm gonna leave your black ass.' I yell back, 'You fucking that bastard who cuts hair in your shop. That's why you're talking about leaving me.' Her face breaks wide open with surprise. 'You accusing me?' she say. She's a pretty woman but her face turn ugly then, her mouth all twisted, and the words come out like slime. 'God knows I need to be fucking somebody,' she say.

"That's when I hit her. My fist is in her face, knocking her front teeth loose. She falls back against the dresser and I'm right on top of her, slamming her hard against the wall. Her mouth is busted open. She sags down to the floor. The dresser drawer has flown open and I snatch the letters and the gun, stand over her. Rosa aint scared, her bleeding mouth still twisted saying, 'Go ahead. Shoot me.' I back away from her and run out of the house, away from the temptation to close her mouth forever."

The junkie was snoring gently. Jethro shook him but couldn't awaken him. The magnitude of what he had done brought tears to his eyes. "I hit her," he moaned. Petey had been wrong about shooting your mother who wasn't revolutionary enough. And yet he had wanted to kill her. Rosa. Who he loved more than God.

He put the gun back into his pocket and as if that was a signal Andy's voice bounced around in his head like a billiard ball. *It's work I here for so count me out. You colored born here, it's like you in a war with your white folks. A war with no end, man. . . . It's that kinda t'ing, so count me out.* But Andy couldn't be counted out. Or Sylvestre. Or the rest of that crew. They were all blocking shit moving freely down the hall, which would suck them under the moment they ceased to be hard-working carriers of little green cards. They had been tilted sideways to fit like he had been tilted out. Strange how not working had filled him with guilt. It had settled in his shoulder blades like a load of cement traveling down his veins to shrivel his balls.

Alex's head tipped forward. A glob of spit glistened in the corners of his mouth. Jethro wiped it away with the back of his hand. Being a recent convert to the walking dead himself he understood with sudden clarity Alex's need for premature oblivion. Finally, he knew what he had to do. Alex fell against him. Jethro inhaled the man's stench as if he were breathing in life itself, gulping the air as a newborn baby does whose backside has just been slapped. He put his arm around Alex's shoulders, pulled him close to his chest. A feeling of peace came over Jethro, an ecstasy of calmness.

The sun rose and the two men still sat there, Jethro cradling the addict's body in his arms. Around nine o'clock he decided that it was time. He laid Alex down on the crate, stood up, and began his walk across town. *You colored born here born here born here . . .*

Kenneth Seabury turned around in his seat at Jethro's entrance, then resumed scanning the worksheets on his desk. "I'm not hiring anyone now," he said. "Got a full crew." Jethro did not answer or leave and the irritated Kenneth Seabury glanced up into the nozzle of a thirty-eight. "My God," he cried, the last words he ever uttered. The bullet left a little round hole in his temple.

Later, still in shock, his secretary told the police, "I was in the outer office and no . . . nobody came through here."

Jethro had not been noticed, leaving the premises as he had entered it through the back door, carrying his hat in his hand. He walked several blocks before he put his visor cap back on, pulling it down on his head at a cocky angle.

TONI MORRISON

Recitatif

My mother danced all night and Roberta's was sick. That's why we
were taken to St. Bonny's. People want to put their arms around you
when you tell them you were in a shelter, but it really wasn't bad. No
big long room with one hundred beds like Bellevue. There were four to
a room, and when Roberta and me came, there was a shortage of state
kids, so we were the only ones assigned to 406 and could go from bed
to bed if we wanted to. And we wanted to, too. We changed beds every
night and for the whole four months we were there we never picked
one out as our own permanent bed.

It didn't start out that way. The minute I walked in and the Big
Bozo introduced us, I got sick to my stomach. It was one thing to be
taken out of your own bed early in the morning—it was something else
to be stuck in a strange place with a girl from a whole other race. And
Mary, that's my mother, she was right. Every now and then she would
stop dancing long enough to tell me something important and one of
the things she said was that they never washed their hair and they
smelled funny. Roberta sure did. Smell funny, I mean. So when the
Big Bozo (nobody ever called her Mrs. Itkin, just like nobody every
said St. Bonaventure)—when she said, "Twyla, this is Roberta. Roberta, this is Twyla. Make each other welcome." I said, "My mother
won't like you putting me in here."

"Good," said Bozo. "Maybe then she'll come and take you home."

How's that for mean? If Roberta had laughed I would have killed
her, but she didn't. She just walked over to the window and stood with
her back to us.

"Turn around," said the Bozo. "Don't be rude. Now Twyla. Roberta. When you hear a loud buzzer, that's the call for dinner. Come
down to the first floor. Any fights and no movie." And then, just to
make sure we knew what we would be missing, *"The Wizard of Oz."*

Roberta must have thought I meant that my mother would be mad
about my being put in the shelter. Not about rooming with her, because as soon as Bozo left she came over to me and said, "Is your
mother sick too?"

◇ 243

"No," I said. "She just likes to dance all night."

"Oh," she nodded her head and I liked the way she understood things so fast. So for the moment it didn't matter that we looked like salt and pepper standing there and that's what the other kids called us sometimes. We were eight years old and got F's all the time. Me because I couldn't remember what I read or what the teacher said. And Roberta because she couldn't read at all and didn't even listen to the teacher. She wasn't good at anything except jacks, at which she was a killer: pow scoop pow scoop pow scoop.

We didn't like each other all that much at first, but nobody else wanted to play with us because we weren't real orphans with beautiful dead parents in the sky. We were dumped. Even the New York City Puerto Ricans and the upstate Indians ignored us. All kinds of kids were in there, black ones, white ones, even two Koreans. The food was good, though. At least I thought so. Roberta hated it and left whole pieces of things on her plate: Spam, Salisbury steak—even jello with fruit cocktail in it, and she didn't care if I ate what she wouldn't. Mary's idea of supper was popcorn and a can of Yoo-Hoo. Hot mashed potatoes and two weenies was like Thanksgiving for me.

It really wasn't bad, St. Bonny's. The big girls on the second floor pushed us around now and then. But that was all. They wore lipstick and eyebrow pencil and wobbled their knees while they watched TV. Fifteen, sixteen, even, some of them were. They were put-out girls, scared runaways most of them. Poor little girls who fought their uncles off but looked tough to us, and mean. God did they look mean. The staff tried to keep them separate from the younger children, but sometimes they caught us watching them in the orchard where they played radios and danced with each other. They'd light out after us and pull our hair or twist our arms. We were scared of them, Roberta and me, but neither of us wanted the other one to know it. So we got a good list of dirty names we could shout back when we ran from them through the orchard. I used to dream a lot and almost always the orchard was there. Two acres, four maybe, of these little apple trees. Hundreds of them. Empty and crooked like beggar women when I first came to St. Bonny's but fat with flowers when I left. I don't know why I dreamt about that orchard so much. Nothing really happened there. Nothing all that important, I mean. Just the big girls dancing and playing the radio. Roberta and me watching. Maggie fell down there once. The kitchen woman with legs like parentheses. And the big girls laughed at her. We should have helped her up, I know, but we were scared of those girls with lipstick and eyebrow pencil. Maggie couldn't talk. The kids said she had her tongue cut out, but I think she was just born that way: mute. She was old and sandy-colored and she worked in the kitchen. I don't know if she was nice or not. I just remember her legs like parentheses and how she rocked when she walked. She worked from early in the morning till two o'clock, and if she was late, if she had too much cleaning and didn't get out till two-fifteen or so, she'd cut through the orchard so she wouldn't miss her bus and have to wait another hour. She wore this really stupid little hat—a kid's hat with ear flaps—and she wasn't much taller than we were. A really awful little hat. Even for a mute, it was dumb—dressing like a kid and never saying anything at all.

"But what about if somebody tries to kill her?" I used to wonder about that. "Or what if she wants to cry? Can she cry?"

"Sure," Roberta said. "But just tears. No sounds come out."

"She can't scream?"

"Nope. Nothing."

"Can she hear?"

"I guess."

"Let's call her," I said. And we did.

"Dummy! Dummy!" She never turned her head.

"Bow legs! Bow legs!" Nothing. She just rocked on, the chin straps of her baby-boy hat swaying from side to side. I think we were wrong. I think she could hear and didn't let on. And it shames me even now to think there was somebody in there after all who heard us call her those names and couldn't tell on us.

We got along all right, Roberta and me. Changed beds every night, got F's in civics and communication skills and gym. The Bozo was disappointed in us, she said. Out of 130 of us state cases, 90 were under twelve. Almost all were real orphans with beautiful dead parents in the sky. We were the only ones dumped and the only ones with F's in three classes including gym. So we got along—what with her leaving whole pieces of things on her plate and being nice about not asking questions.

I think it was the day before Maggie fell down that we found out our mothers were coming to visit us on the same Sunday. We had been at the shelter twenty-eight days (Roberta twenty-eight and a half) and this was their first visit with us. Our mothers would come at ten o'clock in time for chapel, then lunch with us in the teachers' lounge. I thought if my dancing mother met her sick mother it might be good for her. And Roberta thought her sick mother would get a big bang out of a dancing one. We got excited about it and curled each other's hair. After breakfast we sat on the bed watching the road from the window. Roberta's socks were still wet. She washed them the night before and put them on the radiator to dry. They hadn't, but she put them on anyway because their tops were so pretty—scalloped in pink. Each of us had a purple construction-paper basket that we had made in craft class. Mine had a yellow crayon rabbit on it. Roberta's had eggs with wiggly lines of color. Inside were cellophane grass and just the jelly beans because I'd eaten the two marshmallow eggs they gave us. The Big Bozo came herself to get us. Smiling she told us we looked very nice and to come downstairs. We were so surprised by the smile we'd never seen before, neither of us moved.

"Don't you want to see your mommies?"

I stood up first and spilled the jelly beans all over the floor. Bozo's smile disappeared while we scrambled to get the candy up off the floor and put it back in the grass.

She escorted us downstairs to the first floor, where the other girls were lining up to file into the chapel. A bunch of grown-ups stood to one side. Viewers mostly. The old biddies who wanted servants and the fags who wanted company looking for children they might want to adopt. Once in a while a grandmother. Almost never anybody young or anybody whose face wouldn't scare you in the night. Because if any of the real orphans had young relatives they wouldn't be real orphans. I saw Mary right away. She had on those green slacks I hated and hated even more now because didn't she know we were going to chapel? And that fur jacket with the pocket linings so ripped she had to pull to get her hands out of them. But her face was pretty—like always, and she smiled and waved like she was the little girl looking for her mother— not me.

I walked slowly, trying not to drop the jelly beans and hoping the paper handle would hold. I had to use my last Chiclet because by the time I finished cutting everything out, all the Elmer's was gone. I am left-handed and the scissors never worked for me. It didn't matter, though; I might just as well have chewed the gum. Mary dropped to her knees and grabbed me, mashing the basket, the jelly beans, and the grass into her ratty fur jacket.

"Twyla, baby. Twyla, baby!"

I could have killed her. Already I heard the big girls in the orchard the next time saying, "Twyyyyyla, baby!" But I couldn't stay mad at Mary while she was smiling and hugging me and smelling of Lady Esther dusting powder. I wanted to stay buried in her fur all day.

To tell the truth I forgot about Roberta. Mary and I got in line for the traipse into chapel and I was feeling proud because she looked so beautiful even in those ugly green slacks that made her behind stick out. A pretty mother on earth is better than a beautiful dead one in the sky even if she did leave you all alone to go dancing.

I felt a tap on my shoulder, turned, and saw Roberta smiling. I smiled back, but not too much lest somebody think this visit was the biggest thing that ever happened in my life. Then Roberta said, "Mother, I want you to meet my roommate, Twyla. And that's Twyla's mother."

I looked up it seemed for miles. She was big. Bigger than any man and on her chest was the biggest cross I'd ever seen. I swear it was six inches long each way. And in the crook of her arm was the biggest Bible ever made.

Mary, simple-minded as ever, grinned and tried to yank her hand out of the pocket with the raggedy lining—to shake hands, I guess. Roberta's mother looked down at me and then looked down at Mary too. She didn't say anything, just grabbed Roberta with her Bible-free hand and stepped out of line, walking quickly to the rear of it. Mary was still grinning because she's not too swift when it comes to what's really going on. Then this light bulb goes off in her head and she says "That bitch!" really loud and us almost in the chapel now. Organ music whining; the Bonny Angels singing sweetly. Everybody in the world turned around to look. And Mary would have kept it up—kept calling names if I hadn't squeezed her hand as hard as I could. That helped a little, but she still twitched and crossed and uncrossed her legs all through service. Even groaned a couple of times. Why did I think she would come there and act right? Slacks. No hat like the grandmothers and viewers, and groaning all the while. When we stood for hymns she kept her mouth shut. Wouldn't even look at the words on the page. She actually reached in her purse for a mirror to check her lipstick. All I could think of was that she really needed to be killed. The sermon lasted a year, and I knew the real orphans were looking smug again.

We were supposed to have lunch in the teachers' lounge, but Mary didn't bring anything, so we picked fur and cellophane grass off the mashed jelly beans and ate them. I could have killed her. I sneaked a look at Roberta. Her mother had brought chicken legs and ham sandwiches and oranges and a whole box of chocolate-covered grahams. Roberta drank milk from a thermos while her mother read the Bible to her.

Things are not right. The wrong food is always with the wrong people. Maybe that's why I got into waitress work later—to match up the right people with the right food. Roberta just let those chicken legs sit there, but she did bring a stack of grahams up to me later when the visit was over. I think she was sorry that her mother would not shake my mother's hand. And I liked that and I liked the fact that she didn't say a word about Mary groaning all the way through the service and not bringing any lunch.

Roberta left in May when the apple trees were heavy and white. On her last day we went to the orchard to watch the big girls smoke and dance by the radio. It didn't matter that they said, "Twyyyyyla, baby." We sat on the ground and breathed. Lady Esther. Apple blossoms. I still go soft when I smell one or the other. Roberta was going home. The big cross and the big Bible was coming to get her and she seemed sort of glad and sort of not. I thought I would die in that room of four beds without her and I knew Bozo had plans to move some other dumped kid in there with me. Roberta promised to write every day, which was really sweet of her because she couldn't read a lick so how could she write anybody. I would have drawn pictures and sent them to her but she never gave me her address. Little by little she faded. Her wet socks with the pink scalloped tops and her big serious-looking eyes—that's all I could catch when I tried to bring her to mind.

I was working behind the counter at the Howard Johnson's on the Thruway just before the Kingston exit. Not a bad job. Kind of a long ride from Newburgh, but okay once I got there. Mine was the second night shift—eleven to seven. Very light until a Greyhound checked in for breakfast around six-thirty. At that hour the sun was all the way clear of the hills behind the restaurant. The place looked better at night—more like shelter—but I loved it when the sun broke in, even if it did show all the cracks in the vinyl and the speckled floor looked dirty no matter what the mop boy did.

It was August and a bus crowd was just unloading. They would stand around a long while: going to the john, and looking at gifts and junk-for-sale machines, reluctant to sit down so soon. Even to eat. I was trying to fill the coffee pots and get them all situated on the electric burners when I saw her. She was sitting in a booth smoking a cigarette with two guys smothered in head and facial hair. Her own hair was so big and wild I could hardly see her face. But the eyes. I would know them anywhere. She had on a powder-blue halter and shorts outfit and earrings the size of bracelets. Talk about lipstick and eyebrow pencil. She made the big girls look like nuns. I couldn't get off the counter until seven o'clock, but I kept watching the booth in case they got up to leave before that. My replacement was on time for a change, so I counted and stacked my receipts as fast as I could and signed off. I walked over to the booth, smiling and wondering if she would remember me. Or even if she wanted to remember me. Maybe she didn't want to be reminded of St. Bonny's or to have anybody know she was ever there. I know I never talked about it to anybody.

I put my hands in my apron pockets and leaned against the back of the booth facing them.

"Roberta? Roberta Fisk?"

She looked up. "Yeah?"

"Twyla."

She squinted for a second and then said, "Wow."

"Remember me?"

"Sure. Hey. Wow."

"It's been a while," I said, and gave a smile to the two hairy guys.

"Yeah. Wow. You work here?"

"Yeah," I said. "I live in Newburgh."

"Newburgh? No kidding?" She laughed then a private laugh that included the guys but only the guys, and they laughed with her. What could I do but laugh too and wonder why I was standing there with my knees showing out from under that uniform. Without looking I could see the blue and white triangle on my head, my hair shapeless in a net, my ankles thick in white oxfords. Nothing could have been less sheer than my stockings. There was this silence that came down right after I laughed. A silence it was her turn to fill up. With introductions, maybe, to her boyfriends or an invitation to sit down and have a Coke. Instead she lit a cigarette off the one she'd just finished and said, "We're on our way to the Coast. He's got an appointment with Hendrix." She gestured casually toward the boy next to her.

"Hendrix? Fantastic," I said. "Really fantastic. What's she doing now?"

Roberta coughed on her cigarette and the two guys rolled their eyes up at the ceiling.

"Hendrix. Jimi Hendrix, asshole. He's only the biggest— Oh, wow. Forget it."

I was dismissed without anyone saying goodbye, so I thought I would do it for her.

"How's your mother?" I asked. Her grin cracked her whole face. She swallowed. "Fine," she said. "How's yours?"

"Pretty as a picture," I said and turned away. The backs of my knees were damp. Howard Johnson's really was a dump in the sunlight.

James is as comfortable as a house slipper. He liked my cooking and I liked his big loud family. They have lived in Newburgh all of their lives and talk about it the way people do who have always known a home. His grandmother is a porch swing older than his father and when they talk about streets and avenues and buildings they call them names they no longer have. They still call the A & P Rico's because it stands on property once a mom and pop store owned by Mr. Rico. And they call the new community college Town Hall because it once was. My mother-in-law puts up jelly and cucumbers and buys butter wrapped in cloth from a dairy. James and his father talk about fishing and baseball and I can see them all together on the Hudson in a raggedy skiff. Half the population of Newburgh is on welfare now, but to my husband's family it was still some upstate paradise of a time long past. A time of ice houses and vegetable wagons, coal furnaces and children weeding gardens. When our son was born my mother-in-law gave me the crib blanket that had been hers.

But the town they remembered had changed. Something quick was in the air. Magnificent old houses, so ruined they had become shelter for squatters and rent risks, were bought and renovated. Smart IBM people moved out of their suburbs back into the city and put shutters up and herb gardens in their backyards. A brochure came in the mail announcing the opening of a Food Emporium. Gourmet food it said—and listed items the rich IBM crowd would want. It was located in a new mall at the edge of town and I drove out to shop there one day—just to see. It was late in June. After the tulips were gone and the Queen Elizabeth roses were open everywhere. I trailed my cart along the aisle tossing in smoked oysters and Robert's sauce and things I knew would sit in my cupboard for years. Only when I found some Klondike ice cream bars did I feel less guilty about spending James's fireman's salary so foolishly. My father-in-law ate them with the same gusto little Joseph did.

Waiting in the check-out line I heard a voice say, "Twyla!"

The classical music piped over the aisles had affected me and the woman leaning toward me was dressed to kill. Diamonds on her hand, a smart white summer dress. "I'm Mrs. Benson," I said.

"Ho. Ho. The Big Bozo," she sang.

For a split second I didn't know what she was talking about. She had a bunch of asparagus and two cartons of fancy water.

"Roberta!"

"Right."

"For heaven's sake. Roberta."

"You look great," she said.

"So do you. Where are you? Here? In Newburgh?"

"Yes. Over in Annandale."

I was opening my mouth to say more when the cashier called my attention to her empty counter.

"Meet you outside." Roberta pointed her finger and went into the express line.

I placed the groceries and kept myself from glancing around to

check Roberta's progress. I remembered Howard Johnson's and looking for a chance to speak only to be greeted with a stingy "wow." But
she was waiting for me and her huge hair was sleek now, smooth
around a small, nicely shaped head. Shoes, dress, everything lovely and
summery and rich. I was dying to know what happened to her, how she
got from Jimi Hendrix to Annandale, a neighborhood full of doctors
and IBM executives. Easy, I thought. Everything is so easy for them.
They think they own the world.

"How long," I asked her. "How long have you been here?"

"A year. I got married to a man who lives here. And you, you're
married too, right? Benson, you said."

"Yeah. James Benson."

"And is he nice?"

"Oh, is he nice?"

"Well, is he?" Roberta's eyes were steady as though she really
meant the question and wanted an answer.

"He's wonderful, Roberta. Wonderful."

"So you're happy."

"Very."

"That's good," she said and nodded her head. "I always hoped
you'd be happy. Any kids? I know you have kids."

"One. A boy. How about you?"

"Four."

"Four?"

She laughed. "Step kids. He's a widower."

"Oh."

"Got a minute? Let's have a coffee."

I thought about the Klondikes melting and the inconvenience of
going all the way to my car and putting the bags in the trunk. Served
me right for buying all that stuff I didn't need. Roberta was ahead
of me.

"Put them in my car. It's right here."

And then I saw the dark blue limousine.

"You married a Chinaman?"

"No," she laughed. "He's the driver."

"Oh, my. If the Big Bozo could see you now."

We both giggled. Really giggled. Suddenly, in just a pulse beat, twenty years disappeared and all of it came rushing back. The big girls (whom we called gar girls—Roberta's misheard word for the evil stone faces described in a civics class) there dancing in the orchard, the ploppy mashed potatoes, the double weenies, the Spam with pineapple. We went into the coffee shop holding on to one another and I tried to think why we were glad to see each other this time and not before. Once, twelve years ago, we passed like strangers. A black girl and a white girl meeting in a Howard Johnson's on the road and having nothing to say. One in a blue and white triangle waitress hat—the other on her way to see Hendrix. Now we were behaving like sisters separated for much too long. Those four short months were nothing in time. Maybe it was the thing itself. Just being there, together. Two little girls who knew what nobody else in the world knew—how not to ask questions. How to believe what had to be believed. There was politeness in that reluctance and generosity as well. Is your mother sick too? No, she dances all night. Oh—and an understanding nod.

We sat in a booth by the window and fell into recollection like veterans.

"Did you ever learn to read?"

"Watch." She picked up the menu. "Special of the day. Cream of corn soup. Entrées. Two dots and a wriggly line. Quiche. Chef salad, scallops . . ."

I was laughing and applauding when the waitress came up.

"Remember the Easter baskets?"

"And how we tried to *introduce* them?"

"Your mother with that cross like two telephone poles."

"And yours with those tight slacks."

We laughed so loudly heads turned and made the laughter harder to suppress.

"What happened to the Jimi Hendrix date?"

Roberta made a blow-out sound with her lips.

"When he died I thought about you."

"Oh, you heard about him finally?"

"Finally. Come on, I was a small-town country waitress."

"And I was a small-town country dropout. God, were we wild. I still don't know how I got out of there alive."

"But you did."

◊ 253

"I did. I really did. Now I'm Mrs. Kenneth Norton."

"Sounds like a mouthful."

"It is."

"Servants and all?"

Roberta held up two fingers.

"Ow! What does he do?"

"Computers and stuff. What do I know?"

"I don't remember a hell of a lot from those days, but Lord, St. Bonny's is as clear as daylight. Remember Maggie? The day she fell down and those gar girls laughed at her?"

Roberta looked up from her salad and stared at me. "Maggie didn't fall," she said.

"Yes, she did. You remember."

"No, Twyla. They knocked her down. Those girls pushed her down and tore her clothes. In the orchard."

"I don't—that's not what happened."

"Sure it is. In the orchard. Remember how scared we were?"

"Wait a minute. I don't remember any of that."

"And Bozo was fired."

"You're crazy. She was there when I left. You left before me."

"I went back. You weren't there when they fired Bozo."

"What?"

"Twice. Once for a year when I was about ten, another for two months when I was fourteen. That's when I ran away."

"You ran away from St. Bonny's?"

"I had to. What do you want? Me dancing in that orchard?"

"Are you sure about Maggie?"

"Of course I'm sure. You've blocked it, Twyla. It happened. Those girls had behavior problems, you know."

"Didn't they, though. But why can't I remember the Maggie thing?"

"Believe me. It happened. And we were there."

"Who did you room with when you went back?" I asked her as if I would know her. The Maggie thing was troubling me.

"Creeps. They tickled themselves in the night."

My ears were itching and I wanted to go home suddenly. This was all very well but she couldn't just comb her hair, wash her face and pretend everything was hunky-dory. After the Howard Johnson's snub. And no apology. Nothing.

"Were you on dope or what that time at Howard Johnson's?" I tried to make my voice sound friendlier than I felt.

"Maybe, a little. I never did drugs much. Why?"

"I don't know; you acted sort of like you didn't want to know me then."

"Oh, Twyla, you know how it was in those days: black—white. You know how everything was."

But I didn't know. I thought it was just the opposite. Busloads of blacks and whites came into Howard Johnson's together. They roamed together then: students, musicians, lovers, protesters. You got to see everything at Howard Johnson's and blacks were very friendly with whites in those days. But sitting there with nothing on my plate but two hard tomato wedges wondering about the melting Klondikes it seemed childish remembering the slight. We went to her car, and with the help of the driver, got my stuff into my station wagon.

"We'll keep in touch this time," she said.

"Sure," I said. "Sure. Give me a call."

"I will," she said, and then just as I was sliding behind the wheel, she leaned into the window. "By the way. Your mother. Did she ever stop dancing?"

I shook my head. "No. Never."

Roberta nodded.

"And yours? Did she ever get well?"

She smiled a tiny sad smile. "No. She never did. Look, call me, okay?"

"Okay," I said, but I knew I wouldn't. Roberta had messed up my past somehow with that business about Maggie. I wouldn't forget a thing like that. Would I?

Strife came to us that fall. At least that's what the paper called it. Strife. Racial strife. The word made me think of a bird—a big shrieking bird out of 1,000,000,000 B.C. Flapping its wings and cawing. Its eye with no lid always bearing down on you. All day it screeched and at night it slept on the rooftops. It woke you in the morning and from the Today show to the eleven o'clock news it kept you an awful company.

I couldn't figure it out from one day to the next. I knew I was supposed to feel something strong, but I didn't know what, and James wasn't any help. Joseph was on the list of kids to be transferred from the junior high school to another one at some far-out-of-the-way place and I thought it was a good thing until I heard it was a bad thing. I mean I didn't know. All the schools seemed dumps to me, and the fact that one was nicer looking didn't hold much weight. But the papers were full of it and then the kids began to get jumpy. In August, mind you. Schools weren't even open yet. I thought Joseph might be frightened to go over there, but he didn't seem scared so I forgot about it, until I found myself driving along Hudson Street out there by the school they were trying to integrate and saw a line of women marching. And who do you suppose was in line, big as life, holding a sign in front of her bigger than her mother's cross? MOTHERS HAVE RIGHTS TOO! it said.

I drove on, and then changed my mind. I circled the block, slowed down, and honked my horn.

Roberta looked over and when she saw me she waved. I didn't wave back, but I didn't move either. She handed her sign to another woman and came over to where I was parked.

"Hi."

"What are you doing?"

"Picketing. What's it look like?"

"What for?"

"What do you mean, 'What for?' They want to take my kids and send them out of the neighborhood. They don't want to go."

"So what if they go to another school? My boy's being bussed too, and I don't mind. Why should you?"

"It's not about us, Twyla. Me and you. It's about our kids."

"What's more *us* than that?"

"Well, it is a free country."

"Not yet, but it will be."

"What the hell does that mean? I'm not doing anything to you."

"You really think that?"

"I know it."

"I wonder what made me think you were different."

"I wonder what made me think you were different."

"Look at them," I said. "Just look. Who do they think they are?

Swarming all over the place like they own it. And now they think they can decide where my child goes to school. Look at them, Roberta. They're Bozos."

Roberta turned around and looked at the women. Almost all of them were standing still now, waiting. Some were even edging toward us. Roberta looked at me out of some refrigerator behind her eyes. "No, they're not. They're just mothers."

"And what am I? Swiss cheese?"

"I used to curl your hair."

"I hated your hands in my hair."

The women were moving. Our faces looked mean to them of course and they looked as though they could not wait to throw themselves in front of a police car, or better yet, into my car and drag me away by my ankles. Now they surrounded my car and gently, gently began to rock it. I swayed back and forth like a sideways yo-yo. Automatically I reached for Roberta, like the old days in the orchard when they saw us watching them and we had to get out of there, and if one of us fell the other pulled her up and if one of us was caught the other stayed to kick and scratch, and neither would leave the other behind. My arm shot out of the car window but no receiving hand was there. Roberta was looking at me sway from side to side in the car and her face was still. My purse slid from the car seat down under the dashboard. The four policemen who had been drinking Tab in their car finally got the message and strolled over, forcing their way through the women. Quietly, firmly they spoke. "Okay, ladies. Back in line or off the streets."

Some of them went away willingly; others had to be urged away from the car doors and the hood. Roberta didn't move. She was looking steadily at me. I was fumbling to turn on the ignition, which wouldn't catch because the gearshift was still in drive. The seats of the car were a mess because the swaying had thrown my grocery coupons all over it and my purse was sprawled on the floor.

"Maybe I am different now, Twyla. But you're not. You're the same little state kid who kicked a poor old black lady when she was down on the ground. You kicked a black lady and you have the nerve to call me a bigot."

The coupons were everywhere and the guts of my purse were

bunched under the dashboard. What was she saying? Black? Maggie wasn't black.

"She wasn't black," I said.

"Like hell she wasn't, and you kicked her. We both did. You kicked a black lady who couldn't even scream."

"Liar!"

"You're the liar! Why don't you just go on home and leave us alone, huh?"

She turned away and I skidded away from the curb.

The next morning I went into the garage and cut the side out of the carton our portable TV had come in. It wasn't nearly big enough, but after a while I had a decent sign: red spray-painted letters on a white background—AND SO DO CHILDREN****. I meant just to go down to the school and tack it up somewhere so those cows on the picket line across the street could see it, but when I got there, some ten or so others had already assembled—protesting the cows across the street. Police permits and everything. I got in line and we strutted in time on our side while Roberta's group strutted on theirs. That first day we were all dignified, pretending the other side didn't exist. The second day there was name calling and finger gestures. But that was about all. People changed signs from time to time, but Roberta never did and neither did I. Actually my sign didn't make sense without Roberta's. "And so do children what?" one of the women on my side asked me. Have rights, I said, as though it was obvious.

Roberta didn't acknowledge my presence in any way and I got to thinking maybe she didn't know I was there. I began to pace myself in the line, jostling people one minute and lagging behind the next, so Roberta and I could reach the end of our respective lines at the same time and there would be a moment in our turn when we would face each other. Still, I couldn't tell whether she saw me and knew my sign was for her. The next day I went early before we were scheduled to assemble. I waited until she got there before I exposed my new creation. As soon as she hoisted her MOTHERS HAVE RIGHTS TOO I began to wave my new one, which said, HOW WOULD YOU KNOW? I know she saw that one, but I had gotten addicted now. My signs got crazier each day, and the women on my side decided that I was a kook. They couldn't make heads or tails out of my brilliant screaming posters.

I brought a painted sign in queenly red with huge black letters that said, IS YOUR MOTHER WELL? Roberta took her lunch break and didn't come back for the rest of the day or any day after. Two days later I stopped going too and couldn't have been missed because nobody understood my signs anyway.

It was a nasty six weeks. Classes were suspended and Joseph didn't go to anybody's school until October. The children—everybody's children—soon got bored with that extended vacation they thought was going to be so great. They looked at TV until their eyes flattened. I spent a couple of mornings tutoring my son, as the other mothers said we should. Twice I opened a text from last year that he had never turned in. Twice he yawned in my face. Other mothers organized living room sessions so the kids would keep up. None of the kids could concentrate so they drifted back to *The Price Is Right* and *The Brady Bunch.* When the school finally opened there were fights once or twice and some sirens roared through the streets every once in a while. There were a lot of photographers from Albany. And just when ABC was about to send up a news crew, the kids settled down like nothing in the world had happened. Joseph hung my HOW WOULD YOU KNOW? sign in his bedroom. I don't know what became of AND SO DO CHILDREN****. I think my father-in-law cleaned some fish on it. He was always puttering around in our garage. Each of his five children lived in Newburgh and he acted as though he had five extra homes.

I couldn't help looking for Roberta when Joseph graduated from high school, but I didn't see her. It didn't trouble me much what she had said to me in the car. I mean the kicking part. I know I didn't do that, I couldn't do that. But I was puzzled by her telling me Maggie was black. When I thought about it I actually couldn't be certain. She wasn't pitch-black, I knew, or I would have remembered that. What I remember was the kiddie hat, and the semicircle legs. I tried to reassure myself about the race thing for a long time until it dawned on me that the truth was already there, and Roberta knew it. I didn't kick her; I didn't join in with the gar girls and kick that lady, but I sure did want to. We watched and never tried to help her and never called for help. Maggie was my dancing mother. Deaf, I thought, and dumb. Nobody inside. Nobody who would hear you if you cried in the night. Nobody who could tell you anything important that you could use. Rocking, dancing, swaying as she walked. And when the gar girls pushed her down, and started roughhousing, I knew she wouldn't scream, couldn't—just like me—and I was glad about that.

We decided not to have a tree, because Christmas would be at my mother-in-law's house, so why have a tree at both places? Joseph was at SUNY New Paltz and we had to economize, we said. But at the last minute, I changed my mind. Nothing could be that bad. So I rushed around town looking for a tree, something small but wide. By the time I found a place, it was snowing and very late. I dawdled like it was the most important purchase in the world and the tree man was fed up with me. Finally I chose one and had it tied onto the trunk of the car. I drove away slowly because the sand trucks were not out yet and the streets could be murder at the beginning of a snowfall. Downtown the streets were wide and rather empty except for a cluster of people coming out of the Newburgh Hotel. The one hotel in town that wasn't built out of cardboard and Plexiglas. A party, probably. The men huddled in the snow were dressed in tails and the women had on furs. Shiny things glittered from underneath their coats. It made me tired to look at them. Tired, tired, tired. On the next corner was a small diner with loops and loops of paper bells in the window. I stopped the car and went in. Just for a cup of coffee and twenty minutes of peace before I went home and tried to finish everything before Christmas Eve.
"Twyla?"
There she was. In a silvery evening gown and dark fur coat. A man and another woman were with her, the man fumbling for change to put in the cigarette machine. The woman was humming and tapping on the counter with her fingernails. They all looked a little bit drunk.
"Well. It's you."
"How are you?"
I shrugged. "Pretty good. Frazzled. Christmas and all."
"Regular?" called the woman from the counter.
"Fine," Roberta called back and then, "Wait for me in the car."
She slipped into the booth beside me. "I have to tell you something, Twyla. I made up my mind if I ever saw you again, I'd tell you."
"I'd just as soon not hear anything, Roberta. It doesn't matter now, anyway."

"No," she said. "Not about that."

"Don't be long," said the woman. She carried two regulars to go and the man peeled his cigarette pack as they left.

"It's about St. Bonny's and Maggie."

"Oh, please."

"Listen to me. I really did think she was black. I didn't make that up. I really thought so. But now I can't be sure. I just remember her as old, so old. And because she couldn't talk—well, you know, I thought she was crazy. She'd been brought up in an institution like my mother was and like I thought I would be too. And you were right. We didn't kick her. It was the gar girls. Only them. But, well, I wanted to. I really wanted them to hurt her. I said we did it, too. You and me, but that's not true. And I don't want you to carry that around. It was just that I wanted to do it so bad that day—wanting to is doing it."

Her eyes were watery from the drinks she'd had, I guess. I know it's that way with me. One glass of wine and I start bawling over the littlest thing.

"We were kids, Roberta."

"Yeah. Yeah. I know, just kids."

"Eight."

"Eight."

"And lonely."

"Scared, too."

She wiped her cheeks with the heel of her hand and smiled. "Well, that's all I wanted to say."

I nodded and couldn't think of any way to fill the silence that went from the diner past the paper bells on out into the snow. It was heavy now. I thought I'd better wait for the sand trucks before starting home.

"Thanks, Roberta."

"Sure."

"Did I tell you? My mother, she never did stop dancing."

"Yes. You told me. And mine, she never got well." Roberta lifted her hands from the tabletop and covered her face with her palms. When she took them away she really was crying. "Oh shit, Twyla. Shit, shit, shit. What the hell happened to Maggie?"

MARGARET PORTER

Sugarman

for my father, Davis C. Porter

> who is that cigar mouthed man
> beside the chimney
> in khaki pants
>
> sugarman?
>
> you say i followed him
> to the toilet
> put too much salt in
> his grits
>
> where did he go muhdeah?
>
> you say he sat with you
> on front porches at night in summer
> hibiscus stroked your nose
> in rocking chairs muhdeah
>
> who is that man who lured you
> into his world at thirteen years
> that man gray haired in khaki pants
> davis muhdeah
> dad muhdeah
>
> he left you with stairstepped
> children to remind you
> of his eyes his hair
> his perfect mouth
> his temperament
> a house with eighteen windows

that man in the ambulance
who died and left his photograph
on the shelf
why did he go
before i could remember
the smell of tobacco
in his mouth
the coffee on his breath
or taste the salt
of his sweat

or love him
or hate him

why did he have to leave.
my memory so early?

when i rite

soap
toilet paper
a grocery list begins
a poem
creeping & crawling
up a hand
sneaking up on
a word
screeching a train
rakes thru poetic
brainstorms

i don't want nobody
peeping over my shoulder
when i rite
looking over

◊ 263

metaphors just now
train rushing
a gush of words spilled
over eyeballed paper

inflation

i am declaring war
on my refrigerator
whose rancid mouth
devours seventy dollars worth of food
like it was an appetizer
drinking all my juices with
not even a thank you
to sweeten its halitoxic breath
i am kicking its ass!

Aishah Rahman

Transcendental Blues

Transcendental Blues was originally produced by the Frederick Douglass Creative Arts Center at the Manhattan Theatre Club in an Equity showcase, August, 1976, directed by Kimako Baraka, with the following cast:

(in order of appearance)

WILMA: Starletta D'pois
JULIAN: Count Stovall
ABORTED CHILD: Madeline Murray
ABORTED CHILD: Erich Berg
FOSTER MOTHER: Yvonne Warden
SHADOW FATHER: Richard Gant
KELVIN: Peter Wise
BOB: Skip Waters
AKBAR: Akin Babatunde
GUEST: The Audience

Place: In the mind, memory, and thought of WILMA

The action takes place in the cosmos of WILMA's mind, thought, and memory. It is a mind searching over its own surfaces and burrowing deep into its depths. No scenery is needed . . . only actors shifting in and out of a three-level stage, appearing and disappearing instantaneously like thoughts in one's mind. Actors will freeze and/or lie down as the focus changes and blackout occurs; the dialogue will make it clear who is "alive" at any moment. WILMA is a shy, gentle, velvet woman who hides under the cover of self-assured aggressiveness. This woman is full of inner conflicts, self-doubts; yet there is a stillness, almost a deep peace within her that makes her a bit mysterious. A woman of approximately forty with a ripeness that threatens to overflow. Wilma's beauty is hidden under years of subconscious self-abuse. Attractive in an eccentric kind of way, her clothing reveals imagination, design, and color if not much neatness. She always dresses as if going to a ball. She is self-questioning . . . trying to grasp the meaning

◊ 265

of her reality . . . It's as though her life was a very tangled, knotted piece of string and she has set out to untangle it . . . knot by knot.

WILMA (*Emerging from the bottom level, extending a graceful hand toward the audience. Lights reveal her slowly*): Actually, I called you on the spur of the moment, half hoping that you wouldn't make it. . . . No, no, please stay . . . I need someone to talk to. Be my guest. (*Suddenly looking around, eager to please*) What can I get you . . . wine? Smoke? Well (*laughing to herself*), even if I don't have a damn thing in the house I can still offer it to you . . . you know, just to show my hospitality. Please, I really want you to stay. You know, we've known each other a long time but somehow you never wanted to look at me . . . you kind of wished that I would vanish . . . I guess I was just fat black mama with lie-gap teeth, smelling strong like damp earth. You know, the kind of woman everyone loves but no man wants. . . . Please . . . don't take it personally . . . but there's a crisis in my life . . . I'm losing someone I love . . . again. My man is leaving me and I said this is the last man that I could ever have. Why? For twenty years I gave pieces of myself to random bodies that rubbed against me with unseeing eyes, and then Julian came searching me out when he was young and I was already old. . . . I came to him with a belly full of baby whose father I wasn't sure of, not that it mattered: I finally had someone to love growing inside of me. When I came to him I was strangely happy though there was no happiness inside of me, and he flooded my flesh with dreams! When we first made love, I was returning from an orgy, still tingling and filled with strange urgings. I passed him on the street, caressing his image. He smelled my heat and chose me. . . . But he was young and I was already old and I strung my blues like beads, counting off each one. You remember how the old folks warn, "Watch out for them old womens, boy . . . they give you worms!" Well, it wasn't worms that I gave my young man but a . . . chilling . . . kind of despair. He brought me love, pure and strong, while I in turn brought him . . . my life . . . memories. And now he wants to leave me and I must play the role of the understanding, mature woman. Big ma-moo, mother earth will smile, move aside, and "unselfishly" wish him love.

JULIAN (*Appearing on the top level, slowly descending toward* WILMA *but looking past her. He moves on the balls of his feet, lightly. There is an air of tenderness and strength about him*). I've got to go now, baby, got to go. I'll be back someday but I've really got to go.

WILMA: He watered my body with his love, making the child within me take root between us. I overflowed. Full up with his juice I soaked into the universe and caught fire to the sun. His green spirit almost chased my years away but his young fire was no match against my pain. Memories were too strong and I fingered my blues like a rosary, counting off each one.

ABORTED CHILDREN (*Unfinished, grotesque* ABORTED CHILDREN *roll around on the second level blocking* JULIAN, *wailing and tossing a chant between them*):
You stifled our breaths
Before they hit the air
Burst our beginnings
And broke our births!

WILMA (*To* GUEST): I don't know why I bring them up at this moment. (*Calling out to* ABORTED CHILDREN *as they vanish*) How much shame do you want me to feel? I hate what I did . . . but I've explained . . . I felt like nothing!

FOSTER MOTHER (*Facing front, beside* WILMA, *as if she is speaking to an invisible little girl*): Nothing . . . that's what you are . . . less than nothing. Here I take you out of the garbage can off the streets where your own mother threw you and this is the thanks I get. . . . Well, like I always say, you can't get a silk purse out of a sow's ear.

WILMA (*Remaining, facing* GUEST): I'm sorry, Mama, I didn't mean to be bad (*ducking an invisible blow from* FOSTER MOTHER); I'm sorry, sorry that my mother didn't want me. Can't I be your little girl for real?

◊ 267

VOICES OF ABORTED CHILDREN (*Taunting*):
Tell your mama give me some
Whole damn block say she is fun
Who's your real ma, don't you know?
I'm your mama
Your daddy tole me so!

FOSTER MOTHER (*Striking out at the invisible voices, becoming strangely alive*): GET OUT, trash. (*Caressing* WILMA) You're just as good as they are. . . . It's not your fault. Trash . . . Soon we'll be moving away from here. . . . Shhhhh. Shhhhh, don't cry, darling; those children are trash. We may live in Harlem but we're not common niggers. When I was a young girl in Barbados living in my father's house we had people doing our laundry. White people. Stand still and let me fix your clothes. Your behind is so big your skirts are always hiked up in the back.

(*Lights up on* SHADOW FATHER, *who is standing on a box with the American flag planted beside him. He is playing "Onward Christian Soldiers" on a clarinet.*)

FOSTER MOTHER (*Calling across to him*): A jackleg preacher . . . I won't have it. Not in my family. We've belonged to the Church of England for years!

SHADOW FATHER (*Looking upward*): I am praying, great Jehovah, to be atoned. Atoned for her hatred . . . Forgive me, sweet Jesus, for her shame when she looks at me.

FOSTER MOTHER: Look at me. . . . Look at me. . . . Look at me, I said. . . . Man, I'm talking about money. I NEED MONEY. . . .

SHADOW FATHER (*Looking at her*): No . . . I'm not afraid. . . . At last I'm prepared to face the world. I've got the call, woman . . . and this time I'm going to answer.

FOSTER MOTHER: You fool . . . you fool . . . I've forgiven you many things. (*To* WILMA) I was in my father's house in Barbados where we had white folks doing our laundry and I come to this.

◊ 268

Lord! I come to this. . . . He told me he was going to be a musician . . . a big-time musician like Louis Armstrong. I come to this
country to get rich and now I have to take in strangers . . . foster
children . . . to make ends meet. He had a good job stoking fires
for General Motors . . . a good company . . . and he give it all up
to try and play music. . . . (*To* FATHER) I've forgiven you. . . .
Do you hear me, I don't hold that against you. (*To* WILMA)
Then he tried . . . of all things . . . I was so ashamed . . . magic . . .
my husband . . . a magician . . . a low, common trickster . . .
Black Herman, traveling from town to town, telling people how
to balance an egg or burn a handkerchief with their breath, or
grow hair, selling miracle tonics . . .

SHADOW FATHER (*Interrupting*):
My dreams were always beautiful
My thoughts were high and fine
No life was ever lived on earth
To match these dreams of mine
(*Continues to play "Onward Christian Soldiers"*)

FOSTER MOTHER: And now . . . a jackleg preacher . . . No, I won't
let you. . . . I'll have, I'll have you arrested.

WILMA (*Miserably*): Stop talking, mama.

FOSTER MOTHER: He was such a good-looking man . . . when he
took me from my father's house in Barbados where white folks
were doing our laundry. He wore a top hat, a gray striped suit,
and spats. How I loved his spats and his silver walking cane.
(*Calls to* SHADOW FATHER, *who has been playing hymns
in the background*) Haven't I loved you all these years . . . haven't
I stuck it out with you? We've loved each other! We used to. . . .
Why don't you ever hold up your head? You never look at me.
You used to look me in the eyes.

SHADOW FATHER: Woman, I am a gentle man and although you
have made my home a battleground and I shrink against your

warring tongue ... I am strong. You have won the war, but I have gained peace. Peace, be still, woman ... let me be.

(*They all disappear, leaving* WILMA.)

JULIAN (*Suddenly appearing, continuing toward her*): Please ... try and understand ... I've got to go. Got to be free. (*Vanishes suddenly*)

WILMA (*Holding up her hand as if to abort these images, says to* GUEST): Why do I keep thinking of things falling apart?

KELVIN (*Calls across to* WILMA *from the second level*): Here I am, Mother, over here, look. (*Vanishes*)

WILMA (*In anguish*): Not yet, honey, it's too soon. ... I'll get to it. ... I'll get to it.

FOSTER MOTHER (*Appearing next to* WILMA *again*): Pregnant? After all I've done for you, you've gone and turned out just like your mother. ... Well, like I always say ... ungratefulness is worse than witchcraft ... you whore. (*Lights up on* SHADOW FATHER) Is it yours? ... Oh, you're not fooling me. ... I know what you two have been doing when I go out. ... I know you've been doing it with her, I know your kind, (*spitting the words out viciously*) jackleg preacher!

WILMA (*Appealing to* GUEST): Shall we lay it all to mothers? Can there be some beginning before them ... some beautiful kind of cosmic birth before we are murdered into this life and so much depends on what kind of luck we have with our parents. ... Is that the reason I feel like crying all the time? I awoke very early this morning and the new day's flesh was soft and indefinable ... leaving me suspended between yesterday and now ... a prisoner of my own memory ... a victim of my own survival. (JULIAN *enters;* WILMA *turns and goes toward him*) Gradually, the morning caressed me and dawn broke softly against my face. I drained my mind of all memories and knew only you dared to live without hating. When you found me my breasts were already ripened with mother's milk, ready to fall, and still I was without a man and had lived through all the promises. I was a woman of worn soil and bitter harvest, yet you loved me, sucking the pain out of me. Yes, it was only you that could love without hating. The others were so helpless (*looking past* JULIAN) yet they all wanted to be saviors. All of them wanted to rescue me, to save this poor Black woman from their own hatred, trying to save me from their own condemnation.

BOB (*Appearing suddenly*):   She had blond hair like rope. We stretched out in the sun so she could dry her hair after I washed it for her. She ran off with another man and left me with our two children. Once, I caught them together . . .

WILMA (*Stopping in front of* BOB, *remembering*):   You'd look at me and call out her name. You'd beat me in your sleep dreaming that it was her next to you and wake up and look at me, your eyes full of a lost love. You taught me that while you would rather feast on her white flesh, my black meat would do as long as you were starved.

BOB (*Taking* WILMA *in his arms*):   Oh, Black girl, queen of the universe, I know not that you are beautiful with your pouting eyes and magic wiggle and hair like, oh, oh, let me sing inside of you . . . (*completely caught up in orgasm*) give me that good white pussy!

WILMA (*Pulling away from him, addressing* GUEST):   I was so young, so new to it all. All I wanted was everything that was you. You were the first and I wanted you to be an absolute Black truth. But the world wouldn't recognize you and soon I couldn't stand what I saw in your eyes when you looked at me.

BOB: If only I hadn't been born into slavery. If only I was free to love you. I wanted to love you, knew I should love you. You were my

◊ 271

mother, my sister. You were me, my Black woman, womb of the universe, mother of mankind. But every time I looked at you I felt so inadequate and frail. My passion for you wasn't love but hate. Hatred for making me fear you.

(BOB *exits;* JULIAN *enters.*)

WILMA: He looked at me, trying to reach back to a time when I must have been young and beautiful; he toiled in me, watering my child, filling me up with sweetness, singing inside of me, but the years proved too strong. (*Continuing toward* JULIAN) Oh, how I wanted to love newly, how I wanted to forget, to laugh at myself and doubt my existence before your love. Please don't leave; I'm afraid my spirit will die if I lose you; it will be the end of me, the death of all love.

JULIAN (*Calling across to* WILMA):   I've been trying to tell you, just because I'm leaving doesn't mean you're losing me. When I met you I was on my way to freedom. I only stopped to love you because you needed love so badly.

WILMA (*Angrily interrupting*):   Who do you think you are? Who do you think I am? I'm not a beggar. I'm a woman and I want love, not pity. Who do you think you are, a savior, a charity worker? A . . .

JULIAN: I'll tell you who I am, not much, a natural man. A rule unto my own law, which is simply love. I take love wherever I run into it. Woman . . . I am a natural man who loves many things and many people—

WILMA: Oh, please. You don't have to brag . . . I know all about her. I know all about your greenhearted woman that you are leaving me for. Well, I've had others too . . . it was not so much a matter of revenge as it was exorcism. Any man would have done as long as he dug deep inside of me and released me from you . . . pressed you into the shade, put distance between us . . .

JULIAN (*Continuing as if he was not interrupted by* WILMA's *tirade*):   And I love you. Though my feet touches this earth my heart is in an eternal sunland and heaven is in your thighs. And yet? Though I was born a man, who expects me to be one? I am Black, strong, uneducated, and not capable of being moral or rational. And I likes my rum. I am a Black man in an imperfect world. But luckily my ancestors' spirits ride me and I step to the beat of the ogun gun drum. I'm a stranger here . . . a captive from sunland and to hell with the new gods and the things that imprison a man! Wilma . . . you must understand . . . that I must go . . . not toward anyone or away from you . . . my freedom is the going . . .

WILMA: Go, go. Leave, leave. Leaving is easy. When are you *all* going to learn how to stay?

JULIAN: When are you all going to learn to love with no questions asked . . . just love for the pure joy of loving? No questions asked . . . no contracts signed.

WILMA: It wasn't as though I wanted to marry you . . . or even live with you . . . but I've got to have something . . . sometime.

JULIAN: I'm not rich and I can't promise you forever. . . . I can't, would never promise you anything. . . . I am young. How many times must I tell you that I am still so far beneath you. . . . I have so far to go. . . . It doesn't mean that I am unworthy but it does mean that I need time and space to grow at my own rate. . . .

WILMA: Oh God, Oh Goddamn . . . how you drag me down. . . . How dare you be an abstract, irresponsible nigger when my life is imprisoned in realities. . . . For God's sake DO SOMETHING. . . . I've got to pay the rent, feed the baby . . .

(*Suddenly,* FOSTER MOTHER *appears.*)

WILMA/FOSTER MOTHER: I'm talking about money, man. I NEED MONEY.

◊ 273

WILMA (*Calling across to* SHADOW FATHER, *who has suddenly reappeared*): Oh God ... Daddy ... I promised myself I wouldn't be like her ... I wouldn't let it happen to me ... and look at me ... just listen to me, Daddy. ... Why didn't you stop her ... why didn't you help me?

SHADOW FATHER:
My dreams were always beautiful
My thoughts were high and fine
No life was ever lived on earth
To match these dreams of mine

JULIAN (*As if continuing where* SHADOW FATHER *stopped*):
And I too am a stranger here
A captive from sunland
To hell with the new gods
And the things that imprison a man
Take my hand, mama, use my love
Bathe in it, heal, and don't be afraid
But tell me ... once you were delicate
And soft to a man's touch
Now you are all wrinkled and rough. ...
What did they do to your soft nature?
Tell me if you can ... tell me ...

WILMA: I burst the heads of babies growing within me and gave away my firstborn child in order to cleanse my blood of a Black woman's curse!

(ABORTED CHILDREN *and* KELVIN *reappear.*)

ABORTED CHILDREN (*making loud breathing sounds*):
Every breath you take
Is one you denied us

KELVIN: Don't leave me. ... I am your son. ... Don't throw me away.

◊ 274

(ABORTED CHILDREN *suddenly vanish.*)

WILMA (*Continuing*):   The curse of "Oh God, if only I had someone to help me raise these children." The curse of "Wait till the check comes and I'll buy you some food." The curse of sleeping with the highest bidder. (AKBAR *appears, a rather short square African-garbed man with a walking stick and an air of intensity that borders on madness*) I watched someone I loved go mad and became part of his insanity trying to fight the shadows in his mind. . . .

AKBAR (*Performs the following, bobbing and weaving his body as if he were a jazz musician playing a sax.*):
Black womannnnnnn, womannnnnnn, womannnnnnn
With your blue salt, too salt salt tears, salt tears,
salt tears
Bursting into red, green, magenta smiles
Splashing coolly, bluely, into my soul
Passion! Passion! Passion!
Seed of Life
I am youuuuuuuuuuuuuuuuuuuuuuuuuuu
You are meeeeeeeeeeeeeeeeeeeeeeee
Black womannnnnnnnnnnnnnnnnnnnnnn
(*Pausing*) I am God and since you're my queen that makes you God-ess. I'll dedicate my poems to you.

WILMA (*To* GUEST):   Why am I grateful for being loved . . . why couldn't I have just said . . . of course you love me . . . because I am so lovable . . . if you don't love me you don't know your place in the universe. (*Calling to* AKBAR, *who is moving away from her*) And you won't ever look at any other woman . . . right? I'll be all woman to you. . . . (*Incredulously*) You raped a woman . . . in our house. . . .

AKBAR: Why? Because I told you I am God . . . Allah . . . Allll ahhh!

WILMA (*To* GUEST):   I married him because I wanted . . . poetry! His words were like hot liquid blaring away, making my blood pop, but sweet like the taste of a lover's sweat. I wanted his poems . . . to be close to them . . . to touch them . . .

◊ 275

AKBAR (*Interrupting*):   To smother me ... (*Grows progressively more out of control*) To drain my poetry like some some fucking Black vampire! You sucked my poetry from my head, drained my energies, making me play nursemaid to you because you are an emotional cripple ... and you said you loved me. Yes I raped a woman in our own bed ... and you dare ask me why? Because I give my people my poetry and they don't even know who I am.... They eat up my poetry without recognizing that I have been declared Allah, yet they worship at the temple of my words. I am the most well-known obscure poet living.... Why? Because I am going mad with fat frustrations ... and the mad commit holy rapes! You women ... I want to consume you all and make you part of my greatness. Instead you stand separate and afraid of me, trembling and in your nakedness waiting to devour me.... Maybe I should just say fuck it and get jabbed in the ass by some dude with voluptuous muscles, but I confess ... I lust after pussy ... I want to capture the mystery of you women ... and that is why I rape, my queen, and anyone is subject to my lust. (*Disappears suddenly*)

WILMA (*Calling to* JULIAN ... *struggling toward him*):   Are you listening, my man? Do you hear the things I'm telling you? I have dreamed of loving soft young women ... their ripe wombs quivering against my tongue.... I have been to Hopeless Town where woman marry woman because there are no men and I.... and I ...

KELVIN: And you saved me for last ... although I happened first ... you saved me for last.... It's time, (*sarcastically*) mother.

WILMA: Yes, I know. (*To* GUEST) And so we're back to the beginning again. (*Suddenly appealing to* KELVIN *as if she were the child and he the parent*) Do we have to ... talk about this ... after all, I've exposed myself enough.

KELVIN (*Relentlessly*):   But have you told the truth? You and I know the truth, don't we, Mother dear, and it's time you admit it.

◊ 276

WILMA: Go away.... I don't know you, child.... It was so long
ago.... Why do you keep bothering me?

FOSTER MOTHER (*Appearing and disappearing suddenly*):   Pregnant? After all I've done for you!

WILMA (*As if in a trance*):   When I knew I was pregnant I hated you.
You were some evil thing growing inside of me, choking off my
life ... you were a curse that ran in my blood and took root in my
body. You were fat mamas hanging out top-floor windows waiting
for their checks ... you were fatherless children never knowing
from what source your blood flowed ... you were a woman's cries
beating against the night, searching for her gone-man's ears.... I
wanted to soar, to fly, to go to Paris, to live in a garret, chew
mushrooms, and be the most loved woman in the universe ... I
wanted art, music, love ... I wanted LIFE!

KELVIN (*Relentlessly*):   The truth ... Mother dear.

WILMA: I'd like to pretend ... you arrived for noble reasons on my
part.... The only reason, dear child of mine, that you were born
is because I was afraid that if I had an abortion I would die also.

KELVIN: Later on, you just got wiser and crushed my brothers and
sisters before they could escape your womb ... but me ... your
firstborn ... you just dumped me on charity ... gave me away to
a state that couldn't care less about unwanted Black babies.

WILMA: They told me it was best. (*To* GUEST) I never believed
that he would be born ... I remember being surprised and annoyed when the pains began. I remember being astonished at his
warm wetness, his weight in my arms when they brought him and
said, "Here's your son."

KELVIN: Go on. What happened then ... did your mama's love
come tumbling down in one happy torrent?

◊ 277

WILMA (*Continuing*):   I looked at you, freshly born . . . new soul swaying in the wind . . . my son. I knew that I would leave you and all my life be doomed to lose the people I loved. . . .

KELVIN: It's time to admit your big secret, Mother dear.

WILMA (*Continuing, ignoring him*):   And at three months while he was wearing a mint-green suit I . . . (*in a toneless voice*) voluntarily and of my own free will give up all rights to my son Kelvin Randolph and will not attempt to claim him in any manner now and forever more.(*Appealing to him suddenly*) But they told me you would be adopted. By a nice professional colored family with matching skin tone and a yard and a bicycle for you to play with.   .

KELVIN: The truth . . . the truth after all these years . . . admit your secret. Go on . . . admit . . . all your life . . . all these years you never loved anyone.

WILMA: That I am incapable of love?

KELVIN: That you are incapable of love. That each man who comes into your/ life is all the evil in the world, all the betrayal, all the broken hopes, all the murderous revenge. That/ you are the deadly she animal inflicting your/ "love" upon men, weakening them with your unhappiness, setting them up for the death of love. That down through the years you used men like toilet paper . . . flushing away the endless line of men. . . . You never loved any of them. . . . You got rid of your children, gave away your son and left your men. . . . Go on . . . admit that you are incapable of love and you hate men!!

(BOB, AKBAR, *and* JULIAN *appear, tumbling and somersaulting over one another . . . now a talented group of gymnasts. They toss the following dialogue among them while performing . . . locking in* WILMA.)

◊ 278

AISHAH RAHMAN

AKBAR:

    All I was trying to tell her
    Was I can't stand still
    In no where air
    Got to get where I can breathe
    Got to make it
    Take care of bizness now!

JULIAN:

    Here's to makin, makin, makin it
    Ain't no big thing
    Sounds like a slamming door
    Fading footsteps
    into white nights
    of Emptiness
    Heavy sound of empty pockets
    Taking care of bizness
    Just trying to take care
    Of a little bizness

BOB:

    Mmmmmmmmmm mmmmmmmmmm mmmmmmmmmm
    Sure is fine

AKBAR:

    Lady of mine

BOB:

    Big ass

JULIAN:

    Nice mouth
    Can I have a word with you in private?

AKBAR:

    No need for us to . . .

◊ 279

BOB:

I'll take the bottom
Was always a leg man myself
Now how come she couldn't understand?

JULIAN:

There are 360 ways of lookin at a man
She only knew two
"Correct" and "incorrect"
(*Mimicking a female voice*)
You are sure one incorrect nigga!
There are at least twenty-one dimensions
Fools like us only see three!

BOB, JULIAN, AKBAR:

Wow, I'm gone
Yes, I'm gone
Got to take care of bizness now!!!!

JULIAN:

All I'm trying to tell you, woman
You're my sweet baby

AKBAR:

In love

BOB:

Around love

JULIAN:

Out of love

BOB:

Under love

AKBAR:

Before love

◇ 280

AISHAH RAHMAN

JULIAN:
On top of love

BOB:
Past love
Found love
Left love

JULIAN, AKBAR, BOB:
Got to make it, baby
But your buns are the best

AKBAR:
Now, all I'm trying to tell you, Mama

JULIAN:
Is that I grew up on you

AKBAR:
You raised me

JULIAN:
Cut my man-teeth
on yo soft titties

AKBAR:
Yo big ass
Yo good pussy

BOB:
Yo hard words

JULIAN:
Yo soft ways

AKBAR:
Yo good love

◊ 281

JULIAN:
> I even took the part of you
> That you were saving for yourself

BOB, JULIAN, AKBAR:
> But I'm gone now
> Yes, I'm gone now
> Can't stand still
> In no where air
> Got to take care
> OF BIZNESS right now

AKBAR:
> Spring-Toned Lady

BOB:
> Black Fantasy Bitch

JULIAN:
> All I'm trying to say
> Is I dig you
> In my own way
> But I'm gone gone gone gone
> Fraid to stand still
> In no where air
> Got to get where I can breathe

(BOB, AKBAR, *and* JULIAN *have* WILMA *locked in with their hands and bodies, forming a prison.*)

WILMA (*In a slow-building tempo*):   That I hate men? No. YOU ARE THE KILLERS; let me out of here. . . . It's not true. Leave me alone, don't, leave me alone . . . stop tormenting me, predatory beasts prowling in the jungle preying on silly women, eating my flesh trying to find love, trying to give love brought me pain . . . pain burning in every vein, sizzling, stinging, starfire pain. Screaming, silent, singing pain. Blues pain. Take me where no pain sings. I hate men? No, it can't be true, finally that day is there when you know it ... the day we finally are what we are ... we have stopped becoming. We see for the first time what we are and what I am simply is ... tired ... I need to be taken care of ... do something. Anything. I need so much that it is really so little. ... I need to fuck in the afternoon. Each of you wanted my love, my concern, but how come you big strong men didn't seem to care what I need when all I really need is yellow roses and music and a man who stays in me after he comes. Trees. I need trees. Need to bathe in liquid roses. My silly little needs are more desperate than yours and I remember the tender moments, soft memories and there is no past, no vendetta, only now, and truth is I can't see myself as old and in the end he leaves as he is leaving in the beginning and that's all right cause now I know that I always have, always will be bout some loving. (WILMA *rises, purified, talking to* GUEST) Thank you, thank you for coming. ... If you hurry you can catch the last bus. ... It's the first time we ever talked in all these years and I needed you to listen so much ... but now I know ... there will be others. ... I will love again after Julian leaves me. ... I will love again, again, and again because now I know I always have and always will be bout some loving. ...

I've conquered the death of love
Lurking inside of me
Waiting to strike like a deadly scorpion
It's love slave that I am
Not men
Through all of you
I found the love in myself
My own love
In all of you
So go or stay
Either way, I'll never lose
Cause who am I not to Transcend Blues?
Who am I
To have known velvet times?

◊ 283

Loving you in soft rooms
Happily licking your smile
With my eyes?
Who am I?
Who am I?
To have loved at all?
As the years fall like rain
And the fire in my blood
Burns rivers

The Lady and the Tramp

CHARACTERS

Opal, A Black Woman
Psyche, A Black Man
Bus Driver's Voice
Bus Passengers

A crawling, crowded bus headed uptown in the hot city. The bus is dimly lighted. BUS PASSENGERS move in slow motion on and off the bus. There is something ghostly, unreal, macabre about them. The bus driver could be a huge papier-mâché figure with a leering grin. Once in a while the bus jerks and coughs, throwing PASSENGERS together, entangling their bodies. The bus is already crowded except for one empty seat, although some folks are already standing. Suddenly, the bus doors yawn open and in the ritualistic getting on and off PSYCHE enters. He is of indeterminate age. He walks erratically, in the manner of a wino. Spying the empty seat he makes a beeline for it. PASSENGERS slowly turn their faces toward him. Once PSYCHE captures the seat, he looks around, stretches out his body. sticking his feet straight out in front of him despite the crowd and crossing them at the ankles, and folds his hands across his chest, laying his chin there and closing his eyes. OPAL enters. She is dressed in New York chic–African-arts-and-crafts fashion. She carries a large portfolio. Spying an empty strap in front of PSYCHE, she looks around to see if

*she has any other alternative. Seeing none, she settles for the spot
in front of* PSYCHE. *Finally, straddling the large portfolio between her legs, she extracts a book with one hand, and hanging
on to a strap she proceeds to read in order to blank out* PSY-
CHE *in front of her.*

PSYCHE: Dja wanna sit down?

(OPAL *ignores him.*)

PSYCHE: Lady, dja wanna seat? Djou wanna sit down, huh?
(*Reaches out to touch her in order to get her attention*)

OPAL (*Recoiling at his touch*):
Ohhhhhhhh!

PSYCHE: Look, lady, I was jesh trying to be a gennulman but if you
don't want to sit down . . . fuck it. . . . (*Begins to scat a bebop
riff*)

OPAL: Oh, no thanks . . . that's all right. . .

PSYCHE: Suit yourself . . . suit yourself. (*Continues scatting. Annoyed that* OPAL *has refused his chivalry, he opens his eyes and
deliberately stares at her for a few beats. Suddenly, breaking into
a smile, he slowly extracts a bottle from his chest. Ceremoniously
opening it, he takes a long slow drink, tilting his head back as far
as he can, drinks deeply. Satisfied, he suddenly sits upright, holding the bottle in front of him.*) Say, lady . . . djou wanna drink?

OPAL: Look, I don't want to sit down, I don't want a drink, and I
don't want to talk. Now will you please stop? Besides . . . you're
DRUNK!

PSYCHE: Madam . . . I admit . . . I did imbibe. . . . I acknowledge
that I did partake of the grape. But to accuse me of being ine-
briated is to slander my character!

◊ 285

(BUS PASSENGERS *crack up at both* OPAL *and* PSYCHE.)

OPAL: I mean, why . . . why me? All the people on the bus for you to mess with, why do you have to PICK ON ME?

PSYCHE: Lissun, lady, I thought with all these packages you would be both tired and thirsty . . . that's all. . . . I didn't mean no harm. . . . Don't you unnerstand?

> When you are tired you rest
> When you are thirsty you drink

I jes ask you to sit an have a lil ole drink with me . . . that's all.

(OPAL *retreats to her book.*)

PSYCHE: What chu reading, lady?

(OPAL *continues to ignore him.*)

PSYCHE: Don't ig me, woman! I don't unnerstan how you could hang all over me . . . knocking up against me and me sitting in front of you, eye level to your crotch, and you still pretend that I'm not real. (*Leaning closer, yelling*) I SAY, WHAT ARE YOU READING?

OPAL (*Coldly*):   You're sure. You're quite sure you want to have a conversation with me?

PSYCHE: What better way for an old drunk riding uptown on a bus to pass his years than to have a conversation with a young lady with clear eyes?

OPAL: You are sure. You are quite sure it's just not your liquor talking?

PSYCHE: Madam . . . I do feel it's my duty to tell you . . . my liquor is me. When I speak . . . the grape speaks. . . . We are inseparable. . . .

(*At this point the bus jerks ... throwing* OPAL *into* PSYCHE's *lap.* PSYCHE *holds his arms out to her as* OPAL *scrambles, trying to recover her composure.*)

OPAL: *Elimination of the Sexes: Toward an Androgynous Society.* The title of the book ... I mean ...

PSYCHE: The title's enough to make me lose my high ...

OPAL: This book is really great. I think in order to be a total person we must be both male and female.

PSYCHE: Ahhhh, I get you, baby. You a big freak, huh. That's okay, some of my best friends ...

OPAL: I'm not talking about lust. Once we eliminate false divisions such as male and female then we can start to relate to each other as people!

PSYCHE: Uh huh.

OPAL: Look, why do you think I refused your offer of a seat? Because you are a drunken bum? No. Of course not. I'm not like that. It's because you only offered me a seat because I'm a woman!

PSYCHE: Look ... I only thought ...

OPAL: All of these men standing and you didn't offer them a seat. Oh, I know what you automatically thought through your drunken stupor. "Poor lady." You felt sorry for me because I am a woman when the truth is you need the seat more than I do!

PSYCHE (*Softly*):   If you want the truth lady, I didn't want you blocking my view with all your packages. I didn't want that thing with the sharp edges slowly boring a hole in my knee like it's doing at this moment!

◊ 287

OPAL (*Moving the portfolio quickly away from* PSYCHE*'s knee*): Oh. I am sorry.

PSYCHE: What's in that thing, anyhow?

OPAL: My sketches.

(PSYCHE *just looks at her, saying nothing.*)

OPAL: Aren't you going to ask me about them? You were the one with all the questions a few seconds ago.

PSYCHE: Yeah. That was before I felt like an endangered species.

OPAL: I'm a designer. . . . I design intersex clothes for the human body. Here, let me show you what I mean. . . . (*Manages to open the portfolio*) Here's my biggest item . . . pants on one leg and skirt on the other. . . . Isn't that lovely? . . . And here's my open-toed high-heel shoes for both men and women. . . .

PSYCHE: Look, lady, you win. . . . I withdraw my offer of a conversation. So WILL YOU PLEASE STOP? I withdraw my offer of a seat. STAND. You can stand there till you grow roots . . . stand there till the hairs on your pussy turn gray. . . . You can . . .

OPAL: YOU DRUNKEN BUM! YOU ARE CRUDE! CRUEL! VULGAR! . . .

PSYCHE: SAVAGE! SADISTIC! SALACIOUS! The nation's nightmare! Everything you invented. The demon you dream of. The Black male heaped in modern myth! Look, it's only me, Psyche . . . what's your name?

(OPAL *does not answer.*)

PSYCHE: Lilith? Eve? Hagar? Jezebel? Delilah?

◊ 288

OPAL: They were all wicked whores and witches!

PSYCHE: Kali? Fatima? Isis?

OPAL: They were all goddesses.

PSYCHE: Which one are you? Let me see. What do you ladies call yourselves these days? Kadeejha? Sayeeda? Naima? I mean, what can I do with a name? Can I hock it? Please, baby. Tell me your name. Ohhhh ha! I get it. . . . You're afraid I'll find you in the telephone book and make "Hello, baby, you wanna fuck?" phone calls to you. . . .

OPAL: OPAL! MY NAME IS OPAL!

PSYCHE (*Tipping his hat and bowing slightly*):   Pleased to meet you, Miss Opal. . . . You didn't ask me what my name is but I'm Psyche. Now that we're on a first-name basis, Miss Opal . . . tell me . . . where do you live? That's right. Speak right up.

OPAL: UPTOWN. . . . I live uptown. . . .

PSYCHE: Where uptown? Oh, come on. . . . I'm not in any frame of mind to rob you tonight. What street?

OPAL: Uptown.

PSYCHE: Lenox? Seventh? Eighth?

OPAL: Of course not! Convent. Convent Avenue.

PSYCHE: Of course. Convent Avenue. Ritzy, ain't we?

OPAL: Relative. Everything is relative. I suppose from your vantage point it would look good to you.

◊ 289

PSYCHE: I'll ignore that. Now that we're getting along just fine, I'll
    pretend I didn't hear that last cutting remark. Apartment?

OPAL: Brownstone.

PSYCHE: Own? Rent?

OPAL: Own.

PSYCHE: What street?

OPAL: One Hundred Forty-fifth Street.

PSYCHE: I bet it's that house on the corner.

OPAL (*Challengingly*):   Which corner? Which house?

PSYCHE: Northeast corner. The house with the brown shutters,
    I bet.

OPAL: How . . .

PSYCHE: And the white awnings?

OPAL: . . . did . . .

PSYCHE: With the window box of red geraniums?

OPAL: . . . you . . .

PSYCHE: With the iron door with filigree.

OPAL: How did you know? You described my house exactly. Who
    are you, anyhow?

PSYCHE (*Taking out his bottle and putting it to his head, wipes his lips
    with the back of his hand*):   Look, lady . . . I'm just a drunken

tramp riding the bus uptown. I do a lot of walking uptown . . . see a lot of houses. Some I remember. Some I don't. No big deal. . . . Besides . . . you talk too much.

OPAL: What? . . . Mister . . . Psyche . . . you are crazy!

PSYCHE: Is that a medical or lay opinion? No matter. I reject it.

OPAL: Look . . . Mister . . . whatever you call yourself. Who are you? What do you do?

PSYCHE: Anything. . . . I'll do anything. But we're not discussing me . . . at least not yet. Let's stick to you since you're the one that's hanging over me. Know what I could do to you? It's so crowded in here that all I have to do is stick out my tongue . . .

OPAL: No!

PSYCHE: No? Then tell me, Opal. Tell me. Who do you live with in that big house on the northeast corner with the white awnings. No. Don't tell me. I'll tell you. Your husband. He's a dull man with a high salary who you married for his potential.

(OPAL *is silent.*)

PSYCHE: No? Then you have children. No. If you do it's just one, isn't it? A boy, I bet. It happened before you were married. But you didn't let it prevent you from being a colored success.

(OPAL *remains silent.*)

PSYCHE: Your parents? No . . . it couldn't be. . . . You left them in some tedious town in their prefabricated mortgage. You came to New York so that you could be loudly anonymous.

OPAL: For your information, Mr. Psyche . . . I live alone.

◊ 291

PSYCHE: But you have several cats.

OPAL: One . . . just one. Dog, that is. Great Dane. Male.

PSYCHE: I bet he's black.

OPAL: Yes. His name is Niger.

PSYCHE: And you have papers on him.

OPAL: And I have papers on him.

PSYCHE: And you have a special butcher where you buy forty pounds weekly of the choicest meat for doggie. You take your tamed wolf to shows where he struts and wins ribbons for you. He licks your face at night in place of everything else.

OPAL: How did you know about Niger's ribbons? . . . I thought you looked familiar. You must have been at the last dog show.

PSYCHE: I was. . . I was first prize. Arf, arf!

OPAL: Why are you rambling on like this?

PSYCHE: Tell me more about you and Niger.

OPAL: Oh, I forgot to tell you about Ronnie, and Herbert, Yusef, David, and Bob. They live with me also.

PSYCHE: Aha!

OPAL: Sure . . . they're my plants. . . . Poor Ronnie . . . he's the fern and he's always thirsty and has to be watered constantly but the Swedish ivy, philodendrons, ficus, and red geraniums in the window box are doing fine, thank you.

PSYCHE: You, the dog, and the plants.

◊ 292

OPAL: You know, before I got the hang of it I used to just look at a plant and he would die. Now, I've finally got the knack of growing them. But before I cultivated my green thumb I would call myself "the Plantkiller."

PSYCHE (*Looks at* OPAL *for a few beats*): I'm getting off right now. (*Yells*) Goddammit, bus driver. Stop this bus right now. I WANT TO GET OFF!

OPAL (*Shoving him back in his seat*): No! You can't leave now. I haven't finished telling you about myself.

PSYCHE: Opal.... I know all about you. Every nook and cranny of you.

OPAL: Don't be too sure. I'm translucent but not transparent. Opals throw off lights in different colors and shapes. How can you be so sure of what you're seeing when you look at me?

PSYCHE (*Takes out his bottle and holds it out in front of him, looking through it as if it's a crystal ball*): Oh . . . I can see right through you. We know each other. I just didn't want to live through it again tonight but . . . (*puts the cap on the bottle decisively after taking a swig and continues*) yes, Opal, I know you. For instance . . . let me tell you what you'll do when you get off this bus. As soon as you step off this bus you will put a curse on it, hoping that it smashes to smithereens before the next stop, and tell yourself that you really must take a cab next time in order to avoid drunks like me. You will walk along the streets, hugging the curb, afraid, looking at the unlighted eyes of men that grow from sidewalks like bent trees. Secretly laughing when they sing their broken songs or dance. You hurry away from them, stepping on broken tears while avoiding the dog shit. You will hide your flesh from some passing admirer, denying him the magic of lust. But your juice overflows and hiding inside your face, you lurk behind your eyes, measuring the pants of each man passing by, secretly snapping off his penis and spitting it into your perfumed

◊ 293

hankie, coughing daintily, pretending you have a bad cold! Making your way to your house, you curse the air, wishing you were somewhere else, but some radical teacher in some New England college nestled in the peaceful Berkshire mountains told you the ghetto was your battlefield so here you remain, hunting for a Black puritan. Destroying every man that is not the freak of your imagination. You will finally reach your house and put the key in your door, looking over your shoulder to make sure that one of those men whose joint you stole is not following you.

OPAL: Oh, ha ha ha ha ha ha ha! You're a funny man . . . you know. A very funny man. I DON'T WANT TO HEAR ANY MORE!

PSYCHE: You're right, Miss Opal. Excuse me . . . it must be my liquor talking. You got to forgive an old drunk . . . riding the bus uptown.

OPAL: You tramp. You bum. You wino. How dare you talk to me this way? Don't you know I can have you arrested?

PSYCHE: Sure you can. You do that. . . . You're the woman to do it.

OPAL (*Looking around impatiently*): Oh God! Oh God! O God! This bus is so slow!

PSYCHE: Easy, baby, easy. Can't wait to get off, huh? Can't wait to send this bus smashing straight to hell, huh? (*Laughing*) I can't blame you. . . . If I had to stand as long as you have, talking to someone like me with no room to get away from him . . . I'd feel the same way. Don't you want to hear what happens next?

OPAL: When?

PSYCHE: When you put your key in the door. Don't you want to hear what you'll do once you get inside your house?

OPAL: That's enough, Mister. I've listened to you long enough. Who are you?

◊ 294

(PSYCHE *closes his eyes. Doesn't answer.*)

OPAL (*Leaning close to him, whispering*):   You can't fool me anymore. Every shut eye ain't sleep. Every red eye ain't drunk. So
you know who I am . . . well, you are right. There is something in
me so empty, so longing, so full of pain and rage that I hesitate to
speak, for fear of being discovered. But you recognized me and I
know who you are too.

PSYCHE: But we're not talking about me . . . at least not yet. . . . So
you tell me. What *will* you do?

OPAL: I will put the key in my iron door with filigree on it and shut it
against the day. I will pace the rooms of my empty house and
laugh at you who were on this bus, undressing me with your
smile. I will run my hands over my body and scratch my left nip-
ple, thinking of the men I made heavy with lust as I passed them
by. I'll conjure up the images of several possible lovers. I'll feed
Niger and watch his flanks shiver in appreciation and wonder why
all relationships can't be as simple. I'll water my plants and pay
special attention to Ronnie. Poor Ronnie. I lied about him. I told
you that he was a fern but he's not. He's a penis that I cut off and
planted in my window box. He's always thirsty, never satisfied,
but when I feed him he curls up like a prayer plant and takes back
every loving thing he's said to me. Sometimes he flies around the
room, following me to bed. When I put him back in his pot, he
cries. And finally, I sing . . .

I gave my love a poem
I gave my love a baby
He said thank you for the poem
Thank you for the baby chile
I love you sweetcakes
But I'm gonna leave for a while

And so Mr. Psyche, or whatever your name is . . . because of the
men who beat their heads against the sidewalk and mumble in
unknown tongues whenever I come near them, because of the

lover who passes me by with blood in his eyes, an emptiness grows, silent and cruel. . . . But what about you? . . . You haven't told me where you live but I know. . . . You're going to the last stop, to the end of the line . . . and then you'll start all over again. . . . There's no address, no number for you . . . you're free. You sit there in your freedom, having nothing, wanting anything I have, being nothing, wanting to be me. . . .

PSYCHE (*Jumps up from the seat and pulls her down, throwing her into the seat*): SIT DOWN. . . . NOW YOU SIT YOUR ASS DOWN!

OPAL: I know who you are, I know who you are, I know who you are, I know who you are!

PSYCHE (*Removes his disguise, tears it off revealing a handsome, healthy, sober man*): SHUT UP AND LET ME SPEAK. I don't own one house with one dog, several plants, and a potted penis. I have no home. Not New York, America, or Africa. What I do have is several different places to stay, depending on what mood folks are in. And in one of those places (I don't remember which one at the moment) is my briefcase and in that briefcase are . . . let's see . . . numerous bits of paper with names and numbers that have lost their meaning . . . some eight-by-ten glossies showing several of my faces. See, I'm an actor in this world, constantly adjusting to my surroundings. Some "Get out and take your things" letters from women who have begun to catch on that I am only passing through. . . . Oh, don't get me wrong . . . there's nothing wrong with you ladies except that you want me to act out your soap opera fantasies and I can't say who I am unless you agree that I'm real but you don't want me to be real. . . . And in that briefcase in one of those places, I can't remember where, are my dreams. . . . You call me a bum with no ambition? Baby . . . I have dreamed empires into existence! You're right; having nothing myself, I want what you got, I want the world, No. I want the universe. Some nerve for a nigger, huh? You got on this bus and all you could see was a tramp. But I wear disguises so that I can watch the world watching me. My disguises protect my tender insides from the vulgar tongue, from the hard eyes of dream killers, from women like you. (*Goes into his drunken act*) Dja wanna drink lady, keep it moving, keep it moving. Hello, Dolly, this is Satchmo, darling. . . . The names you call me are not mine. . . . The face you see is only a mask. Look at me. . . . Look at me. . . . Are you willing? Do you dare? . . . This is a recording. . . . Leave your answer and get off the bus! (*Sits down wearily in an empty seat next to her*)

OPAL (*Softly*):   I'm thirsty.

PSYCHE: Have a drink . . . of water. (*Hands her his bottle*)

OPAL (*Takes a long slow drink*):   Ahhhhh. That is good. There is seeing and being seen. Which one are you frightened of?

PSYCHE: I want to be seen. . . . Can you see me?

OPAL: Will you come home with me?

PSYCHE: Sure, why not . . . I come when called, go when chased, am grateful when fed.

OPAL: You don't love. . . . You don't hate. . . . There's no such thing as feeling?

PSYCHE: I could hold your hand. And smile at you. I know what. We'll pretend we just met.

OPAL: I'll find myself in your face. In your body.

PSYCHE: I'll see you in the sunlight.

OPAL: We'll smile at each other through the day and night. We'll be a mirror facing each other.

◊ 297

OPAL/PSYCHE: Let's dance.

(*They stand up and face each other. They do a weird sensuous dance stalking each other but do not touch.*)

PSYCHE: What are you afraid of?

OPAL: You ... me ... them ... (*Indicating* BUS PASSEN-GERS) What will you do if they find out we love each other?

PSYCHE: NO. WE CAN'T. STOP IT. IT'S USELESS. I don't want *you* to see me. I know how they see me. But you, you must not see me that way. Don't you understand? That's why I keep running away. I'm running away from you very fast. Because I know what you see.

You see a body without power
A mind without dreams
A man without his name
We're dead to each other before love is born
We're dead to each other before love is born
If they take away your body, you can't work
If they take away your mind, you can't dream
I can work
I can dream
I can't love you!

OPAL:

I'm dead to the world
But I've never been born
We're dead to each other
Before love is born
The world sees a place
To hide its dark desire
You see
Eyes without light
Lips without a song

◊ 298

A woman
Without beauty
I am thirsty
I must drink
I am hungry
I must eat
I will eat
I will drink
I won't love you!

(OPAL *and* PSYCHE *attack each other . . . they stab one another and fall down dead.* BUS PASSENGERS *come alive . . . move off and on the bus, stepping over them.*)

BUS DRIVER'S VOICE: All right, all right . . . keep it moving. Move
    to the rear.

(*Fast curtain.*)

FAITH RINGGOLD

from Being My Own Woman

I found myself longing to paint come the summer of 1969. I had developed a new light in my painting, which I called Black Light, a way of looking at us that came out of our new "black is beautiful" sense of ourselves. My palette was all dark colors. Placed on a white ground they appeared to be only black. But next to each other the dark tones of reds, greens, blues, browns, and grays came alive, no matter how subtle the nuance. It was magic. Ad Rinehardt had done it but I could not find out what method he had used. And, furthermore, he did *abstract* black paintings. Mine were black paintings of black people. I had trouble with the glazes. They produced too much glare, or they made the surface quality of the paint too fragile. I needed time to experiment. My second one-woman show was scheduled for January 1970. The summer would be my only real chance to paint. I had a lot of ideas for new paintings. The subjects taunted me: mask faces, dancing figures of black life, a dark flag with the letters D-I-E in the stars and the letters N-I-G-G-E-R in the stripes. But there was no telling what the summer would produce with two troublesome teenagers stalking my every move. I had to solve that problem first.

The girls, aged sixteen and seventeen, were into rebellion by then. People who didn't have children thought the youth of the day would be our salvation.

"The young people's rebellion is revolutionary," they would say. Revolutionary was a word they used for defiant, youthful, modern, anything for which you could be condemned as too old if you didn't agree with it. Revolutionary could mean practically anything but *a revolution.* They were just doing their thing was another popular explanation for youthful rebellion. That one was more like it. But whose thing was it really?

What made me so upset was that my girls seemed more like they were into doing someone else's thing. They were more the does than the doers. And as their mother and an older woman in her thirties, I

◊ 300

was the target for all the rage they felt for giving up so much for so little. It was as if their brains froze over at the mere sight of a man.

Stokely Carmichael echoed the sentiments they seemed to embrace: "The only position of women . . . is prone."

"But how do you feel about this?" I asked them, trying not to reveal to them the horror I felt that they could repeat this statement without feeling some of the rage they just normally aimed at me. Michele was objective about her feelings: this was his point of view; it had nothing to do with how she felt. Barbara had not been present at the theater group when Stokely spoke so she couldn't really comment.

"Please don't allow yourselves to be used by anyone, male or female," I said. "If you lay your heart out there, it is sure that some creep will come along and step on it. Don't just let life happen to you. Defy *his* ideas as you do mine. Don't just let life happen to you."

But Michele had a super crush on Stokely Carmichael, and Barbara was excited just to hear that she had met him.

"What's he like?" she asked. It was obvious no one heard a word I said.

They had already been told by all the movements that Mother is the undisputed enemy of all revolutionary ideas. Contradictions didn't matter.

"Have a baby for the Revolution!"

Would they then be revolutionary mothers or just more of the old breed, mere women with the added burden of a child to bring up, possibly alone?

Birdie, my husband, was very expressive on the baby issue.

"We don't want a baby, Barbara and Michele. If we did we could have one ourselves. Your mother and I are not as old as we seem. Hold those boys off. The Revolution my ass! All they want to do is fuck and run."

"But, Daddy," said Barbara, "you don't know the boys of today. They are honest. We're not into the lies of your generation."

"We who? You better speak for yourself. You don't know what those little motherfuckas are into!"

The young were in a hurry. They rationalized that Vietnam had given them a sense of urgency. Life was cheap, the death toll a regular feature on the nightly news. Some were even saying that school was a waste of time.

"Drop out!" was high "revolutionary rhetoric." And money was "dirt." Anybody who had it felt guilty and those who didn't were angry, as I was the day I tried to explain to Barbara and Michele our financial situation:

"Even though you girls have had many advantages in life, you must understand we are not rich people like many of your classmates at New Lincoln. We are poor people struggling to see that you . . ."

Michele interrupted me: "The only one who has ever been poor here is you."

Drugs, however, were the pill I could not swallow. There were parents at their school who smoked pot with their children to share the experience. Michele was the friend of a white girl whose mother had a black boyfriend, a jazz musician, and they all got high together. My kids thought that was great—family unity.

"You're too emotional on the subject. Everybody who uses drugs is not a drug addict," they informed me.

I was outraged. Earl and Andrew flashed in my mind. Their deaths were all I could see. The girls standing before me, mere children of thirteen and fourteen at that time, were just a blur. Birdie came between us.

"Don't talk anymore, leave 'em alone. They're just trying to taunt you," he said. "They're young and crazy. They don't understand."

But back to the summer of 1969. I got an idea for a vacation they would like: summer study abroad at the University of Mexico in Mexico City. Barbara could study her favorite subjects, Spanish and Portuguese, and Michele could study hers, art and literature. They could live in a student house where they could be on their own with other young people. A sense of freedom was apparently what they yearned for. Maybe that was just what they needed, an opportunity to show how mature they really were. The trip would be a good test at any rate. They could no longer say that I had babied them and never allowed them to make decisions on their own. The trip would also be a high school graduation present for Michele, and an introduction to college life. She was due to go to Howard University in the fall. Though Barbara was only in her senior year in high school, she was in her fourth year in both French and Spanish at school. Languages were something she "ate up."

Though Mother disapproved of my allowing the girls to go to Mexico by themselves, she admitted that they really had enjoyed studying French at the Alliance Française when she had taken them to Paris in the summer of 1967. It was what saved the trip from total disaster, because they had presented quite a discipline problem to Mother. That summer was a great success for me. Back in New York I had painted my three murals: *The Flag Is Bleeding, U.S. Postage Stamp Commemorating The Advent of Black Power,* and my riot mural, *Die.* Had it not been for Mother taking the girls to Europe *that* summer, I would not have been able to complete those paintings for my first one-woman show.

Birdie and I had been separated since then, since 1967. We had had to have some time away from each other. There was just too much going on: the girls, the art, teaching, and then the house. That was why I walked out the summer Mother took the girls to Europe. I didn't want to spend my summer cleaning the house and cooking, so I moved into Mother's apartment and spent my days at the gallery painting till well into the night. At the end of the summer when the girls and Mother came home from Europe, Birdie had left. Who could blame him? So we had been living apart since then. I needed him, but I needed my freedom too. Maybe later we could get back together again, after things calmed down and we could have some time for ourselves. But if I called him now he would just say, "Don't let those girls go away alone. Keep them with you. Give up the art. Postpone the show. They'll be back at school in a few months anyhow." But then so would I.

They left for Mexico after a thorough briefing: remember to lock your door; be careful when you meet strangers; stay together; and most of all look out for each other. Michele was the oldest by eleven months. She was responsible for Barbara. Kelly, the man I was seeing then, was fluent in Spanish and he knew Mexico City. He contributed to the planning of the trip and he took the girls to the airport to see them off, while I finished my last days of teaching for the year. Right away I began to assemble my canvasses and paints and set about perfecting the glaze formulas I needed to prevent glare on my Black Light paintings. For the first day or two I did nothing but work. Kelly was busy too, catching up with the time he had lost in editing his magazine with helping the girls to get ready to go to Mexico. We talked on the phone and the girls called. They were in Mexico and starting school the next day. Everything was perfect.

Thereafter Kelly came evenings for dinner, and remained with me well into the early morning. I had to stop painting at 4 P.M. to shop and cook in preparation for his nightly visits. He was taking too much time from my work. He argued that I had the summer, but I worried about "the best laid plans" and the "mice" and the girls, not to mention "the men." I told him so. He began to bring the food each night and cook it himself.

The very next evening after our conversation, Kelly arrived early with a package of groceries. I greeted him and returned to my studio. Soon after he called me to eat. But I was right in the middle of a breakthrough, the attainment of a gorgeous metallic blackness. What glazes had I mixed? I was in heaven. My paintings were talking to me. I wanted to share this with Kelly as he had shared with me his writing and his other successes.

"Kelly, let's eat in the studio so I can show you my painting," I said. "I've got something interesting to show you here."

He appeared at the door of my studio wearing my ruffled apron over his shirt, tie, and the pants of his three piece suit. Kelly was a very serious, highly intelligent man with not much of a sense of humor. I could rarely look at him without wanting to laugh. For one thing he had an afro that was more than twice the size it should have been, and for another he wore horn-rimmed glasses. They were just exactly the sort of glasses that someone would wear who had far more brains than brawn. I wasn't laughing this time though.

"See," I said to his impassive face, "you have to look at it from the side. There is a kind of metallic sheen on this black here and it is because I've mixed certain glazes, and I am trying to find out what the underpainting is . . ."

His eyes remained expressionless, two beads in the center of huge horn rims. I tried to go on, "The underpainting is . . ."

He sucked his teeth.

". . . the paint that . . ."

He sucked his teeth again and turned to leave the studio.

"Come outside and eat," he commanded. "Your food is getting cold."

Two A.M. on a hot July morning, Barbara was on the phone. She was in New York at Kennedy airport on her way uptown in a taxi.

"Be downstairs to pay the taxi driver. I'm all out of money," she said and hung up.

Kelly was with me. He was excellent to be with at times like this. He could even be humorous about it. We waited together in front of the building for Barbara. I was facing another hard moment of truth in my life. Kelly was making small talk with the doorman saying something about the long hot summer some dude had predicted from his air-conditioned limousine. I was far away, out of my mind with worry, and talking to myself as if there was no one around.

"Barbara home . . . barely two weeks . . . Where's Michele? Out of money . . . Oh, God, Oh, maybe . . ."

Kelly paid the driver and I embraced Barbara. She looked so young and adorable, my baby, acting so grown up in a new white dress with Mexican embroidery on it. I wanted to hold her and kiss her again and again but she wasn't for it. She was cool, matter of fact, in a hurry to get the greetings over with. She had on her cut-the-kid-stuff, I'm a-woman-now mask face.

Finally Barbara got down to the story. She and Michele had met some "Mexican revolutionary students" the first day of classes and decided to go live with them at their commune in the suburbs of Mexico City. There were three men and two women in their middle to late twenties, except for the leader of the commune who was thirty-two. Michele would not be coming home. She had fallen in love with one of the "revolutionaries," a South American, and had "joined the movement." They would live on at the commune and be happy forever after. I was to send consent for Michele to marry if that would make me feel any better. Otherwise they would just live together. Ramos, a white Mexican and a Jew, the leader of the commune, would take care of everything. Michele had turned over all of their money to him. Barbara came home because she didn't fit in. As for the nature of their "revolutionary activities," the story was vague. They were doing some takes for a movie, in the nude. Otherwise they smoked a lot of pot. The "girls" did housework, though there was a maid, and the men each worked one day a week in town.

I called Michele immediately, ordering her to come home. She was cool too. I could feel her mask through the phone. As far as she was concerned, "I am home," she told me. If I'd feel any better about it I could send permission so that she could get married. That was all she had to say. Ramos, the head of the commune, was there to speak to me if I didn't understand.

Our conversation was hot. He said that I was a reactionary individualist artist, a domineering self-serving woman, a pawn of the capitalist system who had to be destroyed. I was a menace. My children should and must leave me for I was a dangerous negative influence. People like me were beyond hope.

I reached back to my native Harlem street language for what I had to say. That language which used to make me gasp when I heard it spoken. It was now all I knew how to say. A lifetime of careful speech and whitified rhetoric went right through the window. Racial epithets and cultural slurs came on like a river.

"Me? You motherfuck . . . bastard, son of a honky bitch. You have taken advantage of my child. You fucked up pervert. Whoever said a white racist full of shit creep like you . . ."

He was very upset, his hot breath coming through the phone. I could almost feel it.

"Mrs. Ringgold," he said. His Mexican accent was heavier now and his voice was out of control, almost cracking, ". . . your daughter has left you . . ."

"Let me warn you," I screamed. "You're not fucking with a fool. I am a black woman. Your honky ass will be hotter than hell if . . ."

"Mrs. Ringgold," he interrupted me again, "there is nothing you can do. Michele is . . ."

"Listen, you murky, white cracker junkie half-ass revolutionary pimp motherfucker, what have you given her? Some of your dope? My daughter Barbara tells me you have a fucking drugstore there. Well, you dopey freaked-out sack of shit, you better not take me lightly. This "black capitalist bitch" will cause you more trouble than it is worth. What kind of revolutionary are you? You freak. You haven't seen no revolution! The best you can do, you motherfucking drug addict bastard is send my daughter home or . . ."

"Good day Mrs. Ringgold."

On the other end, Michele told me later, Ramos was beet red and trembling uncontrollably. She had never seen a man, a white man so afraid before or since. On my end, I had never been so angry. If words could kill? But Ramos was still alive and Michele was still in Mexico.

I called the American Embassy in Mexico. The ambassador was conveniently out of town. His assistant spoke with me. I told him the story, and that I was rescinding permission for Michele to be in Mexico. I was waving a copy of my letter of consent in my hand. He attempted to explain to me that it would not be possible to make Michele leave Mexico unless she was doing something unlawful.

"Unlawful?" I screamed. "What do you think they are doing over there? Watching the sun set?"

"I don't know Mrs. Ringgold," came the disinterested voice of the assistant.

"And you don't care either, do you? Well, if you know what's good for you, you'll get your ass over there and see what they . . ."

Suddenly I realized I was raving to a dial tone. The assistant had hung up on me.

I had to get a grip on myself. I called the State Department in Washington, D.C. Calmer still, I called the White House and tried to get through to the President, which was, would you believe, Richard Nixon. Then I sent the following telegram to all the appropriate officials.

". . . my daughter is a minor being held in a Mexican commune *against my will.* I am her mother and a black woman, an American citizen, a registered voter, and a taxpayer, and I demand immediate action or any harm that comes to her is the responsibility of all of you who do not assist me in bringing her home immediately. She has a return flight ticket. I expect her in America by sundown tomorrow . . ."

Now the assistant to the ambassador was calling me. He was at the commune. And he wanted to know what Michele looked like.

"She's black!" I bellowed. "Can't you see? Now what are you going to do?"

"Well," he said, "everything looks all right to me here."

"Save your comments," I said. "I'll be there in the morning. At that time you can say that to the proper authorities. You can be my witness, since you are there and see what is going on."

He hesitated. His voice softened, "Well, what do you want me to do?"

"Take her out of there *now*. Put her in a hotel where she will be safe for the night. And tomorrow put her on the first flight home. That is all. Don't leave her there. She is only seventeen, in a strange land alone with strange people, and she does not know what she is doing or whom she is with. She is too young to make such decisions. She does not even speak their language. Can't you see they are adults, taking advantage of a young girl, a young black girl?"

The assistant to the ambassador did as I instructed. One car from the Embassy remained at the commune to see that Michele did not return there. The day Michele boarded the flight to America, she had no ticket, no identification or papers of any kind, and no money. But none were necessary. All she needed was her name and she was given the go ahead. In New York the same was true. She gave her name and she did not have to go through Customs but was sent immediately through a little gate to the side and hustled into a taxi at Kennedy airport.

Michele arrived without notice. She looked as pretty as Barbara had, in a little Mexican dress that seemed to be made for her. She was a little thinner but healthy looking. Her skin and hair glowed. She was hostile, admitting nothing about the drugs: my sore spot. As far as she was concerned I had destroyed her chance for happiness. And like Barbara, she had nothing but contempt for me. As soon as her friends from Mexico came, she would be off again to the commune.

I was most fearful of a drug addiction. Barbara and Michele had been raised on a program of drug prevention. Both Birdie and I had shared with them the accounts of the many friends we both knew who had passed on by the needle. We kept no skeletons in the closet for them to stumble over. Experimenting with drugs was a no-no. Their Uncle Andrew, my brother, and Earl, their father, had done that two decades before them. They were both fatalities, Andrew in 1961 while we were in Rome, and their father in 1966. There was no need to repeat the experiment. It didn't work.

I wanted them both examined for drugs, health—mental and physical. It was as if Earl had come back to haunt us, to take us with him. However, I knew he would have been so disappointed to see what we were going through. He was a very moral man, a musician. Compulsive but not evil. He never wanted to spread his misery around. He didn't need that kind of company.

I searched the Yellow Pages for a community service, someone to talk to who knew more than I did. I found a familiar name, dialed the number. A friendly voice answered in the name of the agency.

"I'd like to talk to someone. I have trouble with my daughters. They, well, have just come from Mexico where they joined a commune and I don't know where to . . . what . . . or if. . . ."

There was an accommodating silence on the other end. Embarrassed, I rambled on, "I don't know why my daughters did this . . . I thought we . . . all knew . . . our struggle was, and what we should be . . . I thought communes were for . . . I didn't think young black people had time for . . . We have so many other important . . ."

She cut me off. "Mrs. Ringgold, please come down to see us. We will talk."

From the way she cut me off, I knew she was a black woman and I could feel that she understood what I was going through.

"But can you tell me why this is happening? Is this not out of character for . . ."

"Please Mrs. Ringgold," she interrupted me again. "Just come in and bring Michele and Barbara the first thing Monday morning."

The conversation ended. The wait through the night began. A quiet desperation crept over me. What would become of us?

Back in Mexico at that very time hundreds of young white Americans were being arrested on marijuana charges, many of whom were forced into heroin addiction in the Mexican penal system, their parents forced to pay thousands of American dollars each year to maintain their board and the habits forced upon them by unscrupulous prison personnel. A large group of them were released in 1979 in exchange for Mexican prisoners serving time in American jails. So I was lucky although I didn't realize it then.

I never saw the black woman I spoke to on the phone. At the social service agency I was greeted by a real cold, pale white, young woman from the old school of social workers. She established my ability to pay and then fell into a dead silence. She had us all figured out before she ever saw us. But I knew enough about the world of social service to know it. Social service organizations and their social workers and psychologists don't have any answers for black girls in trouble. They only have services and only a few of those. And Michele at seventeen was actually too old for what they did have. Little black girls of seventeen are ready for jail. That is the hard truth of the matter. They want us to fit the case study in their book, be the research study they did or the statistic they feel comfortable with. She didn't know the first thing about us. In spite of what she saw and heard, she advised us to go home and wait for all hell to break out then she would feel more comfortable, more in character talking to the police caseworker, or the hospital caseworker, or placing Barbara or Michele with a member of the family while I did time for hurting them or they did time for hurting me.

I was through with talk. I needed help. Michele had to be placed somewhere. She couldn't stay with me anymore. And there was no one else who could keep her. She was, as far as I could tell, determined to turn her life over to the Mexicans, and I was determined that she know full well what she was doing when and if she did that. I would not go through this again. She was going to Howard University in September. If she wanted to leave from there and go back to the commune, so be it. I wouldn't even know when she left. But I wanted her to be somewhere for now. I could not caretake her. I was too potentially violent. I wanted to strike her, to make her feel some of the pain I was feeling.

More than pain, I felt anger for the waste of our energy, time, and resources. It is the ghetto in us that drives so many young women, no matter how richly endowed and carefully brought up, to seek out The Enemy and give themselves over to him. And he is always right there waiting, expecting us to do just that. Can't we disappoint the bastard, leave him standing there as we sashay on by?

At my request, Michele was put in a Catholic girls' home. She had to remain there until it was time for her to go to college in the fall. That would be in five weeks. If she promised not to run away with the Mexicans, she could come home and we would try again. She refused.

It was time for the system to deal with her. It would be either now or later. Somehow she had to learn what it is like to be a black woman in America. Like a doe surrounded by lions, she was fair game and nobody thinks twice about her destruction. She is just another statistic. In fact, they are more prepared to deal with her as a victim, because then they can remand, rehabilitate, hospitalize, or otherwise service her. But to protect, prevent, promote, and prepare her for a good life is the job of her family and those who love her. But who can protect a willing victim?

CAROLYN M. RODGERS

Mannessahs

Echoes. Angels.
Hosannas. Consecrations of mercy.
the tree leaves
fly
away as if they were birds.
something bends. a will, or an idea. And—
a thought becomes
a psalm.

Touch

Translation
Poem 4.

what is want sometimes is specifically
what is need.
what is need sometimes is specifically
what is want.
this is the line.
not thin,
not voluntary nor insignificant—
this is a premise of what it means.
a sun that you
are reaching for but cannot touch.
your hands, a beam in the ark of trust.
your eyes, a lantern in a sea of doubts.
or a cleverness to be defined and then,
a performance in the precisely corrected
span of time.

Touch

Poem 5.

  this is how it is.
  or can be.

 a bird sits on the branch
 of a tree
 and perhaps
 sings. this is not personal.
 nor private.
 but it can touch us.
 the trees
 has no leaves. only a
 web of spiraling branches.
 each branch is a level or degree,
 a wavelength in the air.
 we are building something.
 a ledge. a liturgy in the sky.

Aunt Dolly

 Sitting there on the
 assembly line piecing
 together frocks all alike
 thousands by thousand for
 millions to buy, the same
 cheap pattern duplicated
 all over the world, goes
 home at night and sews

◊ 313

up a storm, a dream that
nobody has "ever" seen
who can deny, when "ever"
she steps out the door,
any day or hour, after work,
after five, she is a *queen.*
She can sew anything you
cannot even imagine.

Folk

Looks like to me
folks ought to mind
they own business, Lula says.
If i want to go around
wading in my hairpins,
up the sidewalks and down
the sky
it's my business due to the
fact
i have paid my dues.
Lulu says, why i'm sending jive
back from where it came,
gon let love & winter go to
the post office c.o.d.
i got a collect on jesus and
some peace is a special delivery
i'm sending for.
you can put the blahs in a no name box & mark it
don't open until never.

◊ 314

Wimmin

One woman say a good man make her want
to shout.
He's my Lazarus, she says. we got UP together.
    Another one says, "a little bit of my
man's molasses goes a long way on my plate."
    What you say, woman?
                    I say—
this discussion falls under
the protection of grace.
                    oh yeah.

SANDRA ROGERS

Waiting For Her Man Too Long

She can't wait for you to knock
so she can ignore you.
She can't wait for you to knock
so she can ignore you and
make you feel the way she feels
now.
She can't wait for you to knock
so that in your hoping to get in
and feel the warmth of her body
all you'll feel is disappointment.
She can't wait for you to knock
so that her silence will tell you
she's not home
because you should have been here
a long time ago.
She can't wait for you to knock
so that her silence will tell you
she's not home even though
she sits here hurting.
She can't wait for you to knock
because in her hurting she will
hurt less because you
hurt too.
She cannot be that selfish in
that she can hurt
by herself.
She cannot be so selfish in
that she will not
share her hurt.
She will not be selfish
She will share and make
you hurt too.

SONIA SANCHEZ

A Poem for Sterling Brown

what song shall i sing you
amid epidemic prophecies
where holy men bleed like water
over the bones of black children?

how shall i call your name
sitting priest/like on mountains
raining incense
scented dancer of the sun?

where shall memory begin you
overturning cradles
rocking cemented eyes
closed flowers
opening like eastern deities under your hand?

and your words.
tall as palm/trees
black with spit
soothing the lacerated mind.

and your words.
scratching the earth
carving dialect men into pyramids
where no minstrel songs
run from their thighs.

your soul. dodging loneliness and
the festivals of Renaissance rhythms
your life
skintight with years
a world created
from love.

◊ 317

you. griot of fire.
harnessing ancient warriors.

    a ye ye ye ye ye ye ye
    a yo yo yo yo yo yo yo
       da a ye loom boom
       da a ye loom boom
       da a ye loom boom
          boom/boom
          boom/boom
          boom/boom
you. griot of the wind
glorifying red gums smiling tom-tom teeth.

Just Don't Never Give Up On Love

Feeling tired that day, I came to the park with the children. I saw her as I rounded the corner, sitting old as stale beer on the bench, ruminating on some uneventful past. And I thought, "Hell. No rap from the roots today. I need the present. On this day. This Monday. This July day buckling me under her summer wings, I need more than old words for my body to squeeze into."

I sat down at the far end of the bench, draping my legs over the edge, baring my back to time and time unwell spent. I screamed to the children to watch those curves threatening their youth as they rode their ten-speed bikes against midwestern rhythms.

I opened my book and began to write. They were coming again, those words insistent as his hands had been pounding inside me, demanding their time and place. I relaxed as my hands moved across the paper like one possessed.

I wasn't sure just what it was I heard. At first I thought it was one of the boys calling me so I kept on writing. They knew the routine by now. Emergencies demanded a presence. A facial confrontation. No long-distance screams across trees and space and other children's screams. But the sound pierced the pages and I looked around, and there she was inching her bamboo-creased body toward my back, coughing a beaded sentence off her tongue.

"Guess you think I ain't never loved, huh girl? Hee. Hee. Guess that what you be thinking, huh?"

I turned. Startled by her closeness and impropriety, I stuttered, "I, I, I, Whhhaat dooooo you mean?"

"Hee. Hee. Guess you think I been old like this fo'ever, huh?" She leaned toward me, "Huh? I was so pretty that mens brought me breakfast in bed. Wouldn't let me hardly do no hard work at all."

"That's nice, ma'am. I'm glad to hear that." I returned to my book. I didn't want to hear about some ancient love that she carried inside her. I had to finish a review for the journal. I was already late. I hoped she would get the hint and just sit still. I looked at her out of the corner of my eyes. She quit and I continued my work.

"He could barely keep hisself in changing clothes. But he was pretty. My first husband looked like the sun. I used to say his name over and over again till it hung from my ears like diamonds. Has you ever loved a pretty man, girl?"

I raised my eyes, determined to keep a distance from this woman disturbing my day.

"No ma'am. But I've seen many a pretty man. I don't like them though cuz they keep their love up high in a linen closet and I'm too short to reach it."

Her skin shook with laughter.

"Girl you gots some spunk about you after all. C'mon over here next to me. I wants to see yo' eyes up close. You looks so uneven sittin over there."

Did she say uneven? Did this old buddah splintering death say uneven? Couldn't she see that I had one eye shorter than the other; that my breath was painted on porcelain; that one breast crocheted keloids under this white blouse?

I moved toward her though. I scooped up the years that had stripped me to the waist and moved toward her. And she called to me to come out, come out wherever you are young woman, playing hide and go seek with scarecrow men. I gathered myself up at the gateway of her confessionals.

◊ 319

"Do you know what it mean to love a pretty man girl?" She crooned in my ear. "You always running behind a man like that girl while he cradles his privates. Ain't no joy in a pretty yellow man, cuz he always out pleasurin' and givin' pleasure."

I nodded my head as her words sailed in my ears. Here was the pulse of a woman whose black ass shook the world once.

She continued. "A woman crying all the time is pitiful. Pitiful I says. I wuz pitiful sitting by the window every night like a cow in the fields chewin' on cud. I wanted to cry out, but not even God hisself could hear me. I tried to cry out till my mouth wuz split open at the throat. I 'spoze there is a time all womens has to visit the slaughter house. My visit lasted five years."

Touching her hands, I felt the summer splintering in prayer; touching her hands, I felt my bones migrating in red noise. I asked, "When did you see the butterflies again?"

Her eyes wandered like quicksand over my face. Then she smiled, "Girl don't you know yet that you don't never give up on love? Don't you know you has in you the pulse of winds? The noise of dragon flies?" Her eyes squinted close and she said, "One of them mornings he woke up callin' me and I wuz gone. I wuz gone running with the moon over my shoulders. I looked no which way at all. I had inside me 'nough knives and spoons to cut/scoop out the night. I wuz a tremblin' as I met the mornin'."

She stirred in her eighty-four-year-old memory. She stirred up her body as she talked. "They's men and mens. Some good. Some bad. Some breathing death. Some breathing life. William wuz my beginnin'. I come to that man spittin' metal and he just pick me up and fold me inside him. I wuz christen' with his love."

She began to hum. I didn't recognize the song; it was a prayer. I leaned back and listened to her voice rustling like silk. I heard cathedrals and sonnets; I heard tents and revivals and a black woman spilling black juice among her ruins.

"We all gotta salute death one time or 'nother girl. Death be waitin' outdoors trying to get inside. William died at his job. Death just turned 'round and snatched him right off the street."

Her humming became the only sound in the park. Her voice moved across the bench like a mutilated child. And I cried. For myself

For this woman talkin' about love. For all the women who have ever stretched their bodies out anticipating civilization and finding ruins.

The crashing of the bikes was anticlimactic. I jumped up, rushed toward the accident. Man. little man. Where you bicycling to so very fast? Man. Second little man. Take it slow. It all passes so fast any how.

As I walked the boys and their bikes toward the bench, I smiled at this old woman waiting for our return.

"I want you to meet a great lady, boys."

"Is she a writer, too, ma?"

"No honey. She's a lady who has lived life instead of writing about it."

"After we say hello can we ride a little while longer? Please!"

"Ok. But watch your manners now and your bones afterwards."

"These are my sons, ma'am."

"How you do sons? I'm Mrs. Rosalie Johnson. Glad to meet you."

The boys shook her hand and listened for a minute to her words. Then they rode off, spinning their wheels on a city neutral with pain.

As I stood watching them race the morning, Mrs. Johnson got up.

"Don't go," I cried. "You didn't finish your story."

"We'll talk by-and-by. I comes out here almost everyday. I sits here on the same bench everyday. I'll probably die sittin' here one day. As good a place as any I 'magine."

"May I hug you, ma'am? You've helped me so much today. You've given me strength to keep on looking."

"No. Don't never go looking for love girl. Just wait. It'll come. Like the rain fallin' from the heaven, it'll come. Just don't never give up on love."

We hugged; then she walked her eighty-four-year-old walk down the street. A black woman. Echoing gold. Carrying couplets from the sky to crease the ground.

Old Words

We are the dead
ones the slow
fast suicides
of our time.
we are the dis
enfranchised ones
the buyers of bread
one day removed
from mold
we are maimed
in our posture

1.

did you hear me start
my herding song that
        summer nite?
it is autumn
now and the nite
multiplies by threes.
can you hear me poet?
        one sound was you
And as i sang you
blue masks marched
from your face
        holy with stains.
O mass produced faces
i have burned myself out
now my ashes have
no place to lean.

sing it billie
    baby.

◊ 322

sing away that ill wind
blowing you no good.
    no good
ill wind.
    spread yo/strange
fruit amid these
stones. we all
strangers here. sing.
    i hear
yo/words quivering with silks
    i smell
your black soul.
    sweet.

2.

it is horrible to be.
gigantic fornicators advance
toward me shrieking
maternity cries.
and as i run i
trip over my deformity.
this is a fool's world
pain is an idiot's ailment
for the wise man knows
how to reconnoiter pain
and make it colloquial.

    go Prez. go man. move
those plastic hands
up and down that sax
blow. man. blow. ride
yo/saxophone cross
the stage and back again
we all riders
here. blow.
    man.
can't you see this

◊ 323

transfixed audience
staring at you while
you bleed.
    blow.
              ride.
bleed . . . blow.

Are we ever what we should be?
seated in our circle of agonies
we do not try to tune our breaths
since we cannot sing together
since we cannot waltz our eyes
since we cannot love.
since we have wooed this world
too long with separate arias of revolution
mysticism hatred and submission
since we have rehearsed our
deaths apart. Now. let us abandon
past heresies. now.
when small men stretch for greatness
via wars on poverty,
(in the twentieth century at a time of Punitive
Contaminated
Repressive Wars)

when men disfigure their bodies
to become holy in space and walk
without footsteps;
(in the twentieth century at a time of
grinning life-Copyrighted-Astronauts)
when men stuff their mouths with
murderous soliloquies and urinate
on hungry faces;
(in the twentieth century at a time of
illiterate adulterous industrious hungers)

we have come to
believe that we are
not. to be we
must be love or
touched and proved
to be. this earth
turns old
and rivers grow lunatic
with rain. how i wish
i could lean in your cave
and creak with the winds.

Present

This woman vomiting her
hunger over the world
this melancholy woman forgotten
before memory came
this yellow movement bursting forth like
coltrane's melodies all mouth
buttocks moving like palm trees,
this honeycoatedalabamianwoman
raining rhythm of blue/black/smiles
this yellow woman carrying beneath her breasts
pleasures without whose body weaves
desert patterns,
this woman, weary with wandering,
reviving the beauty of forests and winds
is telling you secrets
gather up your odors and listen
as she sings the mold from memory.

       there is no place
for a soft/black/woman.
there is no smile green enough or

summertime words warm enough to allow my growth.
and in my head
i see my history
standing like a shy child
and i chant lullabies
as i ride my past on horseback
tasting the thirst of yesterday tribes
hearing the ancient/black/woman
me, singing   hay-hay-hay-hay-ya-ya-ya.
                                         hay-hay-hay-hay-ya-ha-ya.

like a slow scent
beneath the sun

         and i dance my
creation and my grandmothers gathering
from my bones like great wooden birds
spread their wings
while their long/legged/laughter
stretches the night.
         and i taste the
seasons of my birth. mangoes. papayas.
drink my woman/coconut/milks
stalk the ancient grandfathers
sipping on proud afternoons
walk like a song round my waist
tremble like a new/born/child troubled
with new breaths
         and my singing
becomes the only sound of a
blue/black/magical/woman. walking.
womb ripe. walking. loud with mornings. walking.
making pilgrimage to herself. walking.

SONIA SANCHEZ

Kwa mama zetu waliotuzaa[1]

death is a five o'clock door forever changing time.
    and it was morning without sun or shadow;
a morning already afternoon. sky. cloudy with incense.
    and it was morning male in speech;
feminine in memory.
but i am speaking of everyday occurrences:
of days unrolling bandages for civilized wounds;
of gaudy women chanting rituals under a waterfall of stars;
of men freezing their sperms in diamond-studded wombs;
of children abandoned to a curfew of marble.

as morning is the same as nite death and life are one.
    spring. settling down on you like
green dust. mother. ambushed by pain in
rooms bloated with a century of cancer.
yo/face a scattered cry from queequeg's wooden bier.
    mother. i call out to you
traveling up the congo. i am preparing a place for you:
        nite made of female rain
        i am ready to sing her song
        prepare a place for her
        she comes to you out of turquoise pain.

        restring her eyes for me
        restring her body for me
        restring her peace for me

      no longer full of pain, may she walk
      bright with orange smiles, may she walk
      as it was long ago, may she walk

[1] for our mothers who gave us birth

◊ 327

abundant with lightning steps, may she walk
abundant with green trails, may she walk
abundant with rainbows, may she walk
as it was long ago, may she walk

at the center of death is birth.
in those days when amherst fertilized by
black myths, rerouted the nile.
you became the word. (shirley, graham, du bois)
        you were the dance
         pyramidal sister.
you told us in what egypt our feet
were chained
you. trained in the world's studio
painted the day with palaces
and before you marched the breath
of our ancestors.
        and yo/laughter passing
through a village of blacks
scattered the dead faces.
        and yo/voice lingering
like a shy goat fed our sad hungers.
and i. what pennsylvania day was i sucking dry
while you stuttering a thousand cries
hung yo/breasts on pagodas?
and i. what dreams had i suspended
above our short order lives
when death showered you with bells.
        call her back for me
        bells. call back this memory
        still fresh with cactus pain.

        call her name again. bells.
        shirley. graham. du bois
        has died in china
        and her death demands a capsizing of tides.
olokun.[2]

[2] Goddess of the sea

                she is passing yo/way while
                pilgrim waves whistle complaints to man
olokun.
                a bearer of roots is walking inside
                of you.
                prepare the morning nets to receive her.

before her peace, i know no thirst because of her
behind her peace, i know beauty because of her
under her peace, i know not fear because of her
over her peace, i am wealthy because of her

death is coming. the whole world hears
the buffalo walk of death passing thru the
archway of new life.

                the day is singing
                the day is singing
                he is singing in the mountains

                the nite is singing
                the nite is singing
                she is singing in the earth

i am circling new boundaries
i have been trailing the ornamental
songs of death (life)
a strong pine tree
dancing in the wind

i inhale the ancient black breath
cry for every dying (living)
creature

come. let us ascend from the
middle of our breath
sacred rhythms
inhaling peace.

JUDY DOTHARD SIMMONS

Minority

I am the downtrodden
I am the poor and deprived
that got star billing for a decade

I am the snarl of Afro hair and mulatto mouth,
a frantic dancer of defiance in my
sun-raped wrappings reminiscent of some
racial home denied me by the
cataracts of time

I am the mind that is a
terrible thing to waste, the blacker berry
with the sweeter juice, the Matriarch of
impromptu families and the automatic suspect
for light-fingered crimes

mine is not a People of the Book/taxed
but acknowledged; our distinctiveness is
not yet a dignity; our Holocaust is lowercase

I am dream blown and anchored by anger,
a switchblade of frustration, a
time bomb of hunger and pain;
I am reason ravaged and bone cold

I feel life glide through me like a sinister lynx
angling for deep shadows and I know
I am endangered but I am not only prey;
I recall cat rhythms and the sleek expanding muscle slide
of limbs night-hunting their existence

hatred is my curved compassion
I am tender
I am proud

Equal Opportunity

"You ought to do a book, Miss Me;
You write so very well."

"Thank you, Mister Man," I said,
(And may you rot in hell)

"You have a lot to say, you know—
A credit to your race."

(Did he really use that phrase
Today! right to my face?)

"It's wonderful the progress
That we're making all the time
To wipe out every trace of what was
Once our greatest crime."

"Oh, I appreciate the work;
This firm is very fair."
(If you have a penis and a
Thatch of near-blond hair)

"So I've been keeping tabs on you;
You're just the kind we need
To make this firm exemplar
Of our nation's highest creed."

"I'm flattered, Sir, I've tried to learn
The proper steps to take."
(To get your money, skill, and split
Before my guises break)

◊ 331

"We need your high intelligence"
(I need a friggin' gun)
"To keep our tried ways up-to-date."
(Your murder will be fun)

"My door is always open."
(You poor bastard—you're sincere)
"Thank you, Sir."

And that's how slaves
Are pacified this year.

Linseed Oil and Dreams

  early April he began to sniff it:
  linseed oil and dust from the base paths,
  bat wood and musty tee shirts—
  smells he borrowed from the coming June
  or remembered from past September

  he got up earlier, stopped sitting
  in the kitchen reading the back
  of the Wheaties box, breakfasting
  on champions, being eight years old
  and hard to get to school

  his mother missed him, called
  upstairs and through the house, heard only
  bird talk through the back door letting in
  spring's chill; it opened up her memory
  of early April's meaning to her son

  getting ready for his season
  he was sitting on the back steps
  in the soft sun of early April
  rubbing linseed oil and dreams
  into his baseball glove

Eleanor W. Traylor

The Fabulous World of Toni Morrison: Tar Baby

Today, around the schools, they speak of *cultural transmission*. Back then before I went to school, we called it *Grandma say* and *Grandpa say*. In the Pear Orchard—which, to me, was the blackberry patch as well as the peach and fig tree grove or the cornfield or the yard of morning glory, honeysuckle, tiger lily, sunflower, mimosa tree, and elephant ear or the garden of cabbage, collards, peppers, tomatoes, watermelon, and butter beans—was Grandma's house. Grandpa had built it, before he died, out of sentient oak, and he had built the pigpen and the chicken coop and the outhouse, had planted the cornfield and placed the big black pot right square in the middle of the backyard.

On Mondays, my Grandma and me (then) I (now) washed and boiled and starched white sheets and pillowcases handworked in Grandma's embroidery; we scrubbed large gingham aprons and tiny dresses (with underpants to match) and doilies and linen napkins that Grandma made on a washboard that sounded like the sea. We washed Miss Darlene's clothes separate from ours. Our clothes bubbled in the big black pot filled with bluin' water where Grandma churned them with the flatwood battlin' stick 'til they sloshed out cleaner than new.

On Tuesdays, we damped down and rolled smooth the starched-crisp wash that my Grandma flat-ironed to first-wear perfection. And the sound of Tuesday was the crackle of Grandma's spit-fingers testing the surface of the smoothin' iron heated in charcoal just "pert" for the heavy starched ginghams and blued-out sheets. And the smells of Tuesday were the sweet odors of starch and charcoal fire and hot, wet, clean, pure steam on damped-down brighter-than-bleach starched clothes.

Wednesday was weeding day in my Grandma's collard-rich garden behind the big black pot square in the middle of the backyard, but not if it rained. If it rained, Wednesday was piecing day. The piecing trunk stood at the foot of Grandma's carved brass bed dressed in the North Star quilt that she had made. On piecing day, we laid out the million-teenth scraps of flour-sack prints, muslins, burlap, lace, monk's cloth, linen, crepe de chine, velvet, wool, silk stockings, and gingham that

Grandma saved to make her rugs and doilies and quilts and dresses with matching underpants for me. And on piecing day, the silence between my Grandma and me, broken only by the sound of raindrops on a shingled roof, was an immensity of space in which we were inseparable forever. Unlike washing or ironing or weeding day or even Friday baking-day evening, when Miss Cora came from 'cross the road and she and Grandma sat and rocked on the front porch and I swung in the oak tree swing that my Grandpa had built for my Daddy just off the front porch where the grown folks could watch, piecing day was different. It was different even from Saturday cleaning day and early morning store-boughten shopping or even Sunday when, in church, I never sat in the children's section, for everyone knew me not as a child but as Grandma's *Grand*. Those days, not piecing day, were days of *Grandma say* and Grandma songs and me saying, "Grandma, you 'member 'bout the time when . . ." and her saying, "One day when I was a tiny thing like you . . ." And that is when I knew about all the things that now they call folklore, folktale, legend, fairy tale, myth. To me, those things are what my Grandma told me in our yard, on our porch, in her kitchen, and at night before we fell asleep.

"He got stuck," she said. Brer Rabbit got stuck on Farmer Brown's tar baby. I think now that she meant me to understand that I should never get stuck. And if I ever did, I should be smart enough, as the rabbit was, to plea-bargain or battle my way back to the Pear Orchard, which was really the rural section of Thomasville, Georgia, a legion time ago, but which, for me, is the place where on piecing day, my Grandma and I together in an enormity of silence laid out the patchwork designs that yet dress my mother's bed and mine and laid out the patchwork design that is now my life.

Like the rain of color drenching the patchwork collages of Romare Bearden, the crystalline images governing the brilliant fiction of Toni Morrison invite us to absorb experience with multitextured vision. Both the writer and the painter reschedule our imagination and alter the way we see by contracting the distance between the familiar and the strange, finding the point of juncture. What is apparent on the canvases of Bearden is certainly obvious in the novels of Toni Morrison. For instance, "the evocations and associations in Bearden's works are indeed so strong, and so deliberately and specifically and idiomatically either downhome rural or up-north urban, that his preoccupation with imagery from Afro-American experience ... appears to be surpassed only by his commitment to the esthetic process."[1] That process for Bearden is one that "gives his painting the quality of a flat surface painted by hand."[2] That process for Morrison is one that gives her novels the quality of the signifyin' oral tale of Afro-American folk tradition. A flat surface painted by hand is, of course, a wall, much like the historical and mythological walls that Aeneas saw everywhere in the ancient-modern city of Carthage or like the wall painted in 1967 by the OBACHI painters of Chicago or like the walls of our grandparents' houses in south Georgia decorated in newsprint. Bearden's story-murals are made for homes whose walls, no longer restrictors of rooms, would open outward upon the history of the world. Likewise, a tale recounted from mouth to mouth personalizes experience, making it not the possession of any teller but the possession of the whole wide community whose tale it is, much as the blues singer's task invites the world to dance.

The fate of Brer Rabbit, the imported wise scamp of the Afro-American bestiary, and the evocation of the title *Tar Baby*, is not quite the fate of the poor hapless river on Isle des Chevaliers. That island, the primary setting of the story told in *Tar Baby*, "three hundred years ago, had struck slaves blind the moment they saw it" (p. 8).[3] On that island, signifying a virgin world, civilization by forced labor had disturbed the balance of nature and "the land, clouds and fish were convinced that the world was over, that the sea-green green of the sea and sky-blue of the sky were no longer permanent" (p. 9). This perception is precisely what had blinded the first one hundred slaves who looked upon the land. "A rain forest already two thousand years old and scheduled for eternity" had been felled to accommodate "magnificent winter houses on Isle des Chevaliers" (p. 9). But the forest had shielded the river and equalized the rain, and now with the earth "hollowed ... where there had been no hollow," the poor river had "crested, then lost its course, and finally its head. Evicted from the place where it had lived, and forced into unknown turf, it could not form its pools or waterfalls, and ran every which way" (p. 9).

The tale of the hapless river, crashing "headlong into the haunches of hills with no notion of where it was going, until exhausted, ill and grieving, it slowed to a stop just twenty leagues short of the sea" becoming "a swamp . . . a shriveled fogbound oval seeping with a black substance that even mosquitoes could not live near" (pp. 9, 10), foreshadows one half of the story of *Tar Baby*. A variant of the "tar baby" tales featuring the fabulous escapades of Brer Rabbit, by turns a practical joker, a braggart, a wit, a glutton, a ladies' man, and a trickster whose essential ability to outwit eviction and flourish in unknown turf prefigures the other half. Thus, a new fable, the tale of the river, and an old one, the fable of Brer Rabbit and the tar baby, play point counterpoint, and weave, like fine patchwork, threads of a multitude of stories, legends, and tales into the fabulous collage. *Tar Baby* is a modern fable of society in which humanity, like the faces on a Bearden scape, is Black.

A man standing on the deck of a ship is the image opening Toni Morrison's *Tar Baby*; the scene calls to mind a similar one from a book written 194 years ago. The man, whose name we learn to be Son, about to jump ship in *Tar Baby*, is reminiscent of a man called Equiano in *The Life of Olaudah Equiano or Gustavas Vassa, the African* (1789). Equiano's tale is a slave narrative recounting the historical and mythical, the terrifying and mighty passage of the African from the oldest world to the newest. Standing on the deck of a slave ship, the young Equiano recalls his beloved homeland, contemplates means of escape from the dreadful ship, and concludes that he will learn to "navigate" circumstances that would otherwise destroy him. In *Tar Baby*, Son, a refugee, jumps ship and swims to Isle des Chevaliers, the highly symbolic setting (a virgin world raped by the machinations of man) in which the primary action of the story told in *Tar Baby* takes place. Son arrives on the island, climbs aboard a docked houseboat, searches for food, finds too little, spies a great house not far from the houseboat, and enters it. Thus, the quick brushstroke that opens *Tar Baby* introduces Son, the Brer Rabbit of the story, and outlines, by suggestion, the details of the earlier tale in which the rabbit, foraging for food, enters the fenced-in garden-world of Farmer Brown, the self-appointed keeper of the bounty of the world. Having been introduced in the first six pages, a prologue to the novel, Son, though we are ever conscious of his presence, does not reappear for eighty more pages, during which we learn the ways of Farmer Brown.

This re-created Farmer Brown of Toni Morrison's *Tar Baby* is called Valerian Street. His name is interesting; it derives from the Latin proper noun Valerius, the name of a Roman clan, a number of families connected by a common descent and the use of the same name. One relative of the noun Valerius is *valeo* meaning "to be vigorous," "to have force," "to be strong," "to be worth." Yet another meaning of the same word is "to bid farewell"; it may also be an expression of scorn. According to *Cassell's New Latin Dictionary*, the expression from Cicero "*si talis est deus, valeat*" means "let me have nothing to do with him" and "*quare valeant ista*" means "away with them"! Moreover, Valerian, a farmer, was Roman emperor from A.D. 253 to 260. In *Tar Baby*, Valerian Street is a retired, resigned, no longer vigorous or forceful industrialist, a former candy manufacturer who has inherited and brought to corporate success his family's candy business. Now he has "bought an island in the Caribbean for almost nothing; built a house on a hill away from the mosquitoes and vacationed there when he could and when his wife did not throw a fit to go elsewhere. Over the years, he sold off parts of it, provided the parcels were large and the buyers discreet" (p. 53). Of Valerian Street, we learn that "his claims to decency were human: he had never cheated anybody. Had done the better thing whenever he had a choice and sometimes when he did not" (p. 54). In his prime, "he married Miss Maine" (p. 53), a beauty queen whose name is Margaret and who, he discovers, after years of marriage, has never been and has no possibility of becoming a woman.

In her own mind, Margaret, Miss Maine, wife of Valerian Street, fancies herself an envied beauty as in the fairy tale "Beauty and the Beast," or as Cinderella rescued by a slightly aging (for Valerian is almost twenty years older than she) wealthy prince, or as the uneasy queen of "Snow White and the Seven Dwarfs" who keeps asking the mirror, "Who is the fairest of them all?" For Margaret, though it has not been her intention, is a failed wife and mother. Although her beauty, during her childhood, was a source of pain to her as it made her victim of the begrudgeful, yet her beauty has been her sole claim to personhood since her parents, scared a little by her beauty, "stepped back and let her be. They gave her care, but they withdrew attention. Their strength they gave to the others [of their children] who were not beautiful; their knowledge, what information they had

◊ 337

they did not give to this single beautiful one. They saved it, distributed it instead to those whose characters had to be built. The rest of their energies they used on the problems of surviving in a country that did not want them there" (pp. 56–57).

Thus Margaret, when she met Valerian, was completely won by him when the first thing he said to her was "You really *are* beautiful," and she asked him, "Is that enough?" and he replied, "Beauty is never enough. . . . But you are" (p. 83). Thinking that at last she is loved for *herself*—a *self* that has never developed—she is disabused when married to the elegant, worldly businessman, Valerian Street, and expected to supervise a great house in Philadelphia (so unlike in many ways, but in certain others very like, the trailer home that she was born into), command the respect of servants sophisticated and capable beyond her comprehension though not much older than she, and be the mother of a baby boy. The task is beyond her capability; she expected to be Valerian's valentine, a constant sweetheart: "Margaret lived for the concerts Valerian took her to, and the dinners for two at restaurants and even alone at home" (pp. 58–59). But with Valerian away at business, "it was solitude with the colored couple floating mysteriously through the house" (p. 59). Nevertheless, when Ondine, the wife of Sydney— they are "the colored couple" who efficiently manage the Street household—explains to Margaret the characters in *Search for Tomorrow*, Margaret makes the only real friend that she has ever known. But "Valerian put a stop to it saying that she should guide the servants, not consort with them" (p. 59). Yet, "Valerian was never rude to Ondine or Sydney, in fact he pampered them. No, the point was not consorting with Negroes, the point was her ignorance and origins. It was a nasty quarrel. . . . It frightened Margaret—the possibility of losing him" (p. 59). So it is that when Margaret's first and only child is born, a son, Michael, she loves him, of course; she knows that his birth binds the adoring Valerian to his family. But Margaret, the beautiful child-lady, is resentful of the attention that now she must share with the beautiful baby and cannot resist pricking him, from time to time, with pins or burning him with cigarettes or cutting his flesh, ever so gently, with knives. Valerian learns of this, as we do, years after it has happened. He learns of it on Isle des Chevaliers at Christmas dinner when Ondine can no longer suppress her rage at Margaret and at the circumstances in the Street household and shouts, "You baby killer!

I saw you! I saw you! . . . I used to hold him and pet him. He was so scared. . . . All the time scared. And he wanted her to stop . . . so bad. And every time she'd stop for a while, but then I'd see him curled up on his side, staring off. After a while . . . he didn't even cry. . . . A little boy who she hurt so much he can't even cry" (pp. 208–209).

The servants of Margaret and Valerian Street, Ondine and Sydney Childs, are like members of the family. They have nourished and made stable the Street residences for over thirty years. Indeed, they are so immersed in the ways of the Street family that, except for their accomplished science and style, unremarkable in either Valerian or Margaret, and except for their link with Jadine, their niece, they appear to have had no other nascence. Jadine, the daughter of Sydney's dead sister, has been raised by Ondine and Sydney since she was twelve. Even earlier, Jadine would live with them "at Valerian's house" in the summer. When they had sent her away to school, "they had gotten Valerian to pay her tuition while they sent her the rest" (p. 49). Ondine and Sydney are "good as gold" people whose distinction in life has become their servanthood. They live in a suite of their own within the Street's magnificent house on Isle des Chevaliers; they are both the guardians of the family and the extension of the family ways. They know Margaret and Valerian so well that they not only anticipate their needs and wants but prescribe them. Their own personal rituals—ablutions, eating habits, little ways of being and doing—are in perfect rapport with the Streets.' They even respond to the other two servants, residents of the island, as the Streets do. Gideon and Thérèse, natives of Isle des Chevaliers, do the menial chores of the Street household while Ondine is the cook and Sydney is valet-butler. The Streets and the Childses call Thérèse and Gideon "Mary" and "Yardman"; they do not know their names—they do not inquire. To Ondine and Sydney Childs, Mary and Yardman are shiftless, trifling "niggers" to be dealt with accordingly, for they are proper Philadelphia Negroes in the terms of Dr. Dubois. Indeed, Ondine and Sydney, as they age, are more *valeo* than Valerian: they are stronger than he, who now spends his days sitting in a greenhouse on a tropical island listening to the radio, for agile industriousness has kept them vigorous except for Ondine's arthritic knees and feet; they are more than worthy of their hire and the Streets have rewarded them; they are assured of better than social security as long as they are with and in the family. Like Pauline Breedlove of Morrison's *The Bluest Eye,* Ondine and Sydney work hard, are reliable, aim to please and do. Unlike Pauline, they do not shoo away their niece, Jadine, as Pauline shoos away her daughter, Pecola, in order to lavish attention upon the blue-eyed child of the family she serves, yet Ondine and Sydney give Jadine over to Valerian and Margaret, who guide her choices and mold her ways and steer her thinking in the manner in which they wish to guide and mold and steer their own son, Michael, who rejects them.

Jadine, a "copper Venus" (p. 115), has grown up to become a high-fashion model who is also a "graduate of the Sorbonne . . . an accomplished student of art history . . . an expert on cloisonné . . . An American now living in Paris and Rome, where she had a small but brilliantly executed role in a film" (p. 116). At twenty-five, Jadine is confident of her conclusions concerning the nature of things: "Picasso," she tells Valerian, "*is* better than an Itumba mask. The fact that he was intrigued by them is proof of *his* genius, not the mask makers' " (p. 74). But, after all, she has been taught in the schools what *real* culture is. Assured and confident of the fruits of her assumptions, her choices, her way of life, and her successes, Jadine's self-confidence has been deeply wounded only once. In Paris, at a "Supra Market," shopping for a party celebrating her having been "chosen for the cover of *Elle*" magazine, having received "a letter from a charming old man saying your orals were satisfactory to the committee," and being wooed by "three gorgeous and raucous men . . . in Yugoslavian touring cars" (p. 44), Jadine sees a woman,

> *a woman much too tall. Under her long canary yellow dress Jadine knew there was too much hip, too much bust. The agency would laugh her out of the lobby, so why was she and everybody else in the store transfixed? The height? The skin like tar against the canary yellow dress? The woman walked down the aisle as though her many-colored sandals were pressing gold tracks on the floor. Two upside-down V's were scored into each of her cheeks, her hair was wrapped in a gelée as yellow as her dress. . . . She had no arm basket or cart. Just her many-colored sandals and her yellow robe. . . . The woman leaned into the dairy section and opened a carton from which she selected three eggs. Then she*

> *put her right elbow into the palm of her left hand and held the eggs aloft between earlobe and shoulder. She looked up then and they saw something in her eyes so powerful it had burnt away the eyelashes.*
>
> *She strolled along the aisle, eggs on high, to the cashier, who tried to tell her that eggs were sold by the dozen or half-dozen— not one or two or three or four—but she had to look up into those eyes too beautiful for lashes to say it. . . . The woman reached into the pocket of her yellow dress and put a ten-louis piece on the counter and walked away, away, gold tracking the floor and leaving them all behind. (pp. 45–46)*

In this woman, Jadine catches a glimpse of an essence, a beauty, an assurance, a womanliness, an indwelling elegance, a nurture, an authenticity that she had never known before and certainly not achieved. Jadine follows the woman with her eyes, unable to mask her admiration and even awe, but just as the woman disappears, "she turned her head sharply around to the left and looked right at Jadine. Turned those eyes too beautiful for eyelashes on Jadine and, with a small parting of her lips, shot an arrow of saliva between her teeth down to the pavement . . . below" (p. 48). Hence on Isle des Chevaliers, visiting her "Nanadine" and Uncle Sydney for Christmas at L'Arbe de la Croix, the house of Valerian and Margaret Street, Jadine still ponders the splendid woman holding three eggs aloft in a market in Paris. She sought the woman's approval with her eyes, but the woman spat a rejection that shook Jadine's self-assurance for the first time in her life until she meets Son, the Brer Rabbit whom she, as tar baby of Toni Morrison's modern fable, ensnares.

In a scene recalling Richard Wright's *Native Son*, Morrison's Son, hiding in Margaret Street's walk-in closet, is discovered. Son's entry into the Street household, his reentry into the action of the fable, dissolves all pretensions. Attitudes, buried deep, emerge; hidden fears erupt: Margaret, the aged beauty, is convinced that Son has come to rape her; Ondine and Sydney are outraged at the invasion of "niggerdom"; Valerian, managing style, topples under pressure; and Jadine, embarrassed, contemptuous, and insulted, is now Beauty both terrified by and interested in the Beast. Son has entered the house looking for nourishment. Wet, filthy, and hungry from his sea-change, Son, like the rabbit, has inadvertently entered the bounteous garden-world of Farmer Brown, emperor of abundance. The collision-encounter between Son and the inhabitants of L'Arbe de la Croix and the outgrowth of that form the heart of the tale told in *Tar Baby.*

Tar Baby is a fable, and a fable, for one thing, is a story in which values are juxtaposed and exposed. In the world that a fable creates, persons, places, and things assume strange contours bearing large, small, or no resemblance to persons, places, and things in the world we call reality. Wit, humor, subtlety, irony, and verbal color—exquisite finesse—are the materials that shape the fabulous, which, on canvas or in story, presents an image of a world. The world painted by the opulent palette of Toni Morrison, grand fabulist of our time, is a world as much afflicted by bad ideas as blessed by good ones. Yet the fabulous genius of Morrison does not accuse her world so much as it exposes and defines its moral, emotional, and spiritual quagmire and points to its source of renewal and regeneration. The people who inhabit the world created in *The Bluest Eye* (1970), *Sula* (1973), *Song of Solomon* (1977), and *Tar Baby* (1981) represent the ideas that daily bombard them, for these are solidly twentieth-century people. And what that means, in one sense, is that they receive ideas, good or bad, more rapidly than any other people in human history ever have. They are the inheritors of the industrial age, where by means of stupendous technology, ideas, like medicines, are unleashed, many times insufficiently tested, upon the populace and found only later to be fatal.

The people of this fable-world imbibe toxic ideas like Pauline Breedlove of *The Bluest Eye* swallowing whole the nineteen-twenties extravaganzas of movieland and hating herself, her husband, and her child by comparison. Or like Sula of the novel by that name or First Corinthians of *Song of Solomon* or Jadine of *Tar Baby,* they are miseducated by cant; by historical, cultural, and political bias or ignorance of schoolish books; by insidious daily-diet propaganda sponsored by moneymongers; by the pretensions of those who live in the valleys and islands of abundance in this world; by the surrender to pretensions of those who could but do not call upon mother wit and an ancestry endowing them with extraordinary sensibility to double-sight and pierce the core of bad ideas; by foolish slogans rampant in this world convincing many that "if you White, you right; if you Black, stand back or catch up"; by the perennial lusts of a world where "every/body/wants to be/booozie woozie." An affliction of bad ideas, like a rain of bile, pours down upon the natural landscape and the people of the story-world of Toni Morrison. The deluge makes "the daisy trees marshal for war . . . winds do not trade . . . bees have no sting . . . no honey" and "the avocado tree . . . folds its leaves tightly over its fruit" (*Tar Baby,* passim). People caught in the storm of bad ideas lose their direction and become bemused like Shadrack of *Sula,* or become dangerous to the life of their neighborhoods like Soaphead Church or Geraldine, who scorn little Pecola of *The Bluest Eye,* or unhinged like Hagar of *Song of Solomon,* or disconnected from their life-engendering source like Jadine, or bedazzled like Son of *Tar Baby.* Still worse, others, like Valerian Street, whom many wish to become, are beyond the hope of life at its urgent sources—joy, pain, love, struggle:

> *He had not known because he had not taken the trouble to know. He was satisfied with what he did know. Knowing more was inconvenient and frightening. . . . He had made it up. Made up the information he was waiting for. Preoccupied himself with the construction of the world and its inhabitants according to this imagined message. . . . And all he could say was that he did not know. He was guilty, therefore, of innocence. Was there anything so loathsome as a willfully innocent man? . . . An innocent man is a sin before God. Inhuman and therefore unworthy. No man should live without absorbing the sins of his kind, the foul air of his innocence, even if it did wilt rows of angel trumpets and cause them to fall from their vines. (pp. 242–243)*

Unlike Valerian, Son is not guilty of the crime of unseasonal innocence—a state of spiritual ignorance and vacuity, self-barricaded willfulness, allowing only what one desires to pass for what is. Son, born and raised in Eloe, Florida, knows both the briar patch and the fruit of life. In Eloe, more a neighborhood than a town, people know that life is a nourishing root, sometimes gall and sometimes sweeter than coolest well water at a dogday noon. Such people are the source of nourishment and of renewal in the fable-land of Toni Morrison. They are shelters from the storm of bad ideas that afflict that world; they are not self-righteous, nor are they free from error; they think neither too little of themselves nor too much; they know both anguish and joy—neither overwhelms them; they can hear and taste and touch and see a lie two hours before it manifests, yet they themselves may lie; but they never call it truth. They do not separate character from ability or industry from fraternity or individuality from communality. To them, a person is more than what he or she does; a person is not merely the sum of his or her work or achievement or talents—those are expected of any human being according to his gifts. No, the people who are sources of nourishment and clear vision in this world measure a person in a different way. They measure a man in a certain way: a man is a good man, over all he says and does, if he understands something crucial to his *man-ness*—his own and that of his tribe—and understanding that, acts or does not act, knows or can be instantly reminded of the boundaries of his *can-ness*. Understanding makes him deft, on beat, in time, graphing arcs of movement—soul, mind, body—more arduous and adroit than "grace under pressure"[4] or "purity of line."[5] No, the motion of such a man is more like the invisible ripple of still wings in high flight. The men who teach Milkman in *Song of Solomon* are such men; the father of Claudia and his like in *The Bluest Eye* are such men; Gideon of *Tar Baby* is such a man; and in Sydney reside those qualities and their opposite. Guitar of *Song of Solomon* and Son, the journeymen of *Tar Baby*, have the makings of such men.

The people who are sources of nourishment in this fable-world also measure women in a certain way: a woman is a good woman, over all she says or does, if she knows something crucial to her *woman-ness*— her own and that of her tribe. Knowing that, she moves or does not move; if perplexed, she can instantly be reminded of the inscape of her *is-ness*. Knowing makes her easy, still, resilient, alchemic, salient, protogenic. The motion of a woman who *knows* is very like the sea: tidal, undulating, mirroring the sun or cloud, whichever sustains life at any moment. The people who are guides and measures of moral probity in a world as much afflicted by bad ideas as blessed by good ones are the progenitors of and heirs to the fundamental ethos of African American sensibility untainted by pretension, unpolluted by the storm of bilious thought that pummels the world in which they live.

Son issues from such people; he knows them on sight. Even in the midst of his own transgression, he is able to purify his spirit in the storm. But for eight years, he has traveled far from Eloe. He has fought in Vietnam and seen his world from different shores. He has worked at sea and mingled with all manner of men, but mainly he has been a refugee from transgression caused by transgression and

> *in those eight homeless years he had joined that great underclass of undocumented men. And although there were more of his kind in the world than students or soldiers, unlike students or soldiers they were not counted. They were an international legion of day laborers and musclemen, gamblers, sidewalk merchants, migrants, unlicensed crewmen on ships with volatile cargo, parttime mercenaries, full-time gigolos, or curbside musicians. What distinguished them from other men (aside from their terror of Social Security cards and cédula de identidad) was their refusal to equate work with life and an inability to stay anywhere for long. Some were Huck Finns; some Nigger Jims. Others were Calibans, Staggerlees and John Henrys. Anarchic, wandering, they read about their hometowns in the pages of out-of-town newspapers. (p. 166)*

Son, arriving on Isle des Chevaliers at Christmastime, is a starving man in search of nourishment. He is offered the bounty of Christmas food at the table of Valerian Street; he is not nourished by it. Rather, it is Son, the man in search, who brings a nourishment to the house that it has, heretofore, not known. He unlocks the mental dungeon of Sydney and Ondine; he reveals to Valerian Margaret, who is forced to crack her mirror; he offers Valerian the gift of introspection. Son, in turn, finds his meal, his potion and his portion, at the island home of Gideon and Thérèse, menial servants in the House of Street. But Son finds something else. In the household of the Streets, Son, a man benumbed by a deluge of experience, rediscovers feeling. He discovers desire—intense and delicious. This, he feels, is love inspired by the "copper Venus" of the house. Son is not an ignorant man; he is, like Guitar of *Song of Solomon*, a bedazzled man. Bedazzlement in a world of storm is a common malady afflicting the best of men. The "big white fog"[6] hanging curtainlike over such a world creates illusions that pass for reality. Guitar of *Song of Solomon*, like Bigger Thomas of Richard Wright's *Native Son*, enraged by the deluge of bad ideas that afflicts his world, attempts to murder the deluded. But to rid the land of the deluded is itself an illusion—a bedazzlement. For the fog that is

◊ 345

ubiquitous can be cleared only within the mind, the spirit of those who inhabit the storm-ridden world. And the way to that clearing is through the guides, the sources of nourishment in this world. Son, the Brer Rabbit of *Tar Baby*, sees in Jadine the appearance of something real. He is bedazzled.

If the fable wrought in *Song of Solomon* is about a man, Milkman, overweaned but potentially vivifying, who must make a "journey home" to find his bearings in his world, and if the fable wrought in *The Bluest Eye* is about a community whose greatness is its ability to send forth children of the light, of little Claudia, but whose blight, by surrender to pretension, makes possible its derangement of a lovely child—Pecola—and if the fable wrought in *Sula* is about the offspring of that same community who somehow do not fully comprehend its glory and range askew, then *Tar Baby* is about a woman, Jadine, who, disconnected from the life potential of her origins, has lost the crucial is-ness of her tribe. "She has forgotten her ancient properties" (p. 305). That loss has cast her adrift as in a wide world alone, and even when she meets the issue of the tribe, now lost to her, though she feels the authenticity of its is-ness and though it awakens in her what has slept before, she cannot manage the motion—tidal, undulating, proto-genic—of the knowing women of her tribe.

The communion, the sweet and bitter wine, that Son and Jadine taste together is contained in the very cup of trembling. Those who have tasted from that cup know its baptism. That communion and its affliction are the deep pulse of the heart of *Tar Baby*. The beat of that pulse must be experienced in the blood. On the page, we have not seen its like since the story of Teacake and Janie in Zora Hurston's *Their Eyes Were Watching God*. But in that story, Janie and Teacake are both deep within their shared ancestral source. The distance between Son and Jadine is an immensity not of the flesh, not even of the heart, but of the soul of things. Son is a man whose journey far from home has undernourished him; he sees in Jadine the *look* of home absent of its is-ness. Despite his effort, his diluted strength cannot endow it. In Son, Jadine has found the source from which she is disconnected; the woman in the yellow dress has seen the disconnection and forsworn it. The women of Eloe, for Son, honoring custom and his heart, have brought her to them, have seen the disconnection and rebuked it. These women, like those of *The Bluest Eye*, *Sula*, and *Song of Solo-*

mon, young, middle-aged, and old (among them the mother of Claudia, the Maginot Line; Nell, Eva; Pilate, Circe, the woman whose is-ness revitalizes Milkman; also Thérèse and, in her way, Ondine), despite any flaw, know the crucial thing. Jadine does not. She has seen it in the woman in the yellow dress, and she has drunk of it from Son. She cannot find it in herself. She is, perhaps, an unwilling Delilah sucking at the Samson strength of Son. But more and more terribly, Jadine is the embodiment in language of the carcinogenic disease eating away at the ancestral spirit of the race at the present time. It is that disease at which the pen-knife of Toni Morrison cuts.

Jadinese is the disease of disconnection, whose malignancy causes a slaughter of reality. The disease has a long history, and, in America, has manifested itself often and variously in the life, in the government, and in the literature of the country. Disconnection is the disease from which all who live in the land suffer. Some admit their malady; they may, if they wish, become whole. Others are deluded and call their illness health, for they live invincibly in a slaughter of reality. From time to time, some experience a shock from which, if they recover, they gain recognition and seek wholeness. All American writers have been tortured by the national disease. Some have been victims of the malady of disconnection and have themselves been carriers. Others have been diagnosticians, anatomists, or surgeons. And some have achieved, through the practice of letters, epiphany—a vision of wholeness. Thus, from the birth date of the literature of the country, American writers may be fully understood and finally judged by the record that they have left either of their own affliction or of their perception of the anatomy, symptoms, and effects of the national disease—a slaughter of reality—or by their vision of wholeness and by the implicit audience that their efforts have specifically addressed: those who acknowledge their malady; those who are invincibly deluded (in which case, the writer is representative); or those who may from time to time experience a shock from which, if they recover, they gain recognition and seek and may achieve, like the writer, wholeness.

The presence of the disease of disconnection resulting in the slaughter of reality can be seen in the literature as early as *A True Relation of ... Virginia* by Captain John Smith, published in 1608 and called the birth of American literature. In that epistle-journal, language slaughters reality, as when the captain, speaking gratefully of his reception by the Great Powhatan, father of Pocahontas, "who kindly welcomed me with good words, and great platters of sundry victuals, assuring me his friendship . . ."[7] and who provides him not only the very soul of hospitality but the example of the ways and abundance and opportunities of life in the New World, calls his—the captain's—reception "barbarous."[8] For the captain is the child of the Old World sensibility and must appropriate its language, though it is inept for the task of reporting the reality of the abundant and welcoming sensibility of a grand New World.

By the publication in 1782 of *Letters From An American Farmer* by St. Jean de Crèvecoeur, the problem of unreality is firmly planted in the American soul and in the literature that reveals it. "What then is the American, this new man?" asks Crèvecoeur in the third letter of his volume. He answers:

> *He is either an European or the descendant of an European, hence that strange mixture of blood, which you will find in no other country. I could point out to you a family whose grandfather was an Englishman, whose wife was Dutch, whose son married a French woman, and whose present four sons have now four wives of different nations. . . . The Americans were scattered all over Europe; here they are incorporated into one of the finest systems of population which has ever appeared. . . .*[9]

In this epistle of Crèvecoeur, perception slaughters reality, for twenty-three years before his *Letters* appear, a narrative was published whose existence troubles the very terms of Crèvecoeur's definition. The publication is called *A Narrative of the Uncommon Sufferings, & Surprizing Deliverance of Briton Hammon, A Negro Man . . . Servant to General Winslow* (1760). Yet Crèvecoeur claims, "None among us suffer oppression either from government or religion."[10] Stranger still, in his fourth letter, a description of slavery and an attack, Crèvecoeur observes "the horrors of slavery, the hardship of incessant toils . . . those showers of sweat and of tears which from the bodies of Africans daily drop and moisten the ground they till."[11] What may appear contradictory to a beholder is not at all to Crèvecoeur or to the sensibility of which he is representative, for in his essay "Manners of the Americans" in *Sketches of Eighteenth Century America*, championing the social freedoms that the American enjoys, having escaped "the absurd ordinances" of the Old World, Crèvecoeur says of him (emphasis added):

> *Thus this man* devoid of society learns more *than* ever to center every idea within that of his *own* welfare. *To him all that appears good, just, equitable, has a necessary relation to himself and family.* He has been so long alone that he has almost forgot the rest of mankind except it is when he carries his crops on the snow to some distant market . . . *this introduces him to all* the little mysteries of self-interest *clothed under the general name of profits and emoluments. He sells for good that which perhaps he knows to be indifferent. . . .* Fearful of fraud *in all his dealings and transactions,* he arms himself, therefore, with it. *Strict integrity* is not much wanted *as each is on his guard in his daily intercourse, and this mode of thinking and acting becomes habitual.*[12]

Here, *individualism,* which Emerson was to accept and fully exonerate in "Self-Reliance" (*Essays, First Series,* 1841) but which Melville was to fully condemn as solipsism in his character Ahab in *Moby Dick* (1851), is the conundrum, as early as Crèvecoeur, slaughtering reality in the American place.

By 1845, most of the viral elements involved in the disease affecting the heart of the country are announced in its literature. Terrible oppositions struggle in, say, Franklin and Jefferson, as well as between them and, say, Adams and Hamilton. But in *The Life of Olaudah Equiano or Gustavas Vassa, the African* (1789), another convolution has assumed shape. That narrative raises the question of authenticity. It begins with the author's account of himself as he knows himself within the context of his now lost homeland. He is on the high seas, imprisoned in the belly of a slave ship. His account of himself pivots between a revelation of his own identity and that of an identity assigned to him by the captain and the crew of the ship. Inside and outside, or the opposition between the authentic and the imposed blurring reality—and aiding its slaughter—is another convolution of the national disease. But the insight of Equiano, in a shock of recognition occurring midway through the narrative, is, for him and us, sufficient antidote. He says, "I must learn to navigate."[13] And with the publication of

Narrative of the Life of Frederick Douglass, an American Slave (1845), the measure of the disease of disconnection in the American sensibility is fully taken. To go behind *Narrative* and to come forward in time, examining the materials, the design, and the story substance of American writing to the present is the crucial connection (restoring disconnection) that the criticism of American literature must make.

The Afro-American novelist has consistently attempted connection. Posing at least two cultural traditions and offering a third dimension of synthesis, novelists from William Wells Brown to Ralph Ellison have offered paradigms of wholeness. That offering is a phase of literary history awaiting the critic's full report. Within the wake of the consummation that is Ellison's *Invisible Man* (1952), another phase begins. And from the publication of James Baldwin's *Go Tell It on the Mountain* (1953) to the present time, the history of the Afro-American novel demands a scholarship that must teach itself its duties.[14] Toni Morrison and her contemporaries, exposing the present awful and crucial effects of disconnection, and simultaneously working at possibilities of wholeness in new forms born of old traditions that they and they alone fully possess, await the most serious and fully conscious—whole—investigation that the soul of the critic can mount.

Exquisitely told, *Tar Baby* is a story about nourishment—the devastation caused by its lack and the regenerative power of its presence. It is the story of a man in search of nourishment and of a woman whose nourishing power, cut off from its source, has been defused. It is the story of a world where pretension wars with authenticity and where people who live in that world must choose, for there are guides. And those guides, throughout the fabulous fiction of Toni Morrison, are legion. They are, for instance, women who, like those to whom *Tar Baby* is dedicated, are representative of a culture, of a time, of a magnificence perpetually present in human history. *Tar Baby* is dedicated to

> *Mrs. Caroline Smith*
> *Mrs. Millie McTyeire*
> *Mrs. Ardelia Willis*
> *Mrs. Ramah Wofford*
> *Mrs. Lois Brooks*
> *—and each of their sisters*
> *—and each of their sisters,*

all of whom knew
their true and ancient
properties

The women of the dedication are the grandmother, mother, aunts, and sister of the writer; these, then, are the guides to whom the narrative voice of the writer is accountable. Thus, it is not the narrative voice alone that measures sensibility in the story told in *Tar Baby*. Neither is it the narrator who makes crucial judgments, for, after all, what is judged in the world of the story is the behavior of a woman—of women. That judgment implies a definition exceeding the grasp of any narrator alone. Only the cultural integrity from which the storyteller draws is able to adjudicate, much less to authenticate, crucial aesthetic and moral judgments. So the women of the dedication join, as guides, the woman of the "burnt eyelashes" and Thérèse and the women of Eloe, as well as, by implication, the chorus of women of the Morrison canon. These women, by allusion, figure the warrior women, the market women, the calabash-carrying women, the queen women, the life-bearing, culture-bearing women of their own ancient origins. In their songs, their tales, their reference, these women acknowledge women of other cultures whose paradigms they either approve or reject. Just so, the adroit brush of the narrator shades a faint outline of the Clytemnestras, Cassandras, Penelopes, Helens, Hekubas, Andromaches, Medeas, Sapphos, Salomes, Judiths, Deborahs, Esthers, Cinderellas, Goldilockses, or latter-day Revlon girls: women who sink a culture or save it, who delude it or provide it clarity. *Tar Baby* is a sublime story of a people whose experience, ancestral and present, has prepared them to circumnavigate deluge, and their humanity, the source of nourishment in the world in which they live, like the faces on a Bearden scape, is Black.

Sometimes at dusk of evening
When lightning bugs would glow,
My Grandma told me stories in the dark.
And now at dusk of evening
When city lights burn bright,
I live
The very stories that she told.

◊ 351

Notes

1. Albert Murray, "The Visual Equivalent of the Blues," in *Romare Bearden: 1970–1980*, ed. Jerald L. Melberg and Milton J. Bloch (Charlotte, N.C.: The Mint Museum, 1980), pp. 17–28.
2. Ibid.
3. All quotations from Toni Morrison's *Tar Baby* (New York: Alfred A. Knopf, 1981) are cited only by page number.
4. A phrase used by Ernest Hemingway to describe exemplary behavior in *The Sun Also Rises* (New York: Charles Scribner's Sons, 1926).
5. Another Hemingway phrase descriptive of exemplary behavior in ibid.
6. A phrase of Richard Wright's dominating the landscape of *Native Son*, and the title of Theodore Ward's suggestive play of 1940.
7. Captain John Smith, *A True Relation of . . . Virginia* (Boston: Charles Deane, 1866), pp. 33–38.
8. Ibid.
9. St. John de Crèvecoeur, *Letters From an American Farmer* (London: E. P. Dutton, 1912), p. 13.
10. Ibid., p. 151.
11. Ibid., p. 155.
12. St. John de Crèvecoeur, *Sketches of Eighteenth Century America*, ed. H. L. Boudin et al. (1925; reprint ed., New York: Arno Press, 1969).
13. Arna Bontemps, ed., *Great Slave Narratives* (Boston: Beacon Press, 1969).
14. Full explication of this point is attempted in my study *The Presence of Ancestry: Traditions in Recent Afro-American Fiction* now in progress.

ALICE WALKER

I Said to Poetry

I said to Poetry, "I'm Finished
With You;
Having to almost die
before some weird light
comes creeping through
is no fun.
"No thank you, Creation
no muse need apply.
I'm out for good times—
at the very least,
some painless convention."

Poetry laid back
and played dead
until this morning.
I wasn't sad or anything
only restless.

Poetry said: "You remember
the desert, and how glad you were
that you have an eye
to see it with? You remember
that, if ever so slightly?"

I said: "I didn't hear that.
Besides, it's five o'clock in the a.m.
I'm not getting up
in the dark
to talk to you."

Poetry said: "But think about the time
you saw the moon

◊ 353

over that small canyon
that you liked much better
than the big one—and how surprised you were
that the moonlight was green
and you still had
one good eye
to see it with."

Think of that!

"I'll join the church!" I said,
huffily, turning my face to the wall.
"I'll learn how to pray again!"

"Let me ask you," said Poetry,
"When you pray, what do you think
you'll see?"

Poetry had me.

"There's no paper
in this room," I said.
"And that new pen I bought
makes a funny noise."

"Bullshit," said Poetry.
"Bullshit," said I.

FAMILY OF

Sometimes I feel so bad
I ask myself
Who in the world
Have I murdered?

◊ 354

It is a white man's voice
that asks this question,
coming from nearly inside of me.

It is asking to be let in, of course.

I am here too! he shouts,
Shaking his fist.
Pay some attention to me!

But if I let him in
What a mess he'll make!
Even now asking who
He's murdered!
Next he'll complain
Because we don't keep a maid!

He is murderous and lazy
And I fear him,
This small, white man;
Who would be neither courteous
Nor clean
Without my help.
By the hour I linger
On his deficiencies
And his unfortunate disposition,
Keeping him sulking
And kicking
At the door.

There is the mind that creates
Without loving, for instance,
The childish greed;
The boatloads and boatloads
of tongues . . .

◊ 355

Besides, Where would he fit
If I did let him in?
No sitting at round tables
For him!

I could be a liberal
And admit one of his children;
Or, be a radical, and permit two.
But it is *he* asking
To be let in, alas.

Our mothers learned to receive him occasionally
Passing as Christ. But this did not help us much.
Or perhaps it made all the difference.

But there. He is bewildered
And tuckered out with the waiting.
He's giving up and going away.
Until the next time.

And murdered quite sufficiently, too, I think,
Until the next time.

Each One, Pull One

For Hansberry, Jackson & Bond

We must say it all, and as clearly
as we can. For, even before we are dead,
they are busy
trying to bury us.

Were we black? Were we women? Were we gay?
Were we the wrong *shade* of black? Were we yellow?
Did we, God forbid, love the wrong person!
Were we Agnes Smedley or John Brown?

◊ 356

But most of all, did we write exactly what we saw,
as clearly as we could? Were we unsophisticated
enough to cry *and* scream?

Well, then, they will fill our eyes,
our ears, our noses and our mouths
with the mud
of oblivion. They will chew up
our fingers in the night. They will pick
their teeth with our pens. They will sabotage
both our children
and our art.

Because when we show what we see,
they will discern the inevitable:
We do not love them.

We do not love them.
We do not love what they have made.
We do not trust them.
We do not believe what they say.
We do not love their efficiency.
Or their power plants.
We do not love their factories.
Or their smog.
We do not love their television programs.
Or their radioactive leaks.
We find their papers boring.
We do not admire their cars.
We do not worship their blondes.
We do not envy their penises.
We do not think much of their
Renaissance.
We are indifferent to England.
We have grave doubts about their
brains.

◊ 357

In short, we who write, paint, sculpt, dance
or sing
share the intelligence and thus the fate
of all our people
in this land.
We are not different from them
neither above nor below
outside nor inside
we are the same.
And we do not love them.

We do not love them.
We do not love their movies.
We do not love their songs.
We do not think their newscasts
Cast the news.
We do not love their president.
We know why the white house is white.
We do not find their children irresistible
We do not agree they should inherit the earth.

But lately you have begun to help them
bury us. You who said: King was just a womanizer.
Malcolm just a thug. Sojourner "folksy." Hansberry
a traitor (or whore, depending). Fannie Lou Hamer
merely "spunky." Zora Hurston, Nella Larsen, Toomer:
Reactionary, brainwashed, spoiled by white folks. "minor."
Agnes Smedley, a spy.[1]

I look into your eyes
you are throwing in the dirt.
You, standing in the grave
with me. Stop it!

[1] This poem is not denying that some of our people (black and otherwise) have been brainwashed, reactionary or spies. It is saying that it is hard to live in a thoroughly unjust society without making mistakes. In acknowledging rather than burying our people's errors and studying the struggles they waged around them, we can only improve our own chances of living lives we can respect.

Each one must pull one.

Look, I, temporarily on the rim
of the grave,
have grasped my mother's hand
my father's leg
There is the hand of Robeson
Langston's thigh
Zora's arm and hair
your grandfather's lifted chin
the lynched woman's elbow
what you've tried to forget
of your grandmother's frown

Each one, pull one back into the sun

We who have stood over
so many graves
know that no matter what *they* do
all of us must live
or none.

I'm Really Very Fond

I'm really very fond of you
he said.

I don't like fond.
It sounds like something
you would tell a dog.

Give me love,
or nothing.

Throw your fond in a pond
I said.

◊ 359

But what I felt for him
was also warm, frisky,
moist-mouthed
eager
and could swim away

if forced to do so.

Representing the Universe

There are five people in this room
who still don't know what I'm saying.
"What is she saying," they're asking.
"What is she doing here?"

It is not enough to be interminable
one must also be precise.

MARGARET WALKER

MY TRUTH AND MY FLAME

I am a Black woman
and I hold my head up high,
for I rise with the masses of mankind . . .
with the peoples of the earth;
I rise with the tides of revolution
against the systems of oppression
that hammer me down.

I am a Black woman
and my eyes speak history,
for I stand in the shadows of Time;
ever present from the beginnings,
ever ready for the struggle,
ever forceful with the waters
of perpetual changing time.

I am a Black woman
and my beauty is my power.
In my strength is the turning wind.
I am a flower, a fern, a tree.
I am the spirit in all living things
for I grow with my feet
in the rivers of destiny.

THIS IS MY CENTURY . . . Black Synthesis of Time

I
O Man, behold your destiny.
Look on this life
and know our future living;

◊ 361

our former lives from these our present days
now melded into' one.

Queens of the Nile,
Gods of our Genesis,
Parade of centuries
behold the rising sun.
The dying Western sky
with yawning gates of death,
from decadence and dissonance
destroying false and fair;
worlds of our galaxies,
our waning moons and suns
look on this living hell
and see the rising sun.

II
Speak, heralds of our honored dead
Proclaim the heroes' line.
Declaim the sculptured and created truths
from prehistoric time.
Infinitude is bared to finite eyes:
We see the whirling suns and stars
first fixed and moving space
to shape beginning Time.

III
This is my century
I saw it grow
from darkness into dawn.
I watched the molten lava pour
from red volcanic skies;
Islands and Mountains heave
into the Sea
Move Man into the spiraled axis turn
and saw six suns and sunsets rise and burn.

IV
Osiris, Isis, black and beauteous gods,
whence came your spectacle
of rhythmed life and death?
You gods of love
on pyres of sacrifice
our human hearts become
old hearthstones of our tribal birth and flame:
the hammer and the forge,
the anvil and the fire,
the righteous sparks go wild
like rockets in the sky.
The fireworks overhead
flame red and blue and gold
against one darkened sky.
O living man behold
your destined hands control
the flowered earth ablaze,
alive, each golden flower unfold.

Now see our marching dead
The tyrants too, have fled.
The broken bones and blood
Have melted in the flood.

FIVE BLACK MEN . . .

and ten will save the city. . . .

Douglass, DuBois, Garvey, King, and Malcolm X.
Five black men whose leadership we cherish
in the history books
from Slavery to Segregation and the Age of Integration
down the primrose path to face oblivion.

◊ 363

Five black men . . .
    and ten will save the city.

Douglass was the first
brooding face upon our dark waters
rising out of twilight
clutching stars
daring the sun
casting light from all ages
on our miserable circumstances.

Yes, we know our black brothers in Africa
sold their mothers and sisters into slavery.
Yes, we know our white brothers in Europe
packed us like sardines in cans on their stinking ships
and we died like flies.

"I have known the curse of slavery
and the masters' cruel will
the overseer's lash and the reveille at dawn;
when the freedom talkers came
they called my name
but I was not on the roll of the chained
nor the dead
lying before the merciless pity of the Yankees.
I was long since gone.
Lincoln and Garrison
John Brown and the Alcotts
they were all the same—
aflame with one true mockery
of freedom, truth, and faith
but not for brotherhood.
I tell you my fellow shackled human race
we must strike the first blow.
We must be free
by the blood of our own humanity."

Five black men . . .
    and ten will save the city.

DuBois was Renaissance . . .
ancient Egypt, Thebes, and Memphis
Cush and Temples of Karnak, Luxor, and Parthenon.
They were his temples too.
He stood astride the chasm of yawning worlds
bridging the centuries
holding bolts of lightning
electric in his fists.
First social doctor of our century
analyzing our lives, our cities, our towns and schools;
loving our people
and understanding
how Western man built his system
on the labor of our lives
cheap labor, slave labor, from dusk till dawn;
how they made a myth out of race
joined it to their Christianity
and annihilated our lives.
DuBois reminded us and prophesied:
"The problem of the twentieth century will be the color line."

Five black men . . .
    and ten will save the city.

Marcus Garvey.
Up, you mighty Race!
And clench your fist against the sky.
Black is beautiful.
Say it loud, "I'm black and I'm proud."
Visionary, man of destiny
Black Messiah?
The United Negro Improvement Association lives.
The black star ascends.
The black ships and black cross nurses
all are part of a lost black empire.
They followed Garvey from the grass roots
by the tens, by the hundreds
and then by the thousands;

marched down Lenox Avenue in New York
and State Street in Chicago.
Then the mighty ones saw his power.
Was he really guilty of mail fraud
or was that a way the G-I guys could stop him?
A way to make him rot in jail in Atlanta
in the U.S.A.

Discredited, denounced, deported
but not destroyed.
First black nationalist of this century;
Big Black Man, you were never small.
You gave black men hope and dignity and Face.
Up, I say, Up, you mighty Race!

Five black men . . .
        and ten will save the city.

"The King is Dead. Long live the King!"
He gave us more than life.
"If they ask you why he came
tell them he came
to shake the complacent.
Tell them he came
to wake the conscienceless. . . .
Tell them he came
to teach us how to dream."[1]

Atlanta born
Educated
Pastor of Dexter Street Baptist Church
Downtown in Montgomery
He led us through the bloody streets of Birmingham.
We walked and talked with him
in Mississippi and Iowa
in Cicero and Harlem.

[1] The Reverend Kelly Miller Smith

Our hearts followed him to Oslo.
And we held our breath
to see his meteor in the sky.
Shocked by the assassin's rifle in Memphis
we sorrowed and we spoke
same gun that killed Medgar
same gun that killed Kennedy
same gun.
The king is dead. Long live the king!
A man of peace is immortal
beyond the price of segregation.

Five black men . . .
    and ten will save the city.

The old man had the message.
The old man never went to school
but he sent his sons.
The old man knew the depth of hatred
between the races
and he knew the history of hatred
between Jew and Christian and Moslem.
He preached his message from Allah
The message he received from Mr. Fard.

I remember those early days
when the brothers of Mecca
wore red fezzes
dressed neatly
and walked circumspectly
in our neighborhoods.
I remember when children turned their heads
curiously to see
why they looked so different
so strange among us
and yet were black like us.
Tell me now the old man amassed a fortune.
Tell me now the old man had his lieutenant killed.

◊ 367

Tell me now the brothers killed Malcolm.
And I cannot believe you.
Nothing inside my gut reaction tells me this is true.

Malcolm, the man
Big Cat
was feline in his grace;
leonine head
and cat eyes
and hair to match his lion's sign:
Big Red.
Only when he lay dead
and in his funeral Moslem dress
did we cast Christian eyes of wonder upon him.
"Ye shall know a tree by the fruit it bears."
Too late to know
how measureless for all time was this man.

Five black men . . .
        and ten will save the city.

Martin and Malcolm
were leaders of men.
They made revolutions.
They fought wars.
They drew battlelines
and never once
with loaded guns.
Their words were their weapons.
Their deeds were their monuments.
No two men more unlike
yet in all that matters they were the same.
In one bright, hopeless, fated Cause
they were brothers.

I HEAR A RUMBLING . . .

I hear a rumbling underground.
I hear a rumbling . . .
I hear my brothers underground
I hear a rumbling.

I hear an earthquake underground
I hear a rumbling.
I hear the red man underground
I hear a rumbling.

I hear the dead men from their graves
I hear them speaking
I hear the starving underground
I hear a rumbling.

I hear Chicanos underground
I hear them grumbling
I hear the prisoners underground
I hear a rumbling.

I hear a rumble and a grumble
I hear a rumbling
I hear the yellow and the brown men
I hear a rumbling.

There are rockets in the air
There *is* a rumbling
There is lightning in the sky
There *is* a rumbling.

I hear my children crying "Bread"
I hear my children crying "Peace"
I hear the farmers crying "Bread"
I hear the soldiers crying "Peace"

◊ 369

There is a rumbling . . .

Guns and butter will not help.
We want Peace.
Dollars in the marketplace
We want Bread.

When the volcanoes erupt
We want Peace.
Bread and Peace are not enough;
Freedom too.

I hear a rumbling . . .

They have boxed us in a coffin
Underground
They have chained us to a rock
Underground.

How long will their prices rise
to the skies?
How long must my children cry
to the skies?

How long will my people starve
Underground?
How long will the prisoners cry
Underground?

Christ is coming, so they say
In the skies.
Worlds will all be blown away
To the skies.

Will the earthquake underground
And the lightning in the skies
Peace and Bread and Freedom come
And the dead below arise?

◊ 370

MARGARET WALKER

There's a rumbling in the air
There's a lightning in the skies
There's a rumbling and a grumbling
And the walls of prisons breaking.

I hear rumbling underground
I hear rumbling.
Don't you hear the children crying?
Don't you hear the mothers weeping?

Blown to bits this craven crowd
Underground?
Blown to bits these plastic people
Underground?

Will you laugh or shout or cry?
Will you gloat and scream and die?
From the people everywhere
I have heard them here and there

Give us Freedom, give us Peace
Give us Bread and Freedom, too
I hear rumbling underground
Peace and Bread and Freedom, too.

Will we seize the power-mad
Everywhere
We will seize the guns and bread
Everywhere

Give us Freedom, Give us Peace
I hear rumbling underground
Bread and Peace and Freedom too
I hear rumbling underground.

◊ 371

FANFARE, CODA, AND FINALE

They are not for us any more: green fields where corn stands high;
tasseled and bursting kernels glinting in sunlight, pits of clay
where we went to play at dusk; blades of grass to chew idly
and honeysuckle cups to sip; four o'clocks to string and
morning glories to watch; pretty pansies washing their faces
in dew; these are lost flowers. Here underground we cannot
see them any more. In the jails they will not let us look
again.

Out of my lost laughter where my living once would flow, my
song and my sadness are one. My joy and my pain are bound
one on one . . . In the laughing rhythms of my singing, tears
are part of my living, and my tears rain through my laughing
eyes bitter, bitter, bitter through and through.

I buy bread of bitterness everyday in the markets of the world.
Peace and plenty are never my share; every day I go hungry.
Everyday I walk in fear, and no one seems to care. Black
kings on their thrones who lived a thousand years ago are
part of me now. Even they must share my bitter bread.
When I beg, it is bitter bread they toss to me to eat. When I
work, it is bitter bread I win from my toil. Even the mealy
ash cake I bake in my humble hut is borrowed bread, is bitter, borrowed bread.

Grant me one song to sing, America, out of my hurt and bruised
dignity. Let notes confused and bursting in my throat find
melody. Reprieve the doom descending on my life. Remake
the music stifling in my throat. Before my song is lost re-
sound the tune and hear my voice.

Out of my struggle I have sung my song; found hymn and flower
in field and fort and dungeon cell. Yet now I have constric-
tion in my heart where song is born. Such bitterness is eating
at my vocal cords the bells within me, hushed, refuse to ring.
Oh lift this weight of brick and stone against my neck, and
let me sing.

MICHELE WALLACE

The Envelope

I lived with him. It had been my house and then he moved in,
moved his razor into the bathroom, his shoes into the closet, his cold
milk into the refrigerator. And early in the mornings, his own particular smell hung in the air poised above my head until I was used to it
and did not notice it anymore. And I was glad to have him and them
because I had been not lonely exactly but without purpose, or not
without purpose precisely but without anything to distinguish one day
from the next in its relationship to the end of my life. Not that I
was old.

He would not marry me and so I would live with him, or rather he
would live with me. We split the expenses. He did the laundry. I did
the cooking and there was nothing extra, which saddened me but I ad-
justed.

We made no private vows, not even in jest. I discouraged them. I
discouraged talk of the future, and if and when our future would end.
Initially, I took only one precaution because, as you will probably
guess, I was emotionally involved. The first day he was there and his
things were mine or, at least, in my house, I gave him an unmarked
envelope. He stared at the black traces showing through.

"In that envelope," I said, "is my birth certificate."

"I don't want your birth certificate," he said. "I know how old you·
are."

"That envelope contains my birth certificate," I repeated slowly.
This time he was silent, waiting.

"If you should ever wish to leave me, you need not say a single word.
Take it out, look at it, give yourself time to think, and then put it back
in the envelope and return it to me. In this way, I will know you are
leaving."

"I'll never leave you."

"I hate goodbyes."

"Where would I go? I have everything I want right here."

"Nevertheless, I give you this envelope."

◊ 374

* * *

By the end of the first year of our living arrangement, that envelope had grown tattered and dirty, it had been passed to me so frequently. Left under my coffee cup. Deposited in the center of the palm of my hand as he would leave for work in the morning. Thrown at me from the shower or over the kitchen table. We did not always fight but when we did, we fought intensely. And it helped that we had a ceremony with which to mark the crisis. We never mentioned the envelope. We merely passed it back and forth. Or rather he always passed it to me and I took it, sometimes with reluctance, sometimes without.

By the end of the second year, the envelope had worn away and was unusable and there was just the birth certificate. By the end of the third year, the birth certificate was smudged and torn. By the end of the fourth year, it had been taped together so many times, it was unreadable. He had to know it by heart by then. My mother's maiden name: Amanda Johnson. My father's name: Jeffrey Scott. The date of my birth: December 17, 1952. The exact time of my birth.

He gave it to me and he gave it to me until by the end of the fifth year, it was only a fragment of its former self, a ragged piece of paper that could mean nothing to anyone else. And he always took it back. Need I say we were happy?

It was in the sixth year that he finally asked me.

I no longer noticed his smell or his shoes in the closet or his razor in the bathroom. They had become a part of me and my house. I took them for granted. Although I did not drink milk, I bought it automatically when I shopped, placed it in the refrigerator automatically in the place he liked to find it so that he could reach for it in the dark and without looking.

I knew all his tastes in foods. I knew what he would say in the morning. I knew which of his friends he liked and which he really didn't like. I knew where to find his keys when he didn't know. And I knew he would hide money in books he would never read. I knew what it meant when he called his mother. I knew what it meant when he took a shower twice in one day. I learned and I knew. I knew him.

Nothing happened. He just asked me.

I'll admit that the telephone bill was unusually large that month.

That I had run out of toilet paper twice in one week and we had had to use napkins. I'll admit that I watched more reruns on television that entire year. I'll admit that we hadn't quarreled in weeks. But nothing had really happened to distinguish the future from the past.

Was it a morning or an afternoon? It must have been on a weekend.

I poured his coffee, added just the amount of sugar he had always said he liked.

"Why a birth certificate?" he asked me. Just like that. In all these years, he had never asked me that.

"What?"

"You heard me."

"I didn't hear you."

"I asked you why a birth certificate."

"What would you like for breakfast? You could have pancakes."

"You're not going to answer me?"

"Not after all these years. Of course, if you don't want pancakes . . ."

"Pancakes will be fine."

I made the pancakes. He sat right there in the kitchen, watching me. Studying my back that had never borne a child. Not that I wanted a child.

"It must be of symbolic importance," he said slowly. I had made only two pancakes and was keeping them warm in a low oven. He liked three.

"What?"

"It must be of symbolic importance. Your birth certificate."

"It is of no symbolic importance. It is merely the day I was born."

"It is not the day you were born. It is a piece of paper."

"A piece of paper. Yes."

"My back hurts."

I put his pancakes in front of him. Stood behind him and began to knead his shoulders, his neck as I had done so many times before. But the tightness wouldn't go away.

"You do that well," he said nevertheless. "You do everything well."

"If you say so."

He let his head hang forward. He closed his eyes. I thought he slept.

"Do you love me?" he asked.

"Do you love me?" I asked.

*   *   *

I never saw the envelope again nor the tattered piece of paper that had been my birth certificate. Once again I noticed his smell in the house. It clung to everything I had, to the tiles in the bathroom, to my clothes, to the towels, to my fingers. He hadn't put the piece of paper in my hand. I bought milk for the longest time and let it rot. Need I say he was gone?

REGINA WILLIAMS

ASYLUM

(for Ernestine Lewis)

mourning suns filter thru her
opaque eyes
an inmate clamors
begs, fights for a place
to lay her trauma
straightjacketed smiles
focus in hallucinated reality.

they say she is mad
this red-maned, red-hued
black woman of piercing eye and probing . . .
she says "i may look broken
but i'm anchored in an ancient ebony frame"
she thinks history splintered &
mutters about an ancestry of cuts
cocks her head and walks
in her own lush garden

> *she calms my terror*
> *says redmen are passive*
> *only in movies*
> *blackmen only in whitemen minds*
> *sends me to "lie-berries" to read*
> *between lines   double-dutches me thru*
> *dual histories*
> *skip-ropes to Now*
> *says tomorrow it's hide & (above all) seek*

a bald-faced pharisee
is the rock

◊ 378

shattering her life
so her eyes take on splinters

her life is a legacy
of blood & wired glass
framed
as my window

They say she is mad
and like a mirror
she is.

For our life is a matter of faith

(for Mariah Britton Howard and Almeina Talbert)

she called to say she thought
she'd died
asked if she could expect
an afterlife.
i try to remember

my own passing . . .
the shallow breaths
on which i'd tried to live
                              fully

my fear of movement
the dread of hearing
my own voice

for i'd ridden quicksilver
waves of someone else's dreams
                         so long
                         sucking sand

◇ 379

so long
been the barren midwife
of everyone else's dream
                          so long
i bled/breathed fear
i remember fear's claw
gnashing, slashing
ripping the tight space
of my misplaced pride
and i scream a hungry shudder
            Dear God take me to another place
            where shadows won't circle
            my eyes

through my concave scream
i scavenged, scraped
began to search the marrow
of my soul

genesis was beating

though i could not see
shore
i felt my river swelling
a mighty tide
could not feel sky
but sensed my wings
spanning

and i tell her "yes"
i remember genesis

becoming

REGINA WILLIAMS

I AM NOT MY SISTER'S KEEPER: I AM MY SISTER

(for New York City's 36,000 "counted" homeless—1980)

empty-eyed building reflect nothing
of abandoned life
within
my hungry soul
digging thru trash for a reminder

                                your waste is my survival

i live underground
with blood-eyed empty-veined
passengers
tunnelled in sub-ways
of living

                                i had a family
                                once

children look at me
from under plastic lids closing
nostrils to foul odors
cringe at the wardrobe of winters
i wear

                                there is no vision in their eyes

    i used to have a dog
    he ate the leavings
    warmed my feet in winter
    rousted vagrants
    from public benches

they bark at me now
(the dogs)
eye the bones i've retrieved
challenge me for hovels
or abandoned houses

i live in doorways
of memory
hinged to no one and no thing

still
i do not qualify
the commonweal cannot document my survival
   it is buried in my matted hair
   under oozing sores and layered dirt
   between spaces of hollow teeth
   in fists of limp hands
   birthed behind my veiled eyes

i had a family
once
i even had a name

SHERLEY ANNE WILLIAMS

from "The Iconography of Childhood"

ii
These are tales told in darkness
in the quiet at the ends
of the day's heat, surprised in
the shadowed rooms of houses
drowsing in the evening sun.

In this one there is music
and three women; some child is
messing with the victrola.
Before Miss Irma can speak
Ray Charles does of "The Nighttime"
and *Awww* it Is the fabled

music *yo'alls* seldom given
air play in those Valley towns
heard mostly in the juke-joints
we'd been toold About; and so
longed for in those first years in
the Valley it had come to

seem almost illicit to
us. But the women pay us
no mind. We settle in the
wonder of the music and
their softly lit faces listening
at the songs of our grown.

iii
Summer mornings we
rose early to go
and rob the trees

bringing home the
blossoms we were told
were like a white girl's
skin. And we believed
this as though we'd
never seen a white
girl except in
movies and magazines.

We handled the
flowers roughly
sticking them in oily
braids or behind
dirty ears laughing
as we preened ourselves;
savoring the brown
of the magnolias'
aging as though our color
had rubbed off
on the petals' creamy
flesh transforming some
white girl's face into
ornaments for our
rough unruly heads.

v
The buildings of the
Projects were arrayed
like barracks in
uniform rows we
called regulation
ugly, the World in
less than one square block.
What dreams our people
had dreamed there seemed to
us just like the Valley
so much heat and dust.

◊ 384

Home training was
measured by the day's
light in scolds and
ironing cords; we
slipped away from chores
and errands from
orders to stay in
call to tarry in
the streets: gon learn what
downhome didn't teach.

And
Sundown didn't hold us
long. Yet even then
some grown-up sat still
and shadowed waiting
for us as the sky
above the Valley
                    dimmed.

vi
Showfare cost a lot
but we ran the
movies every chance
we got, mostly grade
B musicals that
became the language
of our dreams. Baby
Lois sang in the
rain for the hell of
it; Helen was a
vamp. Ruise was the
blood-red rose of
Texas, her skin as
smooth and dark as a
bud with just a hint
of red.

◊ 385

Sweating and
slightly shamefaced, we
danced our own routines
seeing our futures
in gestures from some
half remembered films.
We danced crystal
sidewalks thrilled in the
arms of neighborhood
boys and beheld our
selves as we could be
beyond the Projects:
the nine and ten year
old stars of stage and
screen and black men's hearts.

you were never miss brown to me

I
We were not raised to look in
a grown person's mouth when they
spoke or to say ma'am or sir—
only the last was sometimes
thought fast even rude but daddy
dismissed this: it was yea and
nay in the Bible and this
was a New Day. He liked even
less honorary forms—Uncle,
Aunt, Big Mama—mamma to
who? he would ask. Grown
people were Mr. and Miss

admitting one child in many
to the privilege of their
given names. We were raised to
make "Miss Daisy" an emblem
of kinship and of love; you
were never Miss Brown to me.

II
I call you Miss in tribute
to the women of that time,
the mothers of friends, the friends
of my mother, mamma
herself, women of mystery
and wonder who traveled some
to get to that Project. In the
places of their childhoods, the
troubles they had getting grown,
the tales of men they told among
themselves as we sat unnoted
at their feet we saw some image
of a past and future self.
The world had loved them even
less than their men but this did
not keep them from scheming on
its favor. It was this that
made them grown and drew from our
unmannerly mouths "Miss"
before their first names.

I call
you Daisy and acknowledge
my place in this line: I am
the women of my childhood
just as I was the women of
my youth, one with these women
of silence who lived on the
cusp of their time and knew it;
who taught what it is to be grown.

◊ 387

a record for my friends

I
It was a season
when even music
was expensive; dimes
pennies even nickels
appeared beside turn
tables
      We learned the
price of old favorites
and paid it, citing
Allen each time we
dropped that dime—College
brotha knoow the
value of records
had a stereo
And a collection

He had risen above this.

once in a moment
of passion paying
$.35 to
      steady the tone-arm
so Watson & Duke
could blow the stomp down
Blues listening like
every revolution
of the record was
his own

      his love was
our cloak and our crown.

◊ 388

2
War is Eldridge's next
reincarnation
laid back and funky
turned dippty dip and
one note

"Why can't we be friends?"
and Mao in the
moon: the shiek of freak
on jesus this is
the last cliche They
have snickered at
Fidel and he out
lived them.

ii
We flicker
the same way we flame
briefly *"real is real"*
One always do know;

All they say about
California is
true.

coda
I have come to
hear Monk
forever funky
and laid glowing Growing
solo and gold giving
birth to no one
so much as himself.

III
I have lived without
music except what

I could play in my
head—O radio
defended me, the
Happy Harolds of
the ghetto, souling
in a grubby war
with silence and sales
the mean substitute
for song

Its about
someone saying what
the next theme will be
and spe*ech R*each.
                    for
it
And we do. driven
on gypsy chords to
root the word now
fluid
        well
No. the mind
is not music Get

what you love by heart
Play this for your friends.

this city-light

Oh, I see myself as I was
then skinny little
piece a woman dying to
get to Frisco and change. I
couldn't see the worn patches on
my coat, only the suede and

once late at night I climbed through
a window into a room.
It was bare the pot up in
smoke and the nigga was gone.

I see myself as I was then
skinny little woman-girl
sitting in a third floor room
a voice floats up from the street
calling me to prayer and once
in answer I went to the
door. There was an old woman
there crying Belle. Belle. Belle I
wet myself and falling up
the stairs.
       (He asked once to tease
what I did *jes fo* fun. You
don't smoke you don't drink you don't
fuck, was the way it was phrased
and the words, no I don't fuck
unless it's with you, never
got said and I passed it all
off as one more hip joke.
              Oh,
I could say more—there was
the day we crossed the Bridge, we were
perched on the back of the truck.
I never saw the bay quite
like that again: Oakland a
dream city I was leaving
behind; Frisco a city
of dreams I wanted to make
mine—but these three things would still
stay the same. I came to the
city to live on a hill.
I am the bird that was plucked.
I am the woman that was

the wishon line

i
The end of a line
is movement the
process of getting
on, getting off, of
moving right along

The dank corridors
of the hospital
swallowed him up
(moving right along
now—from distant
sanatorium
to local health care
unit—the end of
that line is song:
*T.B. is killing
me* We traveled some
to see Daddy on
that old Wishon route
but the dusty grave
swallowed him up.

ii
These
are the buses of
the century running
through the old wealth of
the town, Huntington
Park, Van Ness Extension
the way stops of
servants; rest after

miles of walking and
working: cotton, working
grapes, working hay. The
end of this line is
the County: County
Hospital, County
Welfare. County Home—
(moving right on—No
one died of T.B.
in the 50's; no one
rides that Line for free.

GERALDINE L. WILSON

REFUGEE MOTHER

Sand swirls a halo
   round the dark mother   Africa
   burying her child
      cries stones   in a land
     where there is no water
     vomits grief   there is no food
  famine spreads wings wide
  buzzard touching feet to
  tiny bones/sandy waste   squawking
in triumph over ancient life

OUR CHILDREN ARE OUR CHILDREN

They are ours
fighting mothers with
electric red winds of blue violence
spreading out   fans of
dark predators
    escaping school abuse
    fleeing family misuse   dodging
Running fast concrete trails
noise of transistorized porno
fills their veins   stifles their hearts

They are ours
    snatching weekly wages   fathers shout
    Me, baby! your neighbor!
    they trap grandmothers/screams
    She fed him greens   he raped her
  maimed friends   knifed her
    rent for the room she gave him

◊ 394

GERALDINE L. WILSON

They face white/criminal justice
cuffed in legal bracelets
spilling blood instead of tears.

Watching All *their* Children and Dallas' Cowboys
Our children became strangers   on
Eyewitness News   Tune In.

NZADI ZIMELE-KEITA (MICHELLE McMICHAEL)

Birds Of Paradise

(1)
once

once, the canyons say,
there was but one cloud
there was but one bird
all the land looked to
one great circle of clay
and only the wind knew language
an arrow pierced the circle
the cloud split into nations
and there were many birds
the wind was pleased
and measured out his singing
in pacific threads
the first waters rushed to them
from the hills of god's face
mountains grew to guard them
forests followed the rain
and from desert altars
they littered the sky with hymns

(2)
Wa-Ko-Da

"My words are like the stars that never change . . ."
"There is no death, only a change of worlds . . ."
—Seattle, a Dwamish Indian chief

Grandfather of the four mysteries
draws the end of summer
around my neck
This barren morning

yawns between his
fingers
drumming the rhythm
of a death that only
changes worlds

we sleep longer when
a crow's wing holds the night open
to be blessed by Water's Child,
and the filings from turquoise teeth
lay where
soldiers burned children
and cornfields

Grandfather of the oldest memory
breaks the light into prisms
and makes morning a red cloud before me
     a black hawk before me
      an antelope running before me
this is still your land
  still your land,
     recalling the birds who walked
     defying its metal prongs
     a miracle that won't be moved

(3)

prayer

let rivers tremble again between the breasts
of your women,
 people of earthly grace
and let heathens hear you from winter caves;
   secret as the eagle's eternal smile
   silent as the golden mummy's mouth
   praising the dead with beaded tears—
 your spirits are left when the trees turn away.

people of holy earth,
  the wind rustles in your breath;
  send out canoes to divide the sun,
  and come like a quetzal,
  crossing acres of pain.

long road rhythm

she gives herself to a burning man,
watered and fed
by the passing of days,
syllables and shadows. a
man who folds her name in
blooming oriental shapes—
and knows that
in her face the plains are wide
gold.
yes.
between his brows she can believe
(they are running) she can see
soft feet press resilient green
coming to her (coming to her)
their shadow/names
(coming to her)

in his face, a woman
who will begin them brown
in his face she
can stop running
(be held, rocked, be known)
can hear the fountains
blooming
in his words

NZADI ZIMELE-KEITA (MICHELLE McMICHAEL)

what we know

          years will fall through our fingers
honest to the changes brilliant
        and bleeding their newness
honest to the simple weight
        of Living that wants to be;
sometimes needing all the satin in your
  eyes. sometimes
        grasping at pain or sleepless words
always step to step/ a handmade
  singing song of work,
    teaching us to walk and tell time again

we have what we know: somewhere
in my milk, your name is swimming; children
will cling to us like soil, a jewel
      woven in all our touch
      we have what we know: I uncovered the dawn
      heard You coming. You dropped wine
      for the earth, and my
      morning rain completed your smile

NOTES ABOUT AUTHORS

Janus Adams has written for television and film. Besides her work as a penetrating electronic journalist, she has had plays performed and is working currently with the Negro Ensemble Theater Workshop.

Fatimah Afif is a teacher in the Philadelphia School System, a mother of four, and a graduate student at Cheyney State College. Her activities include filmmaking with Ukweli Msanifu, a film production collective, and the Third World Film and Video Association. She is also affiliated with Project BAIT (Black Awareness in Television/Radio), a radio production group that produces weekly programs on WRTI and WUHY. Her poetry has appeared in *Kitabu Cha Jua (Journal of Black Poetry)* and she has read at various functions and on radio programs in Philadelphia.

Fayola Kamaria Ama is a poet and writer whose illustrations have also gained some recognition, most recently in *The Painted Bride Quarterly*. A graduate of Temple University, she now lives in Philadelphia, Pennsylvania.
  "My view of the creative process is that it flows from that higher divinity, and we are but vehicles for that expression of human struggle and beauty. What comes out on the paper depends on how much we grow inside and learn from our experiences."

Johari M. Amini's poems and other works have been included in many volumes of *Journal of Black Poetry*, *Black World*, and *Pan-African Journal*, among others. More than half a dozen books of her poetry have been published, and she is currently working on a collection of essays in social psychology. A graduate of the University of Chicago, she is a resident of Chicago and is teaching in the area.

Maya Angelou, novelist, actress, singer, dancer, is one of the best-known black women authors in the world. The last installment of her autobiographical work, *The Heart Of A Woman*, was published in 1981. One of her most powerful works was *I Know Why The Caged Bird Sings*. *And Still I Rise* is her most recent book of poetry.

Toni Cade Bambara's past work has appeared in *First World*, *Callaloo*, *American Rag*, *Black World*, *Negro Digest*, *Massachusetts Review*, other small press journals, literary anthologies, and children's readers. Her books include *The Black Woman, Tales and Stories for Black Folks, Gorilla, My Love and Other Stories, The Seabirds Are Still Alive and Other Stories,* and the novel *The Salt Eaters.* She is currently assembling a book on Atlanta between the years 1979 and 1982, readying a new collection of stories to be entitled *The Faith of the Bather,* and scripting a number of teleplays and films. (She can be reached at 991 Simpson Street, NW, Atlanta, Georgia 30314.)

Amina Baraka (Sylvia Jones) was born in Charlotte, North Carolina, and raised in Newark, New Jersey. A former painter, dancer, and actress, she published her first book of poetry, *Songs for the Masses,* in 1979. Her work has appeared in *Black Scholar, Main Trend, Unity & Struggle,* and a number of leftist and other publications. She is a Marxist-Leninist, married, and the mother of seven children.

Brenda Conner-Bey is a member of the Harlem Writers Guild, the John Oliver Killens Creative Writers Workshop, and Metamorphosis Writers Collective. She is also the founder and director of MenWem Writers Workshop, Inc., a literary information service located in Brooklyn, New York. Recipient of a 1982–83 CAPS grant for poetry, she is working on a collection of prose and poetry called *Thoughts of an Everyday Woman/An Unfinished Urban Folktale.* She is also currently working on a novel, *Vyella's Song,* a story about four generations of women, their struggles, their travels, and their resolutions.

"In my writing, the people I try to make come to life; the places, though inspired by my surroundings and my past, I try to tell something more than just my own story. I try to reach for essences of truth that speak to us as a people."

Gwendolyn Brooks was born in Topeka, Kansas, but has lived in Chicago, Illinois, since the age of one month. She is a member of the American Academy and Institute of Arts and Letters and is Poet Laureate of Illinois. Her awards have included the Pulitzer Prize for poetry, an American Academy of Arts and Letters award, the Shelley Memorial award, the Anisfield Wolf award, the Kuumba Liberation award, two Guggenheim fellowships, and forty honorary doctorates. She has taught at Columbia College, Elmhurst College, the University of Wisconsin at Madison, Northeastern Illinois University, and City College of New York; has lectured at hundreds of colleges and universities in this country; and has read her poetry at universities in Africa and in London. She is the author of fifteen books and has edited two anthologies.

◇ 402

Lucille Clifton is mother of six, a new grandmother as of October 1982, and the author of books for children and adults. She was born in Depew, New York; grew up in Buffalo; attended Howard University for two years; has been married for a quarter of a century and is the 1982–83 Jenny Moore Visiting Writer at George Washington University. She is Poet Laureate of Maryland.

"I hope that my work (and my life) is confirmation of the celebration of the spirit and flesh of what is a whole human. I write what I know. I am Black, a woman, and have been gifted with certain experiences of spirit. I try to act on what I have learned."

Jayne Cortez was born in Arizona and grew up in Los Angeles, California. She is the author of five books of poetry and three recordings. Her poetry has been published in many journals, magazines, and anthologies including *New Black Voices, Mundus Artium,* and *Presence Africaine.* Her latest book is *Firespitter,* and her third recording of poems was released in the winter of 1982. She has traveled and read her poetry throughout North America, Latin America, and Africa. Ms. Cortez lives in New York City and teaches Black Literature and Creative Writing at Rutgers University in New Brunswick, New Jersey.

Alexis De Veaux is a poet, playwright, and novelist born and raised in New York City. She has appeared on a variety of radio and television shows across the country and has given numerous prose/poetry readings. Her plays include *Circles, The Tapestry, A Season to Unravel,* and *"No."* A teacher of writing and performance arts, Ms. De Veaux has published a novel, *Spirits in the Street,* an award-winning children's book, *Na-ni,* and a unique biography of Billie Holiday, *Don't Explain: A Song of Billie Holiday.* Her poems and short stories have appeared in such publications as *Black Creation, Encore, Sunbury, Black Box* (poetry cassette), the *New Haven Advocate, Essence, Nimrod: New Black Writing,* the *Iowa Review, Hoodoo, Midnight Birds* (an anthology), *Conditions,* and *Gap Tooth Girlfriends: An Anthology.* The co-founder of Flamboyant Ladies Theatre Company, she is also a contributing editor at *Essence* magazine and is currently at work on a collection of short fiction and a novel.

"I want my work to reflect the many ways that I am a Black woman: I want it to be crazy, evil, loving, left-handed, sane, short, hard-to-get-along-with, tender, joyous, gap-toothed, riot-full, on time, moody, stepping forward, Black as it could be. I want it to speak in tongues and clear sentences; to have color, guts, and the nerve to be alive. I want it to be a bridge and an airport to other dark peoples. I want my work to be a revolt."

Y. W. (Yvonne Watkins) Easton, born, raised, and educated in New York City, as a single parent raised her only child, worked at administrative jobs, and later became a labor as well as community organizer. That world changed when she moved to Paris to search out and clarify her creative potential. Returning after two years, Easton was determined to be a part of the Black cultural energies that permeate America. Writing is only a third of Easton; she is also a sculptor and graphic artist whose works have been exhibited in New York City, Washington, D.C., and Newark, New Jersey, where she resides.

Mari Evans, a musician, writer, and educator, resides in Indianapolis, Indiana. Currently an assistant professor at the Africana Studies and Research Center of Cornell University, she is the author of numerous articles, four children's books, several theater pieces, two musicals, and three volumes of poetry, including *I Am A Black Woman* and *Nightstar*. She has taught and read at universities and colleges across the country, and her work has been widely anthologized in collections and textbooks.

Lois Elaine Griffith is a writer living and working in Brooklyn, New York. Her plays have been produced by the New York Shakespeare Festival and by El Puerto Rican Playwrights'/Actors' Workshop. She was the recipient of a CAPS grant for poetry. Currently she is writing a play, *Night Song*, about Marie Laveau. A volume of her poetry, *Barbadian Fantasies*, is soon to be published.

Nikki Grimes was born in New York City and studied at Livingston College-Rutgers University, where she taught Creative Writing for a number of years. She has worked in radio production both in New York with WBAI-FM ("The Kid Show") and in Stockholm with Educational Radio (Utbildningsradio) and immigrant programming ("Gränslöst") in both English and Swedish. She has lectured extensively in universities and other educational institutions in America and Sweden on such subjects as Black English History & Literature and Writing Books for Children. The author of *Growin'* and *Something On My Mind*, books for young people, she has been the recipient of a Ford fellowship. Her poems, articles, and photographs have appeared in such publications as the *Greenfield Review, Essence*, the *Amsterdam News, Callaloo*, and *Sturdy Black Bridges*, an anthology, among others. She has been a literary consultant with New York City's Cultural Council Foundation under the CETA Arts Project. Ms. Grimes currently resides in Stockholm, Sweden, where she free-lances as a writer and singer.

"The single most important thing I strive for in my work is integrity. It is my greatest hope of praising God, and why else has He given me this gift?

Writing, for me, has always been one of the most intimate of matters. Through it, I have always sought to express my deepest concerns: the issues about which I was most strongly convinced; the personal hurts and tragedies which wounded most severely; the dreams and visions which were loftiest and seemed most rugged. Poetry, specifically, has been—and remains—the very language of intimacy for me. When I have been successful, it has allowed me to cut straight through to the pain, the vision, the political concern, with laserlike precision, bypassing the superfluous. I do not pretend that I have always been successful. I trust, however, that a steady growth has always been in evidence."

Vértàmàè Smart-Gròsvènòr is a native of the South Carolina lowlands. She is an actress, poet, writer, and culinary historian whose work has appeared in numerous magazines, including *Ebony, Essence,* and *Ms.* She has also written for *The Washington Post, The Village Voice,* and *The New York Times.* Ms. Grosvenor is currently at work translating the Uncle Remus tales from Gullah into English.

Safiya Henderson is tall, black, and fighting back. She lives, works, loves, fights in Harlem, New York. Her poetry has appeared in such places as the *Guardian* newspaper, *Essence, Black Scholar,* an anthology of black women writers *Keeping the Faith,* and the anthology *Woman Rise.* Safiya is a mommy of a sweet daughter, Naimah, born to her and Preston Holmes on September 15, 1979. Safiya is a Harlem Hospital worker, and has just completed her first novel, entitled *Yellow Satin Blooming in the DMZ.*

Akua Lezli Hope is of the third generation of her families in New York. Her work has been included in *Black Scholar, Iowa Review, Woman Poet East, Ordinary Women, LOVECYCLES* (a chapbook), *Sunbury, Essence, Conditions, Pamoja Tutashinda, Hoodoo,* and *Bopp.* She is currently editing and publishing an independent Black literary magazine, *New Heat,* and has an unpublished manuscript, *The Prize Is the Journey.*

"Studying the tenor sax, recording moments with camera, I seek the evolution of a mythos which clarifies, educates, and inspires necessary change."

Mariah Britton Howard is an instructor of English at Bronx Regional High School and the College of New Rochelle. Her works have appeared in a few literary magazines and anthologies, among them *American Rag* and *New City Voices.* In the autumn of 1982, Metamorphosis Press published a collection of her poems entitled *With Fire.*

"I see my efforts as part of the ongoing quest for identification and expres-

◇ 405

sion of what it is like to be here. Sources of inspiration come from my ancestors and the encounter of what it is like to be here, this time. I try to speak in
the language of metaphor and offer the prize or surprise of understanding to
the reader. The poems included here speak to the dynamics of relationships
and the give and take of healing—that is the human experience."

Lateifa-Ramona Lahleet Hyman is a poet living in Philadelphia, Pennsylvania. She is a graduate of Temple University and has attended Howard University's Graduate English program. Lateifa also holds a certificate from the
Howard University Book Publishing Institute. Moreover, some of her work
has been included in *Obsidian, Callaloo,* and *Janus.* She is a member of the
Seshet Poetry Circle.

"I am a sculpturer of the word, and thus, I try to pursue life like an anthro-
pologist seeking a new folk song because I know that 'The words of a dead
man / Are modified in the guts of the living.' For me the job of the writer is
to write about the most passionate aspects of all things: known and unknown,
simple and complex."

Adrienne Ingrum is from St. Louis, Missouri. She is a book editor and lives in
Harlem.

Rashidah Ismaili, born in Dahomey, was educated in Dahomey, France,
Italy, and the United States. She is affiliated with many organizations, among
them Calabash Poets Writers, African Heritage Studies Association, and the
Caribbean Studies Association. Her work, like her education, has been far-
ranging; she has published throughout the world, in Africa, France, Puerto
Rico, and most recently, Turkey. At present she teaches Black Psychology
and English- & French-speaking African Writers at Rutgers University.

Mae Jackson became an almost legendary figure in the 1960s with her book
of poetry *Can I Poet With You?* Born in Earl, Arkansas, she has a young
daughter, Njeri Ayoka.

"I have been inspired by the works of many poets, Carolyn Rodgers, Mari
Evans, Sonia Sanchez, Nikki Giovanni, Amiri Baraka—they are the real leaders, the true liberators, and being in their company has always been healing
and motivating."

Gayl Jones, born in Lexington, Kentucky, received her Bachelor of Arts degree in English at Connecticut College and her Master of Arts and Doctor of
Arts degrees, both in Creative Writing, at Brown University. Since 1969,

when her work began to appear nationally, Dr. Jones has distinguished herself as a prolific and versatile author of fiction, poetry, and drama. In addition to an impressive list of books, her work appears frequently in journals and anthologies and has been translated into several languages. While much of her writing reflects the brutal circumstances of Black life in the United States, a considerable portion is based on the African presence in Brazil and Mexico during the seventeenth and eighteenth centuries. Her historical writings illustrate the rewards of thorough and meticulous scholarship. The recipient of numerous fellowships and awards, including the *Mademoiselle* Award for Fiction in 1975, Ms. Jones is currently teaching at the University of Michigan in Ann Arbor.

Anasa Jordan, born in Newark, New Jersey, is a member of the Frederick Douglass Creative Arts Center's Poetry Workshop under the direction of poet Quincy Troupe. She is also a member, along with Margaret Porter and Gwendolyn Wilson, of the group of women poets *New Bones.* Her first collection of poetry is titled *Trumpet for an Ebony Flute.* She is living and writing in Harlem.

June Jordan is a poet, novelist, political activist, teacher, keynote speaker, and author. She was the recipient of a Rockefeller Fellowship Foundation grant in creative writing, a Prix de Rome Award in environmental design, and a CAPS grant in poetry, and was elected to the board of directors of Poets and Writers, Inc. She is the author of ten books, among them *Who Look At Me, His Own Where, Things That I Do in the Dark, Civil Wars,* and *Passion.* Many of her articles, essays, and reviews have been published in such publications as *Black World, Ms., The New York Times, Essence,* and others.

"I write because it is the best way I know to fight, and to make love, in public. My life work as a poet celebrates the victory I know is coming soon."

Abbey Lincoln (Aminata Moseka) is, of course, the great jazz singer and composer. Her most recent records, *The People in Me* and *Golden Lady,* are incredible additions to an already astonishing life's work.

Audre Lorde teaches at Hunter College in New York City. Her latest books are *Chosen Poems—Old and New* and *XAMI: A New Spelling of My Name,* her first work of fiction.

Esther Louise was born and raised in Brooklyn, New York. Her poetry has been published in journals such as *Essence, Freshtones,* and *American Rag.*

◊ 407

"I'm a black capricorn, a divorced mother of five, a graduate of CCNY, and a poet. I have been published in various publications, literary and commercial. I hope that my poems help to bridge the gap between mind and soul, because our present age threatens to sever these connections and render them helpless in the future. My poems are self-therapy. If they can be of service to anyone, I'm pleased."

Paule Marshall was born in Brooklyn, New York, just as the Depression was beginning. A Phi Beta Kappa from Brooklyn College, she has received fellowships and prize support from the Guggenheim and Ford foundations, the National Institute of Arts and Letters, the National Endowment for the Arts, and the Yaddo Corporation. Her books include the novels *Brown Girl, Brownstones* and *The Chosen Place, the Timeless People* and a collection of stories entitled *Soul Clap Hands and Sing*. As a member of the Association of Artists for Freedom in the mid-1960s, she attacked paternalistic white liberalism and called for a new, more militant, all-Black organization. Having lived for considerable periods in the Caribbean, she now resides with her son in New York.

As a second-generation Black American having grown up with the "Bajun" cultural style persisting in her home, Ms. Marshall confronted both the problems of acculturation and racism at an early age and has used these experiences in her works.

Malkia M'Buzi is a poet and freelance writer. She peers beneath the surface of the mundane in order to illuminate the complexities within the depths of the human experience. She attempts to inspire as she educates through her work which encompasses poetry, journalism, and fiction. She has read her poetry on radio and in numerous places, including the Harlem State Office Building, AfroArts, Bronx Community College, City College of New York, Bennington College, Black Theatre Alliance, Afrikan Poetry Theatre, and C.A.T. Video Gallery. Her poetry has been featured in several anthologies. Malkia is a former member of The Society of Afrikan Poets and has coordinated cultural programs for St. John's Lutheran Church and B.E.S.T. Head Start. She wrote, produced, and performed a one-woman poetry production and coordinated a poetry benefit for the Benin Gallery entitled "Expansions, A Poetic Fusion" at the Harlem Performance Center. Ms. M'Buzi worked as head of Publicity and Public Relations for Afrikan Functional Theatre and was a co-editor of "Benin Art Notes," a newsletter produced by the Benin Gallery. She held a series of workshops for MenWem Writers Workshop in Brooklyn. She also conducted a poetry workshop at Bennington College and held a series of writing/drama workshops in New York City for senior citizens. Ms. M'Buzi has attended the writing workshop of John Oliver Killens and is currently a member of the Harlem Writers Guild.

"Poetry is a priority, just as my family is. I am a woman working. Writing is my job."

Rosemari Mealy lives and works in Harlem, New York. The author of *Lift These Shadows from Our Eyes*, her essays and poems have appeared in the *Black Scholar, Sunbury, Heresies*, and *Black Women and Liberation Movements*. She was editor of the Black Women Writers Section (*Sunbury 10*) among other publications.

"I've been committed to political activism most of my life, even in my work. Poetry became a tool, another craft to be perfected. I've always held the belief that the poet should use his/her pen as a weapon, a fighting tool to awaken, at various levels of the intellect, the reasons and necessity for challenging the material basis of our class enslavement as Blacks and women."

Louise Meriwether is the author of the novel *Daddy Was a Number Runner* and three biographical books for children. Her short stories have appeared in national magazines and several anthologies. At present she teaches writing at Sarah Lawrence College and is at work on a historical novel.

Toni Morrison's *Tar Baby*, her most widely circulated novel to date, got her picture on the cover of *Newsweek* magazine. Following the well-deserved acclaim for her great work *Song of Solomon, Tar Baby* certainly confirms Toni's obvious eminence among American novelists. She is currently working on a musical drama about Storyville in New Orleans.

Margaret Porter was raised in Gloster, Mississippi, and now lives in Harlem with her husband, the poet Quincy Troupe.

Aishah Rahman, playwright and short story writer, is the author of *Lady Day: A Musical Tragedy, Transcendental Blues*, and *Unfinished Women Cry in No Man's Land while a Bird Dies in a Gilded Cage*, which was produced in the New York Theater. Ms. Rahman has taught at Brooklyn College, Queens College, and the University of Massachusetts in Amherst. At present she divides her time between writing and caring for her daughter, Yoruba, to whom all her work is dedicated.

"I internalized society's image of my kind and decided that the only way I could come close to my dreams of being a writer was to romantically link myself with male authors. And so I wrote through my lovers—typed manuscripts, corrected, suggested, criticized, and inspired. Once in a while I would attempt to write my own words but low self-esteem and active discouragement quickly sent me back to my "rightful place." But lovers have a way of moving on and I changed places and traveled to Sierra Leone, Guinea, Senegal, Puerto Rico, Jamaica. I looked at my sisters everywhere and realized that we all needed dreams that could be nurtured instead of hidden. The dream would become a nightmare if it continued to be aborted. I found the strength to confirm myself and my place in the universe. The poems pushed forward."

Faith Ringgold, painter, sculptor, mixed-media artist, has taught art in New York City schools and colleges and lectured and exhibited her art throughout the United States and in Africa and Europe.

Faith Ringgold's art is a manifestation of her consciousness as a Black woman. In the early 1960s she began an extensive treatment of the civil rights movement as a subject for her art. She has continued to work with political themes, including Attica Prison conditions and the mass murder of children in Atlanta. By originating a series of colors called "Black Light," using pigments that relate to Black skin tones, she brought her consciousness to the palette of her work. Ringgold has given new force to a number of media by interpreting them as specifically female forms for creating visual symbols. Her soft sculptures and doll-making incorporate the tradition of women's handicrafts into a politically visionary art, and her masks bring the rich cultural heritage of Africa into the making of images that symbolically urge women to speak out. Ms. Ringgold's unpublished autobiography, *Being My Own Woman*, is her account of the life forces behind her art.

Carolyn M. Rodgers's most recent book of poetry is *The Heart As Ever Green*.

Sandra Rogers is a very young poet from Brownsville, New York. This is one of her first published works.

Sonia Sanchez. Black woman. Mother. Poet. Professor. Playwright. Activist. Author of ten books, including *Homecoming, Love Poems, A Blues Book for Blue Black Magical Women* and, most recently, *I've Been A Woman: New and Selected Poems* and *A Sound Investment.*

"I am the continuation of Black women who have gone before me and who will come after me. I am Harriet Tubman, Fannie Lou Hamer, Queen Mother Moore, Margaret Walker, Assata Shakur, Gwendolyn Brooks, and all the unsung Black women who have worked in america's kitchens. I am the sister who has been abused by men and loved by men. I am my stepmother, a southern Black woman who was taught her place and as a consequence was never able to fulfill herself as a human being.

"The point of me is to treat the souls of Black folk. to be an artist/surgeon and cut out the terrible years of all these slave/years and let Blackness flow healthily, fully, all around us. The way of me is to take our eyes off the ground. to lift us up. to resurrect. yeah. to let us hear the songs waiting to be sung. Hummmmed. Chanted. Love songs for each other. Mother songs for our children. Warrior songs when the feelings of love, survival and *liberation* move us to say:

Ayo-o-o-o-o-o-Aye-eeeee-
A-A-ye-ye-ye-A-A-yo-yo-yo.

"The point is: no one can just 'happen' to be Black in Capitalist/america be they student. pimp. writer. junkie. professor. Mother. Father. Worker. Ain't no 'by chance' for Black people. The Black writer/artist must reflect the times. Must be the technicians of the people. Must be the mind/changers.

"I have tried to be a standard bearer and a guardian against the forces of capitalism that seek to undermine Black people.

"I have tried to continue the Black woman tradition of excellence."

Judy Dothard Simmons is the popular host of WLIB's *Judy Simmons Show.* She is also a poet of growing reputation.

Eleanor W. Traylor is Professor of English at Montgomery College in Rockville, Maryland, and has held visiting professorships at Tougaloo, Hobart, and William Smith colleges, and Cornell University. A Fellow of the Conference on African and Afro-American studies at Atlanta University, she frequently lectures within and outside the United States on Afro-American literary traditions. In addition, her articles have appeared in *First World Magazine* and in several collections of essays on Afro-American literature. Her occasional scripts have been performed at Crampton Auditorium at Howard University and at the Baird Auditorium of the Smithsonian Institution in Washington. Currently she is preparing a critical book on folk traditional bases of Afro-American fiction. Dr. Traylor resides in Washington, D.C.

Alice Walker is an author, poet, and editor. Her published works include three volumes of poetry (*Once, Revolutionary Petunias,* and *Good Night, Willie Lee, I'll See You in the Morning*), three novels (*The Third Life of Grange Copeland, Meridian,* and *The Color Purple*), two collections of short stories (*You Can't Keep a Good Woman Down* and *In Love & Trouble*), a collection of essays (*In Search of Our Mother's Gardens*, and a biography of Langston Hughes for children. In addition, she has edited an anthology, *I Love Myself When I Am Laughing . . . And Then Again When I Am Looking Mean & Impressive*, and has had her stories included in a number of anthologies. Her many awards have included fellowships from the National Endowment for the Arts, Guggenheim Foundation, and the Radcliffe Institute; the Lillian Smith Award, the Rosenthal Award from the National Institute of Arts and Letters, and the Unique New York Award for Literature; and a National Book Award nomination. Her work has appeared throughout the country in such publications as *Ms., Freedomways, Mother Jones, Essence, Black Scholar, American Scholar, Harper's,* and *The New York Times.*

Margaret Walker Alexander is a poet, novelist, and professor of English at Jackson (Mississippi) State University, where she is also director of the Institute for the Study of History, Life and Culture of Black People. Her book of poetry, *For My People,* and her novel, *Jubilee,* have won wide acclaim. She also has published *October Journey* and most recently, *A Poetic Equation: Conversations Between Nikki Giovanni and Margaret Walker.* Mrs. Alexander received the Yale Award for Younger Poets, a Rosenwald Fellowship, and a Houghton Mifflin Literary Fellowship, in addition to being a Ford Fellow at Yale University. She was more recently appointed a Fulbright Hayes Fellow to Norway and won a Senior Fellowship from the National Endowment for the Humanities.

Michele Wallace flew into the public eye with the publication of her controversial first book, *Black Macho & The Decline of the Superwoman.* She has recently been studying at Yale and is readying for publication her first novel, *Former Friends.*

Regina Williams was born, bred, and schooled in Brooklyn, New York; she studied graphics at Brooklyn Community College and English literature at Brooklyn College. Poet, editor, author of short stories and an educational resource guide for young adults, she is one of the founding members of Metamorphosis Writers Collective. Her poetry has appeared in *New City Voices* (an anthology), *NewsArt, Black American Literature Forum, Concern* magazine, and several other journals. Her short story, *'Splanation,* appeared in *Drum.* She is a member of the Frederick Douglass Creative Arts Center's Poetry Workshop directed by Quincy Troupe and is currently writing a resource text for young adults and teachers for the United Presbyterian Church in the United States.

Sherley Anne Williams is the author of *Give Birth to Brightness*, a critical study of the hero in some works by selected Afro-American writers, The Peacock Poems, a 1976 nominee for a National Book Award, and *Some One Sweet Angel Chile*, a second collection of poetry. Her critical articles, stories, and poems have appeared in major periodicals and journals and in anthologies of contemporary literature. She teaches Afro-American literature and lives in Los Angeles, California.

Geraldine L. Wilson was born, raised, and went to school in Philadelphia, Pennsylvania, where she taught school and was director of a settlement house. After working in the Movement in Mississippi, she moved to New York City, where she is a child development/early childhood specialist. She has written reviews of children's books and critical essays, as well as articles on educational issues, Black children and families, and stories for children.

"My muse prescribed the writing of poetry during an illness and while I was experiencing a personal loss. The writing of poetry still comes as a surprise to me, even after two years. It demands of me much needed discipline. It gives back to me the gift of looking at the world through the eyes of a poet."

Nzadi Zimele-Keita (Michelle McMichael) is a Philadelphian who has been doing poetry readings, dramatic performances, and literature workshops in schools, colleges, community centers, and at Graterford Prison. She is a student of poet Sonia Sanchez. She is affiliated with Seshet Poetry Circle and looks forward to operating an independent press for children's books in the next few years.

"I am a woman, a marriage partner (happily so), a worker, a mother (ecstatically so), a student of the craft of writing. Writing is a way to connect people to pictures and places and events and people that may expand their lives in some way. I have been fortunate to have a brother who taught me to read very early on, and since that time reading has been vital to my life. It has brought me in touch with the African-American literary tradition and exposed me to many good influences, most notably Sonia Sanchez, Gwendolyn Brooks, and Margaret Walker.

Elizabeth Catlett is a sculptor and printmaker whose work aims at reflecting Black life and expression in much the same way as that of the writers in this anthology. She has monumental sculptures in Mexico, where she lives and works, and in the United States. Probably her best-known work is the monument to Louis Armstrong in New Orleans.

◊ 413

Grateful acknowledgment is made to the following contributors for permission to reprint the material contained within this anthology:

Janus Adams for excerpt from *St. Stephen: A Passion Play* © 1981, by permission of the author.

Fatimah Afif for "Tanka" by permission of the author.

Fayola Kamaria Ama for "for 'Mamie' (a poem for my grandmother)" by permission of the author.

Johari M. Amini for "There Is No Title: Only Echoes," "The Promise," and "Story for the Remainder" by permission of the author.

Maya Angelou for "The Reunion" by permission of the author.

Toni Cade Bambara for "Madame Bai and the Taking of Stone Mountain" by permission of the author. (Reprint permissions should be addressed directly to the author.)

Amina Baraka for "Soweto Song," "Haiti," "I Wanna Make Freedom," and "Sortin-Out" by permission of the author.

Brenda Connor-Bey for "Pretending" © 1978, "Martha" © 1980, and "The Dancer" © 1981, by permission of the author.

Gwendolyn Brooks for "Primer for Blacks," "To Those Of My Sisters Who Kept Their Naturals," and "Requiem Before Revival" from *Three Preachments*, Brooks Press, Chicago, © 1980, by permission of the author.

Lucille Clifton for "for her," "my dream about being white," and "morning mirror" by permission of the author.

Jayne Cortez for "Rape" © 1982, "There It Is" © 1982, "You Know" © 1982, "Big Fine Woman From Ruleville" © 1982, "For the Brave Young Students in Soweto" © 1982, by permission of the author.

Alexis De Veaux for ". . . And Then She Said" © 1982, "French Doors: A Vignette" © 1981, and "The Woman Who Lives in the Botanical Gardens" © 1981, by permission of the author.

Y. W. Easton for "The Welcome" © 1982, by permission of the author.

Mari Evans for "I Am A Black Woman," "Where Have You Gone," "Speak the Truth to the People," and "early in the mornin" from *I Am a Black Woman*, William Morrow and Company, Inc., New York, © 1964, by permission of William Morrow and the author.

Lois Elaine Griffith for "Prince Harlem" © 1982, by permission of the author.

Nikki Grimes for "Fragments: Mousetrap" © 1979, from *Callaloo* #6 (Vol. 2, No. 2, May 1979) by permission of the author. "Definition" © 1978, from *The Greenfield Review*, Spring 1979, by permission of the author (originally appeared under the title *NIKS: 2*, Vol. 7, Nos. 3 & 4, Spring/summer 1979). "The Takers" © 1979, 1978, from *Callaloo* #5 (Vol. 2, February 1979) by permission of the author.

Vértàmàè Smart-Gròsvènòr for "Skillet Blond" by permission of the author.

Safiya Henderson for "Portrait of a woman artist," "harlem/soweto," and "letter to my father . . . a solidarity long overdue" by permission of the author.

Akua Lezli Hope for "Lament" and "August" by permission of the author. "1." from *Ordinary Woman*, ed. by Jones Miles and Esteves Chiang, Ordinary Woman Press, New York, © 1978, by permission of the author.

Mariah Britton Howard for "reports," "a using," and "solution #9" by permission of the author.

Lateifa-Ramona Lahleet Hyman for "Paraphernalia for a Suicide: a revelation of life" © 1980, by permission of the author.

Adrienne Ingrum for "Loomit" and "Friday the 13th Candlelight March" by permission of the author.

Rashidah Ismaili for "Murderous Intent with a Deadly Weapon," "Dialogue," and "Struggle of Class" by permission of the author.

Mae Jackson for "For The Count," "A POEM FOR ALL THE MENS IN THE WORLD," "On Learning," and "My Last Feeling This Way Poem" by permission of the author.

Gayl Jones for "Ensinança" © 1982, by permission of the author.

Anasa Jordan for "Sweet Otis Suite" © 1981, by permission of the author.

June Jordan for "ON THE REAL WORLD: Meditation #1" © 1980, "Blue Ribbons for the Baby Girl" © 1980, "A Last Dialog on the Left" © 1980, and "Poem Towards a Final Solution" © 1982, by permission of the author.

◊ 416

ACKNOWLEDGMENTS

Abbey Lincoln for "I am the Weaver," "On Being High," "In The Middle," and "A Name Change" by permission of the author.

Audre Lorde for "NEED: A Chorale of Black Women's Voices" © 1979, from *Chosen Poems—Old & New* by permission of the author.

Esther Louise for "enough," "it's all in the name," "running to gone," "for us," and "tokens for 't' " from *swinging doors of knocking-wood cowards* by permission of the author.

Paule Marshall for "Barbados" from *Soul Clap Hands and Sing*, Chatham Booksellers, © 1971, by permission of the author.

Malkia M'Buzi for "Lament" © 1981 and "Tree Women Quest for Sun . . . (for the women of Namibia)" © 1981, by permission of the author.

Rosemari Mealy for "A Love Poem to an African Freedom Fighter," "untitled," and "New Chapters for Our History" by permission of the author.

Louise Meriwether for "A Man Called Jethro" by permission of the author.

Toni Morrison for "Recitatif" by permission of the author.

Margaret Porter for "Sugarman" in *Sunbury* 9 (Fall, 1980). "when i rite" and "inflation" by permission of the author.

Aishah Rahman for *Transcendental Blues* © 1976 and *The Lady and the Tramp* © 1976, by permission of the author.

Faith Ringgold for excerpt from *Being My Own Woman* by permission of the author.

Carolyn M. Rodgers for "Mannessahs," "Touch: Translation Poem 4.," "Touch: Poem 5.," "Aunt Dolly," "Folk," and "Wimmin" from *Translation Part 1*, Eden Press, Chicago, Illinois, © 1980, by permission of the author.

Sandra Rogers for "Waiting For Her Man Too Long" © 1981 by permission of the author.

Sonia Sanchez for "Just Don't Never Give Up On Love" © 1982. "A Poem for Sterling Brown," "Old Words," "Present," and "Kwa mama zetu waliotuzaa" from *I've Been A Woman: New & Selected Poems* © 1978, by permission of the author.

Judy Dothard Simmons for "Minority," "Equal Opportunity," and "Linseed Oil and Dreams" by permission of the author.

◊ 417

Eleanor W. Traylor for "The Fabulous World of Toni Morrison: *Tar Baby*" by permission of the author.

Alice Walker for "I Said to Poetry," "I'm Really Very Fond," "Representing the Universe" by permission of the author. "FAMILY OF" and "Each One, Pull One" from *Freedomways* by permission of the author.

Margaret Walker for "MY TRUTH AND MY FLAME," "THIS IS MY CENTURY ... Black Synthesis of Time," "FIVE BLACK MEN," "I HEAR A RUMBLING ... ," "FANFARE, CODA, AND FINALE" from *This Is My Century: Black Synthesis of Time* © 1982, by permission of the author.

Michele Wallace for "The Envelope" by permission of the author.

Regina Williams for "ASYLUM," "For our life is a matter of faith," and "I AM NOT MY SISTER'S KEEPER: I AM MY SISTER" by permission of the author.

Sherley Anne Williams for "from 'The Iconography of Childhood,' " "you were never miss brown to me," "a record for my friends," "this city-light," "the wishon line" from *Some One Sweet Angel Chile*, William Morrow and Company, Inc., New York, © 1982, by permission of the author.

Geraldine Wilson for "REFUGEE MOTHER" and "OUR CHILDREN ARE OUR CHILDREN" © 1982, by permission of the author.

Nzadi Zimele-Keita for "Birds Of Paradise," "long road rhythm," and "what we know" by permission of the author.

Cover illustration by Elizabeth Catlett